"Recent events in the US and wider world have emphasized just how critical and controversial the use of force by state agents can be in a democracy and in the full glare of contemporary media. Few writers are as well-qualified or experienced as Richard Hough in analyzing these issues and setting them in context. One of the great merits of this highly readable and thoroughly researched book is that while readers might not always agree with all of his answers, it is abundantly clear that he is asking the right questions."

– *Peter Squires, Professor of Criminology & Public Policy, University of Brighton; President: British Society for Criminology 2015–2018*

"The breadth of Dr. Richard Hough's experience and his keen insights show in this unique text, which is a comprehensive examination/presentation of knowledge gained through both practical on-the-street practice and academic study of force. The work is infused with the human view of officers and those in related occupations and shows appreciation for the complicated dynamics, human and otherwise, affecting officers involved in such events. It is a must-have for administrators, trainers, and educators."

– *Chief Charles D. Reynolds (ret.), Past President International Association of Chiefs of Police, International Police Practices Consultant*

"Police use of force has always been a potential hot-button topic, but given greater media attention due to captured recordings of force incidents in recent years, this issue has taken center stage. Enter Richard Hough's examination of police use of force, which approaches the topic from a variety of angles and is a welcome addition to the literature. I encourage those interested in police use of force to check out the book and begin thinking critically about the myriad complexities at hand."

– *William Terrill, Professor, School of Criminology & Criminal Justice, Arizona State University*

"Dr. Richard Hough brings both practical and academic insight to the raw subject of police force. In this captivating work, he wastes no time tackling the pertinent, often uncomfortable issues we must face as a society: Who are the police supposed to be? To what degree is force a component of the profession and why? If force events are each unique and dynamic—and now almost universally captured on video—how do we explain reasonable force to our public, especially when it's ugly? This book is for cops, yes, but it's equally suited to concerned citizens and policy makers. Dr. Hough brings considerable light to otherwise obscured and complicated issues. Highly recommended."

– *Lt. Jim Glennon (ret.), Co-Owner of Calibre Press, Author* of Arresting Communication: Essential Interaction Skills for Law Enforcement *and Co-Author of the 2018 edition of* Street Survival: Tactics for Deadly Force Encounters

THE USE OF FORCE IN CRIMINAL JUSTICE

The Use of Force in Criminal Justice addresses the how, why, and when of utilizing force against citizens in a democracy. This is the first true textbook on this topic, offering students and instructors a balanced, research-based approach to understanding the use of force in law enforcement, as well as in corrections and juvenile justice. Hough includes features to reinforce key concepts, including "What-Why," "Try This," "Going Global," and "Research Results" boxes.

The Use of Force in Criminal Justice combines academic and practitioner perspectives, making the book well-suited for undergraduate and graduate courses in criminal justice as well as professional training and executive education. The text is accompanied by online resources such as PowerPoints, Lesson Notes, and a test bank. *The Use of Force in Criminal Justice* is an invaluable aid for force trainers, risk managers, and attorneys who must understand the research on force and force issues rather than the rhetoric of individual anecdotes and personal system-of-force concepts.

Richard M. Hough is a faculty member in the Department of Criminology and Criminal Justice and is the Coordinator of the Public Administration Program in the Department of Legal Studies, Public Administration, and Sport Management at the University of West Florida. For more than 25 years Dr. Hough has taught criminal justice and public administration courses dealing with the practices and policies of criminal justice personnel for undergraduate and graduate students. As an instructor of defensive tactics, he has taught physical control and defense techniques and force concepts to law enforcement and corrections academy recruits and in-service officers for more than 30 years. Dr. Hough regularly consults as an expert witness in force usage and police and corrections practices in federal and state courts, and has done so for 25 years.

THE USE OF FORCE IN CRIMINAL JUSTICE

Richard M. Hough

Routledge
Taylor & Francis Group

NEW YORK AND LONDON

First published 2018
by Routledge
711 Third Avenue, New York, NY 10017

and by Routledge
2 Park Square, Milton Park, Abingdon, Oxon OX14 4RN

Routledge is an imprint of the Taylor & Francis Group, an informa business

Visit the eResources: www.routledge.com/9781138221451.

Library of Congress Cataloging in Publication Data
Names: Hough, Richard M., author.
Title: The use of force in criminal justice / Richard M. Hough.
Description: New York : Routledge, 2018. | Includes bibliographical references and index.
Identifiers: LCCN 2017054159 (print) | LCCN 2018011896 (ebook) |
ISBN 9781315410418 (master) | ISBN 9781138221437 (hardback) | ISBN 9781138221451 (pbk.) |
ISBN 9781315410418 (ebk)
Subjects: LCSH: Arrest (Police methods) | Prison discipline. | Juvenile justice, Administration of. | Police shootings.
Classification: LCC HV8080.A6 (ebook) | LCC HV8080.A6 H69 2018 (print) |
DDC 363.2/32–dc23
LC record available at https://lccn.loc.gov/2017054159

ISBN: 978-1-138-22143-7 (hbk)
ISBN: 978-1-138-22145-1 (pbk)
ISBN: 978-1-315-41041-8 (ebk)

Typeset in Bembo
by Taylor & Francis Books

CONTENTS

PREFACE

Neither Hollywood nor snippets of video provide the proper context to evaluate the use of force in criminal justice. While vicariously entertaining or personally shocking, neither source has as its intention to fully and accurately explain and present the myriad factors that may be involved in the scenes depicted. The use of force as a response to a situation is hardly the frequent occurrence the casual watcher might believe based on the number of times an incident appears or its prominent location in the news cycle. The conversation about incidents and issues is often not based on sufficient facts or the knowledge to properly evaluate an outcome. Professors, attorneys, public information officers, and trainers are tasked with presenting a more complete picture of what has occurred in a given situation.

Over the many years I have taught courses on policing, corrections, juvenile justice, and management and policy, I was never satisfied with the coverage of the function and dynamics of force usage in text books devoted largely to broader topics. No one argues that the issues of force usage are not important. Nothing less than the public judgment of the legitimacy and accountability of government is implicated in how the policies and protocols of controlling and restraining others are created, implemented, and monitored. Given the attention paid to instances of force usage seemingly gone badly, many in society have sought answers to the questions about when, why, and how force is used by criminal justice employees. There are some high-quality books which largely examine deadly force. Many skilled researchers have studied various facets of force usage by criminal justice professionals as well as the allied concerns of social justice, organizational behavior, public accountability and many others. Professional organizations within the practitioner community as well as governmental agencies have spent time and effort that reflects the high priority given to the many issues surrounding force usage. All of these efforts are needed but can leave many people bewildered, and it was clear there was an unmet need for an in-depth text on the use of force in criminal justice.

Having taught a university course on the subject of the use of force in criminal justice for several years, I did not find the various available documents and sources useful or relevant to the current student of criminal justice or force usage. I have repeatedly found it necessary to supplement any single document (or even several) with extensive readings. And so I wrote this book for the faculty member, trainer, attorney, or administrator who must explain and give guidance to students, officers, the court, and subordinate managers and supervisors about the when, why, and how of selecting response options including force usage by those we entrust with that authority. One of my purposes in writing the book was to provide an instructor the resources to approach the subject with credibility. Text books addressing criminology, criminal justice, corrections, or law and society serve a purpose by presenting the topic *generally* but with limited discussion of force issues *specifically*.

This text examines the use of force by criminal justice personnel in the U.S. The book examines the various types of force and in what ways they are used as well as in which situations. At the opening, the book considers the use of force within criminal justice and then moves to a discussion of legal issues and selected laws and cases. What flows from a grant of authority to government actors by the public, codified and guided by law, is then examined in regards to using less lethal force and lethal force and how these considerations are addressed by agency policies. Agencies create policy and those who lead departments should understand the concepts covered next in the book about physiological and psychological aspects of force usage. Everything considered in the book to this point must be properly conveyed through well-constructed training. While police use of force in the U.S. is typically where news media accounts are generated, the book provides an examination and insights into the correctional world as well. Therefore, full chapters cover the use of force in law enforcement, the use of force in corrections, and force used by tactical teams, showing the context of force usage by criminal justice personnel. The criminal justice field has continued to increase awareness training for officers on the dynamics and considerations of dealing with the various types of impairments frequently encountered by criminal justice personnel. The text chapter on special populations addresses these issues in detail. The final chapter discusses key considerations in force usage by human officers and the relatively new phenomenon of body-worn cameras (BWCs) and the ubiquity of recording of officer actions.

We are in an era that espouses "intelligence-led" strategies and applied research to assist agency administrators and guide policymakers. The book presents many examples of the central role of policy and the need to ensure that it is clearly communicated to employees. It is important to consider policy issues whenever possible in a discussion of operational practices of public agencies.

As a pedagogical matter it was important to provide a scholarly foundation for the examination of force usage by grounding the book in seminal and current literature. This provides readers the opportunity to review additional research. Several recurring chapter features reinforce student learning of concepts: critical-thinking questions; boxed coverage of relevant issues under the title of "What-Why,"; a "Try This" section to suggest further relevant learning activities; a section called "Going Global" examining use of force issues from Western Europe focusing on the United Kingdom as the historical source of much U. S. jurisprudence and the criminal justice system and itself facing concerns about how force is to be used by public safety professionals; and chapter summaries. Student learning objectives (SLOs) are included at the beginning of each chapter. The book includes the ancillaries and features that allow an instructor to effectively teach a course on the use of force in criminal justice. No similar text books provide these or they have only limited ancillaries. The topics addressed in this book are important and of great interest to students and others. The materials, including PowerPoints, chapter outlines, an instructor manual, and more, allow a criminal justice, criminology, or other relevant program the means to offer a popular course that will benefit learners. The material is turn-key. For those who have expertise or familiarity with the subject, the benefit of furnished ancillaries to edit is often quite helpful.

My perspective and approach to this textbook is, I believe, unique. As a hybrid practitioner-academic, it has long been my *raison d'être* to meld the pragmatic and policy issues of criminal justice with the empirical and evidence-based findings of research. I spent my first career as a law enforcement officer working my way up the ranks and subsequently holding many administrative positions while also teaching in the classroom and in the laboratory of defensive tactics rooms as a second and important part of my identity. I had the opportunity to be director of corrections for two Florida counties where I also formed, commanded, and helped train tactical teams, and I was superintendent of two different juvenile detention centers. In addition to my role as a professor, I remain actively involved in consulting and conducting applied research. It is my hope that students, practitioners, instructors, and administrators will find my approach and my thoughts helpful.

ACKNOWLEDGMENTS

My acknowledgments begin where the project began, with consultation and support from my best friend and frequent co-writer Dr. Kimberly McCorkle. I find it hard to imagine completing the project without the moral support as well as editing reviews and content feedback from Kimberly. I am grateful that, as my wife, she provides clarity far beyond the turn of a phrase.

I gratefully acknowledge the effort, time, and acumen provided by the reviewers of the initial proposal. The value that this book ultimately holds is greatly increased by the insights and suggestions these colleagues provided. Every suggestion was carefully considered and many additions and improvements were the result of the reviews. Thanks to Stephen Holmes (University of Central Florida); Daniel Marshall (Anglia Ruskin University, U.K.); Mengyan Dai (Old Dominion University); Howard Williams (Texas State University); Sergeant Ross Hendy (Senior Practitioner Researcher, New Zealand Police, and Visiting Scholar, Institute of Criminology, University of Cambridge, U.K.); and a reviewer from Old Dominion University.

I certainly want to acknowledge my colleagues and friends among the many defensive tactics and force instructors I have shared mat time, coffee, and in-depth conversation with in the more than 35 years that I have taught force concepts and physical techniques to academy recruits and in-service officers in law enforcement and corrections. All of those recruits, officers, and college and university students should also be acknowledged for their efforts and their service. I appreciate the encouragement and support of Greg Moody, Director, George Stone Criminal Justice Training Center, as well as Greg Robichaud and James Cadden, the outstanding defensive tactics coordinators who provide steady leadership and guidance to the cadre of physical skills instructors at George Stone.

I thank Dr. Pam Chester, Editor for Criminal Justice and Criminology at Routledge, for her unfailing warmth and patience and her competent guidance. Looking forward to the next project.

1

CONSIDERING THE USE OF FORCE IN CRIMINAL JUSTICE

STUDENT LEARNING OUTCOMES

- Students will be able to discuss factors observed in use of force situations.
- Students will be able to describe the rate of force usage by criminal justice personnel.
- Students will be able to explain the role of public perception in considering use of force.
- Students will be able to discuss the influence of media in addressing force occurrences.
- Students will be able to explain the authority to use force.

Introduction

Criminal justice practitioners in a democratic society hold unique roles and exercise unique authority. The role of law enforcement officer is at once a servant member of the public and rule enforcer granted the ability to detain others against their will and to use physical force when necessary to do so. Corrections officers in the environment of secure facilities perform the daily task of containing those accused or convicted of violating criminal laws and, again, employ the use of force as deemed necessary in a variety of circumstances. Probation and parole officers interact with offenders in the community, performing duties of counseling, monitoring, and notifying the court when the person under government control but allowed to live in the community violates a condition of his or her probation or parole. Bailiffs and court security officers maintain order in the courtroom and courthouse setting while also being alert to more serious threats. Contract and proprietary security employees in some roles face the potential for resistance within the strict parameters of their jobs. Each of these officers may be called upon or find it necessary to use force while carrying out their responsibilities.

The unique authority exercised by each of these public employees and security employees is the ability to employ force options against others in a free society. Use of force by the state has been contemplated over the last few centuries by political and philosophical thinkers. The rule of law embraced or claimed by most Western democracies includes the need for separating and balancing the powers that govern our public lives. The legislative branch writes laws to permit and restrict actions by public employees. The courts assess compliance with those laws put in place by the various legislative bodies. And although law enforcement officers find their place within the *executive branch*, at the moment force is used or applied the individual uses his *individual* guided discretion to act. In a subsequent chapter we will examine the legal principles, precedents, and basis for the use of force in a free society.

Societies throughout history have needed peacekeepers. Such peacekeepers have taken various forms over the centuries and focus their efforts on many tasks set before them by rulers, governments, and hopefully in modern times increasingly by the citizens themselves. Appropriate markers along the way include roots as far back as Rome's praetorian guard, England's early use of the mutual pledge system made up of tithings and constables governed by shire-reeves, and eventually the first organized police force that was established in London. England is the recognized touchstone for much of America's system of jurisprudence as well as the precursors to developments in policing, jails, and prisons.

American bounty hunters had their origins in the privately employed thief takers paid by the English government for some assignments, though their authority did not extend beyond taking other citizens into custody. Familiar to many people is the image of the British Bobby, the uniformed officer who patrolled the streets of London from the early 1800s forward. The British police force developed as a practical matter as the population in London grew to a point where individual citizens could no longer effectively handle law and order matters with the moderately formal system. A paid force to perform peacekeeping duties and investigate crimes arose to deal with the dense and often impoverished urban areas of large cities entering the industrial era.

The early British police and those of today are still referred to as "Bobbies," named after Sir Robert Peel, England's home secretary largely responsible for getting Parliament to agree to London's first police force. Peel, who lived from 1788 until 1850, also said that administering punishment was not a role for the police but rather for those with special knowledge of corrections. Another Englishman notable for his role in improving the criminal justice system of the day was John Howard, who was born in 1726 and died in 1790. Howard was the high sheriff of Bedfordshire when he toured almost every jail in England, Wales, and Scotland, inspecting their conditions and practices. He argued persuasively that conditions must be improved within prisons and jails and this included an improvement in those individuals selected as the keepers of fellow citizens.

The authority that citizens grant to government extends to a wide range of actions and services. The social contract of Locke, Rousseau and others posits that as citizens we all give up a certain amount of freedom in return for the common goods offered more effectively and efficiently, we suppose, by governmental agencies. Critical among the functions society authorizes a small number of government agencies to carry out is the use of force to accomplish legitimate goals. Kleinig (2014) states that "the social contract authorizes the ethical, efficient, and conditional transfer of a self-defensive and punitive right that we all possess to a social agency or agencies that have been instituted to secure our basic or fundamental rights" (p. 83). We can extend this commentary to add that such agencies develop and employ specialized training and advanced knowledge. With our tacit transfer of authority to such agents and agencies we expect in return competent performance of duty, transparency in policy, and accountability in the use of that authority, especially the use of force.

Kleinig makes extensive use of John Locke's arguments and propositions in addressing legitimate and illegitimate force usage by government agents. This suits our analysis, since jails, prisons, probation, and parole are contemplated in this conceptualization as well as police. The British concept of policing by consent is also representative of the notion of the social contract. The British police were founded by Sir Robert Peel, who inspired the creation of nine principles or instructions to constables. These admonitions emphasized the symbiotic nature of police and the citizenry, and that police must have the respect and trust of the public which comes through cooperation rather than instilling fear.

There are many potential variables in use of force encounters (Bolger, 2015). While categories of use of force encounters can be described for convenient analysis or illustrative purposes, the mix of static and dynamic factors known or present in each individual event are considered when attempting an evaluation after the fact. Consider the following:

> An inmate refuses a correction officer's instruction to move from point A to point B. Is this a somewhat known convicted offender in a prison setting who is already in a cell? Is the subject a completely unknown arrestee in the booking area of a jail? What are the relative sizes of the subject and officer? Are there other officers present? Are there additional inmates in proximity to the encounter?
>
> A patrol officer tells someone he is under arrest and to turn around and place his hands together behind him. Is the arrestee a 13 year-old shoplifter, a bank robber caught after a chase, an angry bar patron who exchanged punches with someone?
>
> The court bailiff notices a man who came in and sat down during an ongoing trial. The man appears to become increasingly agitated. The bailiff asks the man to step out to the corridor to speak for a minute only to receive a blank/hostile/pained/confused stare.
>
> What about the uniformed but unarmed security officer at the local big box retail store? As a shoplifter runs toward the exit, knocking down an elderly female patron on his way, what actions are authorized in that moment? What can be done prior to the arrival of a law enforcement officer?

There is quite literally no way to describe all of the varied circumstances that can make up the officer–individual encounter. With that said, the book will describe the categories and many of the considerations for the use of force in criminal justice and by its personnel and surrogates. This can be referred to as a 360-degree response options model – considering all relevant factors the officer is conscious of when a response or force choice is selected or occurs as a reaction. And it should be noted at this early point that a force encounter is fluid, dynamic, and as such can ebb and flow and fold back on itself as new factors come to bear including second-to-second reactions and decisions made by the person and the officer who is trying to control that person, as well as other individuals who may become involved at any given moment.

We must also consider the actions of quasi-governmental actors working under contract to a governmental entity, such as private security manning the metal detector at your local courthouse, the so-called bounty hunter or skip tracer of a local bail bond company, and the fully private security representatives of companies and corporations. Another obvious, and well-publicized, example includes the employees of the numerous for-profit correctional facilities that exist across the country.

While contemporary public interest in the United States has once again been directed toward the general use of force and specific actions of law enforcement officers, the accountability of our employees has been of interest for many decades. Holding public safety personnel accountable for all of their many actions while carrying out their duties, is a function of elected and appointed leaders, and at times the courts. The actions pass time in the news cycle and are attention-getters for the media, are matters of academic research interest, and are keenly important to the individual who finds himself the recipient of a force action.

Individuals who have the power or authority to exercise control over others are guided by rules and procedures, reviewed against these procedures by supervisors, and potentially held criminally or civilly responsible when they intentionally or carelessly misuse or misapply their authority. Often agencies and individual employees may be held to legal account even when objectively and by policy and law they have not acted improperly. Black (1976, 1980) conceptualized the use of force by police as the application of law.

What We Think We Know about the Use of Force

Most people in society have a view or conceptualization of what they think of as acceptable use of force by public employees or private employees with duties that may require the use of some force. Attitudes about the use of force may vary by demographic group, or by profession, or geographic location within the country, or based perhaps on previous experience with individuals wielding the authority to use force. Contacts between force-employing individuals in the public can form, break, and reform views and opinions with significantly differing results both short-term and long-term.

The consideration of force issues is a complex and prolonged journey – neither a finite trip nor a discrete task. An officer or actor in a force scenario operates within what can be envisioned as a 360-degree response options environment. Inputs are coming in to the human officer in various ways through the conscious and largely unconscious or automatic sensing systems. If the actor is an employee of an agency, a different set of considerations will be utilized by the latter to evaluate the actions of the former. Media reporting and public discourse may ensue that consider an apparently defined "event" (such as someone being shot by a police officer in the course of duty) by yet different criteria of the lay-observer who may also bring a personal bias for or against the concept of government force without regard to particular factual circumstances. Criminal charges may be filed against various persons involved in the force scenario. Subsequent to the resolution of criminal charges, or in their absence, a civil action may follow by one or more parties against one or more other parties including the governmental entity or private corporation that employs the actual people involved. We take up these issues in greater depth in the next chapter.

A nuanced understanding of the dynamics of the force situation in all of its components and fluidity is rarely possible in the media or public discourse environment. The review conducted by an officer's agency, or one called upon by the employing agency, is also not a review that necessarily delves deep into dynamics; it is satisfied instead by an assessment of whether a use of force was within agency policy or established law. While important considerations, these may not suffice for a fuller examination that can come as a further inquiry by a separate government entity (say, the U.S. Justice Department) or a civil action that retrospectively seeks a possible accounting by other than the parameters of *criminal* law and agency policy. In addition, agencies often desire a tactical debriefing to determine if new or revised training is in order, if adjustments to policy should take place, or even whether the addition of new equipment is needed. Always in considering use of force events is the centrality of the actors. This will include the employee as well as one or more subjects with whom the employee interacts.

It would likely be impossible to identify a person in Western democratic society who has not seen a significant number of video replays of officers restraining or using force on someone. Add to this the volume of police procedurals and movies depicting acts of struggling, fighting, and violence Hollywood-style and you have a wide, but not deep, pool of "experience" that informs the average citizen's perception of arrest and restraint by government employees. This is a good spot to remind readers that while an anecdote can serve to illustrate a point, it does not by itself represent the universe of actions on a particular subject. Empirically we have to consider the context of infrequent force usage by officers and the factors affecting those events.

Body-worn camera usage, just as the car camera, has the potential to provide additional information regarding many officer activities, including force usage. Tactical teams in corrections and law enforcement have long encouraged the use of video recording of actions. Such tactical team events are, however, by definition ones that provide some time opportunity to "gear up" including the designated team member to record the operation. Technology cost reduction that occurs for most common devices has come to the personally-worn camera. Before laptops became ubiquitous in law enforcement, mobile data terminals (MDT) sat firmly affixed in many squad cars around the country. Before this, corner call boxes preceded two-way radios in cars and walkie-talkies with adequate range to make them useful. Similarly, dashboard cameras were not dismountable and able to be easily carried about as officers performed their duties. Fixed-placement cameras in correctional facilities captured much of the goings-on in the common areas of buildings and grounds, but blind spots for technology and normal line of sight are the bane of every jail and prison and their staff.

Now comes a point in the evolution of conducting an officer's business that his efforts can be aided and enhanced through computing power, multiple defensive tools, and the body-worn camera. The choice to spend limited department funds on any tools and technology is a policy one made by agency or governmental leadership. It does not necessarily follow that because a device is believed to be helpful that it will be purchased and rapidly deployed. Given the diversity in size and funding resources of the thousands of law enforcement and corrections entities, commitment to such purchases must be carefully considered. Small and mid-sized agencies have accepted public donations of funds for ballistic vests and even canines because no government agency has all of the funds it might need to equip officers with all available technology and tools. While the courts have determined that lack of funds is not a defense to failure-to-train, there are no universal mandates on specific equipment or technology that an agency must purchase or utilize. These are conversations and fiscal decisions that each community and agency must face. The International Association of

Chiefs of Police (IACP) noted in its 2014 Technology Policy Framework: "Just because a technology *can* be implemented, does not mean that it *should* be" (p. 1).

The President's Task Force on 21st Century Policing (2015) has implicitly and explicitly discussed the ramifications of force usage, vis-à-vis the community. PERF's guiding principles (2016) provide strong recommendations to administrators on issues related to force and community relations. What then is proper force? When is force used to excess? And when is force employed by governmental or security actors inappropriate or unlawful?

Wherever You Go, There You Are

The recruitment, hiring, training, development, and retention of employees, in total, is a resource intensive proposition. Evaluating the potential of applicants to perform duties in law enforcement, corrections, or private security positions is foundational to the organization's success. Throughout the on-boarding of criminal justice and security employees, those responsible for selection, training, and supervising those hired want to ensure the employees' success through the right tools for the job. In criminal justice roles, the tools are often soft-skills (e.g., critical thinking, fast adaptation, verbal persuasion, non-verbal recognition and projection). Officers take in information, they arrive on-scene, they observe and perceive further, they react or respond as called for, they reflect and record. Hiring and developing humans to accomplish tasks involving the complexities and problems of other humans is not only challenging, but can be dangerous. Without question, the ability to use force is a factor that shapes an officer and is shaped in turn by that officer.

The selection of officers is guided by state commissions or federal agency policy as to fitness. This encompasses physical, psychological, and background. Often levels of education may be required, as in bachelor degrees for federal law enforcement agencies, and certainly minimum levels of training for local, state, and federal officers before going into the field. Selection is the culmination of assessing potential. Through the various tests employed and the examination of a person's background an agency arrives at a decision to hire a person, complete necessary training of the individual, orient that person to agency policy and approach, and place them into a position to do the work prescribed for the position. Procedural competence in carrying out this process allows a degree of confidence in the initial stages of an employee's time with a department. Field-training programs place the new employee into situations and tasks with varying levels of difficulty while accompanied by a more experienced incumbent with the dual goals of deepening experience and training of the recruit and assessing progress toward the ability to work independently in the job.

RESEARCH RESULTS

In the wake of high-profile shootings of citizens by police, the public, the media, and law enforcement themselves are asking whether lethal force usage by police is on the rise. Campbell, Nix, and Maguire (2017) examined data of the recent past to determine whether there was any credence to claims of such an increase. Their work looked at data which indicated "random short-term fluctuations that are often misinterpreted as evidence of substantively meaningful trends" (p. 1). They observed that there was neither an increase nor a decrease in fatal use of force incidents.

In addition to assessing potential, the agency may have only statistical information about "who" makes the most effective officer. And of course this varies based on what task is under consideration. Carmichel and Kent (2015) studied 15 years of data on police killings across Canada's 39 largest cities indicating an association of minority population size reaching a point at which declines in deaths were found. Their research also supported the expectation that more female officers in agencies were associated with less use of lethal force. This is not a prescription or a simple explanation of force usage, but an interesting correlation found by the researchers.

Who Is In Charge of the Encounter?

From the comfort of our living room couch or judge's chambers, it is impossible to make a sound declaration of evaluative judgment based on a nine-second smartphone snippet that is proxy for all the dynamics and factors affecting an event and process in which force was involved. Yet often this is the level of examination that passes for evaluation in the public or political discourse. Few people are sufficiently educated about the myriad aspects of those jobs where employees are authorized to wield force. Fewer still may routinely exercise the dispassionate objectivity necessary to examine a force usage event and incorporate all relevant factors – physical, legal, policy-wise, and psychological – to arrive at a finding and judgment. This judgment may include whether officer actions were within policy and whether policy or training should be updated.

Important in considering the use of force by criminal justice personnel are the attitudes of a society's citizens. Western democracies, generally, accept the legitimate and occasional use of force by law enforcement and other officers to accomplish legitimate functions, though we look to police to use force in accord with the law and with some sense of proportion or restraint (Cyr, 2016). On the other hand, citizens may resist, criticize, and call for changes when incidents occur that appear to involve exceeding the limits of granted authority or performing control tasks in a way that seems excessive. Waddington et al. (2009) addressed this issue as they examined differences in firearm usage among various countries. Cultures hold unique views on government authority and action. Subcultures within a society can also hold a more sensitized view of police actions based on historical mistreatment.

The various people within each interaction setting have influence on the course of the interaction and the ultimate outcome. Each person, including the officer, is a mix of motivations and attitudes about the issue at hand, but also about subsequent issues that arise as an interaction unfolds. This includes feelings and emotions that may smolder and suddenly burst into flame or be quenched or managed by the actions of the officer in the event. Yet it is the reality of the unpredictable in human behavior that is ever-present in the mind of the officer. Most people would quickly answer the question posed by the section heading with "The officer is in charge, of course." But this is not always the case and the subjective reality of believing one or the other is "in charge" is suspect to begin with. At any moment an individual inside (or outside) an immediate interaction may act. If the action is a hostile one, it may come with little discernible warning. The human officer, unable to read minds or intentions ahead of overt behavior, is left catching up to a fast ball that has already been hurled.

Officers are taught to assert control over situations quickly so that the people involved do not become unmanageable or more out of control. Officers will use verbal directions, including tone and volume, to try and establish the central role of a dispute or authority in communicating with a single person or allied group of individuals. If the communication between an officer and another person is not immediately one of conflict, she will use active listening and demonstrate courtesy while maintaining self-control and hopefully self-awareness of any nonverbal communication that she is giving off or that the subject is revealing. A crisis situation that an officer enters may require strident directions to moderate conflict between parties and attempt to gain control of a situation. The ability of an officer to recognize verbal and nonverbal signals from people is inextricably bound with her ability to guide an interaction to the extent possible and maintain safety in many circumstances. Effective directions and attempts to assert control can be negatively impacted by the emotions, intentions, and mental state of the individuals the officer encounters (PERF, 2012). To many people, an individual may appear to be out of control. What they observe may be the result of intense emotion and behaviors that show an individual is overwrought. The person may be yelling and cursing, waving his arms, or pacing back and forth in a highly agitated state. To someone who is inexperienced in the ways of people in stressful or crisis situations, this behavioral description may lead the person to believe the upset individual needs to be physically controlled. Perhaps the person is in the emergency room waiting area of a hospital and has just learned that a loved one has been seriously injured. Perhaps the person is in his home, and is highly upset about a family matter. Or perhaps an inmate has just learned some bad news about a spouse leaving him or a lengthy sentence being imposed. Each set of circumstances when considered at arms-length as a hypothetical would result in most people quickly understanding why the involved person would behave in an agitated way. It would also be appropriate to assume that the distressed individual is not about to assault someone. Once again, an inexperienced person entering the scene may not immediately grasp the situation from the perspective of the upset individual and believe that he or she should quickly control the person as they are perceived to be a threat to others. The situation may now deteriorate.

Situational awareness by officers is very important when encountering people you already know or believe to be angry or disorderly. The officer's belief may be founded upon the behaviors she observes, or influenced (consciously or unconsciously) by the race or ethnicity of subjects, the numbers of subjects, the immediate environment and time of day, and many other factors. Such factors may be mitigated as time passes during an interaction and the officer gathers greater amounts of information (Kahn, Steele, McMahon, and Stewart, 2016). Given the nature of many interactions that begin with unknown people and circumstances, the use of force to control a situation is not unexpected. A differential response based on race (or gender) may stand out.

Research and Science in the Use of Force

Citizens and law enforcement agencies do not entirely speak past one another, but there are issues of perspective that are important to consider. Statistically it is a fact that the threatened or actual use of force during interactions with the public is small as a percentage of the overall number of officer citizen interactions that occur each year. The Bureau of Justice Statistics (BJS) (2015) reports that for American society as a whole, contact from 2002 to 2011 involved an average of 44 million people aged 16 or older each year. Contact may be initiated by the citizen or by the officer. The BJS notes that contacts may occur in many of the following ways:

> police provide services to community members; residents seek information or report crimes to
> police officers; residents are passengers or drivers during a traffic stop; police could stop residents

in public places for suspicious behavior, make arrests, search residents, their vehicles or their homes ...

(BJS, 'Police–Public Contacts', https://www.bjs.gov/index.cfm?ty=tp&tid=70)

BJS draws a representative sample of the nation's households but does not include data from law enforcement agencies for the survey. During the latest survey period:

An estimated 1.6 percent experienced the threat or use of nonfatal force by police, including shouting, cursing, threatening force, pushing or grabbing, hitting or kicking, using pepper spray, using an electroshock weapon, pointing a gun, or using other force during the most recent contact.

The report goes on to note that 44 percent of those who said they *had* experienced the threat or use of force (1.6 percent),

were more likely to have had multiple contacts with police than those who did not experience force (28%). Nearly 75% of those who said police used force during the contact described it as excessive.

The problems associated with self-report survey data are well known, but even if the 1.6 percent figure is taken as representative, it is clear that force during citizen–officer contacts is not frequent. A national database for force events does not exist. There is not even a standard format of agency collection methods or forms, though there appears to be considerable similarity on items covered by policies and use of force forms (IACP, 2012; Hough and Tatum, 2012).

One might expect that a great deal of research has been conducted into predicting assaults on officers. While there is a broad selection of training materials that speak to pre-attack signals, there is sparse academic research and few validated studies (Johnson, 2015). The information taught in recruit classes and available through in-service officer training is without question beneficial to agencies as they construct policy and train officers. The practical limitation of such knowledge, however, is that much like the dictum regarding statistics, knowing about global issues may not provide specific knowledge to ward off an attack in the instant when it comes. Officers are assaulted and sometimes killed during arrest situations, responding to a variety of disturbances (Swedler, Kercher, Simmons, and Pollack, 2014), and in various circumstances not easily predicted to turn violent. Intimate partner violence (IPV) calls and some other "domestic disturbances" have had deadly consequences for law enforcement, with 116 law enforcement officers being killed in such calls between 1996 and 2010 (Kercher, Swedler, Pollack, and Webster, 2013).

WHAT-WHY

Each year the FBI compiles a report titled "Law Enforcement Officers Killed and Assaulted." The report includes officers killed accidentally while on the job. In 2015, this report reflected data from nearly 12,000 law enforcement agencies policing 75 percent of the US population. For this year recorded assaults on law enforcement officers topped 50,000 incidents. Close to 30 percent of those officers sustained an injury.

The year 2016 saw an increase in the number of officers killed in the line of duty. The number was the highest in the past 20 years. While information of this sort is consistently collected, there is no corresponding central repository for information or statistics about the number of corrections officers, probation officers, or juvenile justice employees assaulted or injured each year.

For research to be comprehensive, and ideally lead to effective recommendations, it is important to combine legal, theoretical, and issues of criminal justice practices together. While it is common to hear the phrase "best practices," the reality is that practices so labeled are merely the ones most frequently seen. Academic research and the research and work of professional organizations contribute much to our understanding of the many aspects of the use of force by various actors in democratic societies. Some researchers apply a single lens to examine this topic or any other topic for that matter. The perspective may be sociological, psychological, legal, or an asserted purely pragmatic one. A deep understanding of the use of force in society requires a holistic view if it can be managed. Much the same way that the modern criminologist avoids a blinkered view of crime causation to that which she is most familiar, many sources must be sampled and weighed to present a balanced and thoughtful view of this topic. It is important to examine all sides and dimensions of the use of force. Public policy analysts, for example, generally pursue factual information in a comprehensive fashion before offering options and recommendations to elected and political leaders who will use value-weighting to make final policy selections.

A comprehensive comparison of the use of force by criminal justice and public safety entities from around the world is challenging. While this book is aimed at a Western democratic audience, it is instructive to examine and compare the use of governmental authority and specifically the use of coercive force from other countries. Even if the book were comparative in nature, the limitations on available data as well as challenging issues in regards to access and transparency would necessarily limit the ability to comment broadly, as we are able to do in the United States and various other stable modern democracies.

The officer operates within the concept of a vulnerable environment. This must be joined with viable and effective defensive/offensive actions. From an academic perspective, accepting certain risks in constructing interaction scenarios is a given. Law enforcement and other officers are not called upon to visit a family picnic for a pleasant meal. Rather, they are summoned to the scene of discord and disorder and tasked with attempting to control the behavior of people in less than ideal circumstances. Though the use of force is statistically infrequent, officers and citizens, including inmates, are injured. Though force usage is relatively rare, this seems in tension with the perception of many members of the public.

Researchers and professional organizations have devoted a great deal of attention to this most visible aspect of the criminal justice officer and agency role. One such effort was the symposium on the use of force conducted by the International Association of Chiefs of Police (IACP) in 2012. The subsequent report, titled *Emerging Use of Force Issues: Balancing Public and Officer Safety*, was issued jointly by the IACP and the Community Oriented Policing Services (COPS) of the U.S. Department of Justice. These symposium participants examined topics including:

- Current use of force issues and concerns of law enforcement leaders
- Use of force policy and training advancement over the past five years

- Recent use of force incidents or issues that have affected law enforcement approach
- Use of force litigation and risk management from a local agency perspective
- New and emerging research on use of force at the university and law enforcement level
- Concerns about use of force that merit further exploration and investigation.

(IACP/COPS, 2012)

The discussants worked with a continuum of "pre-incident, point of incident, and post-incident variables" (p. 7) to use of force. The listing of variables was grouped as follows

Pre-Incident

- Review of policy effectiveness
- Leadership role
- Review of training effectiveness
- Community education
- Citizen input
- Utilization of accountability software
- Research
- Existing standards/case law.

At Point of Incident

- Internal affairs investigation
- Press management
- Criminal investigation
- Community outreach
- Agency transparency.

Post-Incident

- Accountability
- Dissemination of information
- Adjustments/improvements
- Policy upgrades
- Training upgrades
- Public forums/meetings to address incident.

(IACP symposium advisory group, created at the January 5, 2011 planning meeting)

The recommendations summary of the report provides suggested actions and notes that such systemic efforts by agencies would require funding, likely from the federal government. The list in its entirety is copied here from the report:

- Develop a model communications strategy for law enforcement on the topic of use of force
- Develop a national media guide to inform the public regarding the necessity to use appropriate force in furtherance of public safety

- Develop a sustainable online resource library detailing programs and summaries of approaches that have proven to build better relationships between police and their communities
- Propose national use of force reporting standards
- Collect data and conduct annual national use of force analysis
- Conduct evaluation of use of force issues for the mid-size and small police agency
- Charge a single government sponsored entity with responsibility for disseminating real-time data describing violence directed at police
- Develop and fund a use of force management institute for police leaders
- Develop use of force management publication for city/town or municipal governance
- Survey to determine nationally the current spectrum of use of force training
- Develop model in-service use of force training
- Validate use of force in-service training in pilot departments
- Survey to evaluate the use of force mindset of police
- Support efforts such as the Department of Justice's Officer Safety and Wellness Group, IACP's National Center for the Prevention of Violence Against the Police (NCPVAP) and the FBI's Law Enforcement Officer Killed and Assaulted (LEOKA) program to collect, evaluate, discuss, and publish real-time, data that speaks to trends in violence directed against police.

Incidents of violence against police are documented, as almost all data, in a largely decentralized fashion. Similarly, complaints against the police to be read in the proper context and with a broad aim to improve overall performance, would be more effective if gathered in a consistent manner. The Bureau of Justice Assistance (BJA) has made attempts along these lines, but evidence of serious data flaws still persists (Hickman and Poore, 2016). Early warning systems (EWS) gather information on officer activities such as complaints, use of force incidents, arrests, and more. If analyzed and tended to consistently, such methods can be useful in identifying officers for retraining, counseling, or disciplinary efforts and measures.

GOING GLOBAL

Researchers in the United Kingdom examined the use of less lethal force usage by English and Welsh police in the period between 2007 and 2011 (Payne-James, Rivers, Green, and Johnston, 2014). The researchers asked police agencies about the number of deployments of incapacitant spray, TASER, impact rounds, and armed response units (ARU). In addition to the numbers, they looked at any resulting medical issues reported and whether those medical complications necessitated a medical examination.

Of the 50 police services from which information was requested, only two could provide information about medical needs following deployment of less lethal force. The gathering of data on police use of force in the U.K. has similar problems to those of the United States. Given the level of public scrutiny and the need to be able to determine trends and to fashion effective policies, more consistent reporting of force seems warranted.

THE UNFRIENDLY SKIES

A questionable use of physical force captured a good bit of the news cycle early in April of 2017 when security officers/aviation law enforcement officers physically dragged an already-seated airline passenger from an airplane to make room for airline employees. Video by other passengers predictably went viral, drawing attention to many different issues, but also highlighting a judgment to remove a person by force (referred to as being "re-accommodated" by the airline's CEO) in circumstances not involving a physical threat to anyone or falling within a typical force scenario.

This incident was quickly followed with other smartphone videos and reports of friction and occasional violence or angry outbursts between passengers or between passengers and airline employees. If airline employees sought to remove someone from a flight or prevent them from boarding an aircraft, airport security or law enforcement was typically summoned.

What other steps could airline employees and law enforcement have attempted?

Summary

Considering the use of force is not a narrow task that examines or comments on the specific application of a technique or the taking of an action during a lone interaction between an employee who is legally authorized to use force and a person living in or incarcerated in democratic society. Considered reflection involves appreciation of historic pathways to the present day, knowledge of psychological and physiological factors affecting humans – nested within a specific event context, and intellectual grasp of the limitations of human officers and individuals to start, stop, or redirect actions once they are set in motion.

Officers, agencies, citizen advocacy groups, labor unions and their representatives, elected and appointed government officials, media organizations, medical and mental health professionals, and others all have a voice in the important conversation about the authority, responsibility, and accountability of using force to compel or suppress the behavior of people in the community. People in a community may support their public safety entities to a greater or lesser degree based on their perceptions of those agencies' professionalism, transparency of policy and practices, and pursuit of procedural justice (Wells, 2007). A jail or prison corrections worker may try to break up a fight or conduct the forced removal of an inmate from one location to another. A patrol officer may face a person who foresees impending incarceration and reacts with violence. A probation or parole officer or court bailiff may suddenly be faced with an uncooperative individual in the typically well-ordered environs of an office situated in the community or in the courtroom.

Policy must provide guidance on implementing or applying force that the law allows. Training must accompany the entrustment of the authority and tools to use force as well as specific procedures on *how* to use that force or device. Reviewing individual instances of force usage and monitoring to ensure that if a pattern of force usage develops it is examined in a timely fashion to protect citizens, officers, and agencies as well as to maintain the trust of the community. Review must be systematic not sporadic, and such activities should contribute to a sound agency culture of professionalism and integrity, as well as serve as feedback to training staff, researchers, and policy-makers.

It is appropriate to note briefly that some consider that the use of investigative or arrest authority by law enforcement or probation officers, or the bringing of rule violation sanctions by correctional officers, may in some ways be considered a use of force even without a physical restraint component. The private use of force has been viewed, at least by various legislatures, with permissiveness, without clear boundaries around what may be defended by force and when and how this may be constrained by the authority to use force historically granted to government (Dsouza, 2015). Over the past 50 years, research into police procedures has increased. Specific law enforcement and corrections tactics have not been well studied. There are no magic formulas for ensuring safety for either the officer or others.

KEY TERMS

Use of force
Order maintenance
Social contract

Discussion Questions

1. What does the public understand about order maintenance?
2. How would you characterize what most people think they know about the use of force in criminal justice?
3. What are some of the reasons why it is important that people understand the dynamics involved in the use of force?
4. What impact can research have on policies that address force usage in criminal justice?

TRY THIS

Examine several law enforcement and correctional agency websites. Try to locate the use of force policy. List and discuss the factors that you found within the policy.

References

Black, D. J. (1976). *The behavior of law.* New York: Academic Press.

Black, D. J. (1980). *The manners and customs of the police.* New York: Academic Press.

Bolger, P. (2015). Just following orders: a meta-analysis of the correlates of American police officer use of force decisions. *American Journal of Criminal Justice*, 40(3), 466–492.

Campbell, B. A., Nix, J., and Maguire, E. R. (2017). Is the number of citizens fatally shot by police increasing in the post-Ferguson era? *Crime and Delinquency*, 1–23. doi:10.1177/0011128716686343.

Carmichael, J. and Kent, S. (2015). The use of lethal force by Canadian police officers: assessing the influence of female police officers and minority threat explanations on police shootings across large cities. *American Journal of Criminal Justice*, 40(4), 703–721.

Cyr, K. (2016). Police use of force: assessing necessity and proportionality. *Alberta Law Review*, 53(3), 663–679.

Dsouza, M. (2015). Retreat, submission, and the private use of force. *Oxford Journal of Legal Studies*, 35(4), 727–753.

Hickman, M. J. and Poore, J. E. (2016). National data on citizen complaints about police use of force: data quality concerns and the potential (mis)use of statistical evidence to address police agency conduct. *Criminal Justice Policy Review*, 27(5), 455–479.

Hough, R. M. and Tatum, K. M. (2012). An examination of Florida policies on force continuums. *Policing: An International Journal of Police Strategies and Management*, 35, 39–54.

IACP (International Association of Chiefs of Police). (2012). *Emerging use of force issues: balancing public and officer safety.* Alexandria, VA: Author.

IACP (International Association of Chiefs of Police). (2014). *Technology policy framework.* Alexandria, VA: Author.

Johnson, R. R. (2015). Perceptions of interpersonal social cues predictive of violence among police officers who have been assaulted. *Journal of Police and Criminal Psychology*, 30, 87–93.

Kahn, K. B., Steele, J. S., McMahon, J. M., and Stewart, G. (2016). How suspect race affects police use of force in an interaction over time. *Law and Human Behavior.* Online first, October 21. doi:10.1037/lhb0000218.

Kercher, C., Swedler, D. I., Pollack, K. M., and Webster, D. W. (2013). Homicides of law enforcement officers responding to domestic disturbance calls. *Injury Prevention* (1353–8047), 19(5), 331–335.

Kleinig, J. (2014). Legitimate and illegitimate uses of police force. *Criminal Justice Ethics*, 33(2), 83–103.

Payne-James, J., Rivers, E., Green, P., and Johnston, A. (n.d). Trends in less-lethal use of force techniques by police services within England and Wales: 2007–2011. *Forensic Science Medicine and Pathology*, 10(1), 50–55.

PERF (Police Executive Research Forum). (2012). *An integrated approach to de-escalation and minimizing use of force* (Critical Issues in Policing Series). Washington, DC: Author.

PERF (Police Executive Research Forum). (2016). *Guiding principles on use of force.* Critical Issues in Policing series. Washington, DC: Author.

President's Task Force on 21st Century Policing. (2015). *Final report of the President's Task Force on 21st Century Policing.* Washington, DC: Office of Community Oriented Policing Services.

Swedler, D. I., Kercher, C., Simmons, M. M., and Pollack, K. M. (2014). Occupational homicide of law enforcement officers in the US, 1996–2010. *Injury Prevention* (1353–8047), 20(1), 35–40.

U.S. Department of Justice (2015). *Police use of nonfatal force, 2002–2011.* NCJ 249216. Washington, DC: Bureau of Justice Statistics.

U.S. Department of Justice, Federal Bureau of Investigation, Criminal Justice Information Services Division. (2016). *Law enforcement officers killed and assaulted, 2015.* Washington, DC: Bureau of Justice Statistics.

Waddington, P. J., Adang, O., Baker, D., Birkbeck, C., Feltes, T., Gerardo Gabaldón, L., and Stenning, P. (2009). Singing the same tune? International continuities and discontinuities in how police talk about using force. *Crime, Law and Social Change*, 52(2), 111–138.

Wells, W. (2007). Type of contact and evaluations of police officers: the effects of procedural justice across three types of police-citizen contacts. *Journal of Criminal Justice*, 35, 612–621.

2

LAW AND THE USE OF FORCE

CHAPTER OUTLINE

Introduction
U.S. Constitution
Federal law
State law
Summary
Features: What-Why, Going Global
Key Terms
Discussion Questions
Try This
References

STUDENT LEARNING OUTCOMES

- Students will be able to analyze force situations for legal ramifications.
- Students will be able to contrast federal and state legal mandates regarding the use of force.
- Students will be able to critique case law influence on criminal justice practices.
- Students will be able to interpret trends in legal decisions addressing force usage.
- Students will be able to explain the hypothesized dynamic of extralegal factors in the use of force.

Introduction

The concepts and techniques of use of force within criminal justice are typically referred to as one of the four high liability areas of training officers to fulfill their duties. The other three are emergency vehicle operation, medical first responder, and firearms. Each of these components of training at basic recruit academies is accorded a significant block of hours to reflect the importance and complexity of the topics. Training officers in the use of firearms generally receives the greatest number of hours even with the recognition that most officers will not use their firearm to combat a threat during their career. As with other areas of the law, statutes and administrative codes addressing the use of force provide broad guidance that may be expanded at successive levels of jurisdiction and through agency policies.

The ideas found or interpreted within the legal structure of the United States act as guidance to criminal justice employees as well as the basis for liability sanctions, both criminal and civil. The law constrains. The law changes. Criminal justice personnel must know the law. Yet the law did not spring forth whole in its commentary or mandates on the actions of governmental actors. For most of the country's history, law enforcement has been the responsibility of state and local officers. This, among many other peculiarities of American jurisprudence, left officials at the federal, state, and local levels adhering to a variety of rules, laws and practices until well into the 20th century. English common law was the foundation of the system of laws in the United States. That influence still permeates the American system in a variety of ways. In the early days of the Republic, a relatively weak central government as well as a commitment to state sovereignty on most issues of governance resulted in little interaction with federal courts regarding the exercise of public safety functions throughout the country. Common law gave way to stricter guidance by the courts based on the U.S. Constitution.

Laws have also acted as the manifestation of reform efforts brought on by the abuse of power, the lack of clear direction to public agencies, or the general trend of professionalization within the public service more broadly. Citizens make judgments about the legitimacy of their criminal justice agencies based on how they conduct themselves as well as how effective they are in carrying out tasks. Administrations within cities and counties, in state capital houses, and in Washington DC change with some regularity, which emphasizes the importance of the legal basis for action and restraint realized through the legal codes. It is generally the case that the development of law takes time and cooperation among lawmakers to arrive at consensus. The time frame typical of legislation imposes an important check on swift changes of policies and rules that the executive branch may attempt.

Applying the U.S. Constitution

Under the concept of federalism, the U.S. system of government consists of shared power between the federal and state governments. At the core of this shared system is the U.S. Constitution, which established through Article VI, also known as the Supremacy Clause, that it would serve as "the supreme law of the land." This means that no state law can violate the U.S. Constitution. There are numerous provisions of the Constitution that are relevant to a discussion of the legal complexities of the use of force. With the 1868 adoption of the 14th Amendment came the beginning of the due process provisions protecting "life, liberty or property" extending to *states'* citizens. After the adoption of the 14th Amendment, Congress passed legislation to implement protections of life, liberty, and property. Title 42 of the U.S. Code, Section 1983, and Title 18, Sections 241, and 242, followed a few years later in 1871 to provide for civil and criminal remedy, respectively, of violations of the 14th Amendment. Due process considerations around issues within or addressed by the Bill of Rights began to be addressed, and over the next century touched on a variety of concerns, with specific relief for states' citizens as Section 1983 addressed violations by agents acting "under color of state law."

The Supreme Court eventually began to selectively incorporate portions of the Bill of Rights into the 14th Amendment to bind the states as well as the federal government. Importantly, 4th Amendment searches and seizures were incorporated and had to stand the test of objective reasonableness. In the United States, a firmly established (if not easily defined) concept in the use of force by law enforcement is that of "objective reasonableness." We want to know: was the subjective decision/action of an officer, objectively reasonable? This is not to be based on the movie-going public's "understanding" of the use of force. Rather, a careful review of everything known to the officer at the moment he or she acted can help provide a basis for making a determination of whether a use of force was justified.

The use of force by law enforcement is considered a seizure and so constitutionality turns on the reasonableness of the force (seizure). *Monroe v. Pape* effectively blocked most federal suits against state and local agencies as these entities were not considered "natural persons." In the 1967 case of *Pierson v. Ray*, the U.S. Supreme Court espoused a defense of qualified immunity to individual officers acting in good faith within the scope of their employment by a law enforcement agency. *Monroe v. Pape* was partially reversed in the 1978 Supreme Court decision in *Monell v. New York City Department of Social Services*. Over the past 40 years, *Monell v. New York City Department of Social Services* developed great importance for agencies who the U.S. Supreme Court said could be held liable for their *policies* (or the lack of a policy) which caused a constitutional harm to an individual.

With the number and functions of federal law enforcement agencies increasing, and with no comparable federal statute to serve the purposes of Section 1983, the Supreme Court decided a case that allowed officers in federal agencies to be sued just as their state and local colleagues were (*Bivens v. Six Unknown Named Agents of the Federal Bureau of Narcotics*, 1971).

Correctional Considerations

After an individual is taken into custody, but prior to a conviction, 14th Amendment due process claims arise, which examine an officer's motivation in the use of force rather than the objective reasonableness of the 4th Amendment. The due process clause of the 14th Amendment is generally viewed through a lens of what "shocks the conscience" referred to in Johnson v. Glick (1973). For convicted inmates, 8th Amendment issues arising from claims of cruel and unusual punishment can address the treatment of a *sentenced* person in a correctional facility or program. The Supreme Court established a distinct consideration for those who have already passed the criminal prosecution stage where different rights are provided.

While the courts were generally hesitant to insert themselves into matters traditionally left to correctional administrators, this has changed since the 1970s as it became more obvious that monitoring practices and in some cases reviewing and directing policies would prevent harms and improve overall correctional system outcomes. Estelle v. Gamble (1976) was a Texas prison case that established the legal concept of "deliberate indifference." Deliberate indifference has been invoked in cases challenging health and medical care issues, including the conscious disregard of an injury to an inmate. While this phrase has struggled for clear definition as many such labels do, the court did articulate a contrast with negligence. The Wex legal dictionary of Cornell University's Legal Information Institute defines negligence this way:

A failure to behave with the level of care that someone of ordinary prudence would have exercised under the same circumstances. The behavior usually consists of actions, but can also consist of omissions when there is some duty to act (e.g., a duty to help victims of one's previous conduct).

Some of the suits initiated by inmates under Section 1983 concern the conditions of their confinement, access to the courts, and excessive force, among others. Ross (2013) puts it this way:

> Prisoners commonly file section 1983 lawsuits seeking to gain some type of monetary award or equitable relief. In these lawsuits, the prisoners generally complain about the manner in which officials treated him or her, challenging the constitutionality of the treatment or conditions of confinement, or contesting a correctional practice or rule. Other prisoners may file lawsuits to break up the monotony of prison life.
>
> *(p. 307)*

Use of force that occurs in a prison or with convicted inmates may be challenged by a suit alleging denial of due process under the 14th Amendment or cruel and unusual punishment under the 8th. An argument may be made that when officers used force that they used too much and that this may or may not constitute cruel and unusual punishment (Whitley v. Albers, 1986). In Hudson v. McMillian (1992), the Court stated that force used "maliciously and sadistically," whether or not an inmate's injuries were significant, may be an 8th Amendment violation.

Litigation and lawsuits continue to affect both law and agency policies. Liability is when an officer or an agency is held legally responsible in court. And while civil litigation can alert an agency to gaps in training and performance, this is not a direct line. A suit may be frivolous, or a plaintiff may see opportunity if a previous criminal case against him was declined by the prosecutor. That is, if a person is arrested but not prosecuted, he may decide to sue law enforcement for the arrest or conditions surrounding the arrest. An agency or its insurance provider may be known to settle law suits to avoid higher legal costs incurred by fighting the suit. The incident may be so removed in time as to offer little utility as cautionary tale or agency or officer behavior modification method. It may, however, represent redress for some who have suffered due to excessive or bad behavior by law enforcement. Compare this to people or patients harmed or who die each year as the result of medical personnel errors.

Until around 20 years ago, federal actions in cases of possible constitutional violations were pursued as criminal under 18 U.S.C. §§241–42. The Violent Crime Control & Law Enforcement Act of 1994 provided the Department of Justice (DOJ) the ability to effectively investigate and take binding legal actions against police agencies that engaged in a pattern or practice of unconstitutional acts (42 U.S.C. §§14141 and 14142). The U.S. Department of Justice investigates cases that may involve the violation of civil rights of an arrested or deceased person by public safety employees. 18 U.S.C. 242 states, "Whoever under color of any law … willfully subjects any person … to the deprivation of any rights, privileges, or immunities secured or protected by the Constitution or laws of the United States [shall be guilty of a crime]."

The Constitution of the United States provides the broad parameters of what is both permitted and prohibited. These dicta are built upon to formulate federal statutes that proscribe various acts. The Supreme Court only began to specify application of the Bill of Rights through the 14th

Amendment's Due Process Clause in the mid-1900s. These decisions created the context of "reasonableness" that agencies and officers were subsequently held to in regards to searches and seizures.

In its landmark decision addressing the use of force, the U.S. Supreme Court in *Tennessee v. Garner* (1985) established rules for allegations of police excessive force, including the use of deadly force. Notable language of the court was that use of deadly force would only be appropriate if an "officer has probable cause to believe that the suspect poses a significant threat of death or serious physical injury to the officer or others" (p. 1). Before this Supreme Court decision a majority of states still had so-called fleeing felon laws allowing deadly force to be used by law enforcement in cases where little if any immediate threat was posed by the offender. Even following the *Garner* decision, not all states immediately adopted a *Garner* standard that completely abandoned the common law. The Court made clear that states should move away from the common law and that deadly force "not be used unless it is necessary to prevent the escape and the officer has probable cause to believe that the suspect poses a significant threat of death or serious physical injury to the officer or others" (*Tennessee v. Garner*, 1985). This was not an all-inclusive condemnation of deadly force, and the Court noted further that if an officer did believe the subject posed a threat of serious physical harm that "it is not constitutionally unreasonable to prevent escape by using deadly force" (*Id*. at II (B) para. 4).

In fact, most agencies had already instituted policies more restrictive than the common law even before *Garner*. At the time of the *Garner* decision, some states had some component of common law, and most others had law that was more restrictive than the common law (*Tennessee v. Garner*, 1985). Failure to update such policies or the inadequacy of managerial practices can also have a significant impact on serious force usage in an agency (Lee and Vaughn, 2010).

Four years later, the Supreme Court ruled on the use of non-deadly force in Graham v. Connor (1989). The Court moved evaluation of such force by federal courts from one guided by the substantive due process clause of the 14th Amendment, to the 4th Amendment's treatment of searches and seizures, saying, in part, that "excessive force in the course of arrest, investigatory stop, or other 'seizure' of a person are properly analyzed under the Fourth Amendment's 'objective reasonableness' standard" (p. 386). (explaining that excessive use-of-force claims under 42 U.S.C. Section 1983 should be analyzed using specific constitutional rights). In establishing the 4th Amendment as the basis for such evaluations, the Court held in part that force should be examined "from the perspective of a reasonable officer on the scene, rather than with the 20/20 vision of hindsight" (p. 396). Included in the decision were factors to help determine if force was used reasonably: (1) severity of the current crime, (2) whether the suspect poses an immediate threat to officer safety, (3) whether the suspect is actively resisting arrest, and (4) whether the suspect is attempting to flee to evade arrest. On this point of force used when a suspect flees, the Supreme Court in *Brosseau v. Haugen* (2004) asserted that the use of deadly force to stop someone posing an imminent threat of danger to others is not automatically a violation. A few years later in *Scott v. Harris* (2007), the Court reiterated this view on using deadly force when, during vehicle pursuits, the fleeing driver endangered officers or others.

Along with these factors, the Court cited the need to examine the totality of the circumstances surrounding an arrest, and noted the inability to precisely define or mechanically apply this concept of reasonableness. Rather, "The reasonableness of a particular use of force must be judged from the perspective of a reasonable officer on the scene, and its calculus must embody an allowance for the fact that police officers are often forced to make split-second decisions about the amount of force necessary in a particular situation." The Court provided further clarification in the 1986 case of *Malley v. Briggs* when it stated, "The objective reasonableness test is met if 'officers of reasonable competence could disagree on the legality of the defendant's actions'" (p. 475).

Also in 1989, the Court decided in *Canton v. Harris* that aspects of failure to train officers may leave cities, counties, and other entities exposed to liability under Section 1983. In *Canton v. Harris*, the Court stated, in part, "failure to train amounts to deliberate indifference to the rights of persons with whom police come into contact" (p. 378). It is clear that training employees in their duties is important. When the functions are ones that may infringe on rights or cause physical harm, the need is even more obvious. Another mechanism tied to the training of individual officers is to hold officers accountable through regulations in the form of police officer standards and training (POST) boards in the various states to prescribe the training curricula of criminal justice academies and establish procedures to suspend, restrict, or terminate the state certification of an officer who commits specified acts.

Theories of Supervisory Liability

One legal theory that has been used in lawsuits is supervisory liability. Aside from the actions of a suspect or inmate, or even an officer in a use of force incident, there are considerations of agency policy (discussed in the next chapter) and the actions and practices of other agency personnel. While the individual officer's actions are evaluated based on objective facts known to the officer at the time along with the reasonableness of his force choice, there are a number of theories under which liability may attach for what the agency did or did not do in relation to the officer before the moment of the force usage. Negligent hiring, negligent assignment, negligent entrustment, failure to direct, failure to supervise, negligent failure to discipline, and the negligent retention of an officer are of importance as agency administrators, counsels general, risk managers, and others work proactively to support officers in their work and protect the agency and government entity from liability.

As an example of negligent hiring, if the agency is considering hiring Mr. Smith as a patrol officer, and finds that he has been found responsible for several improper uses of force during previous employment but hires him anyway, there is a basis to sue the department if now-Officer Smith once again is found to violate policy or law in a force usage. Similarly, if the agency failed to even check with former employers, the same situation or negligent hiring may exist because the agency *should have known*. Perhaps Patrol Officer Brown works at a small municipality that maintains a small jail to hold arrestees until they can be transferred to the county jail facility. The single jail officer who works the shift calls in sick and the shift supervisor assigns Patrol Officer Brown to "handle the jail" which has six inmates. Officer Brown has had no training on jails or the risks and challenges of recently incarcerated individuals. Brown turns on a television near the front of the cell block and remains there for most of the shift before deciding to walk through the cell area at 6 a.m. before his relief arrives. He finally notes in the log book that someone has labelled one of the inmates as a suicide risk. Brown walks to the cell and finds that the man has hung himself sometime overnight. Negligent assignment.

Negligent entrustment can be found with an officer being allowed control of potentially harmful equipment though he is not trained in its use. The new officer with no training or certification with a shotgun arrives at a large-scale disturbance and the sergeant thrusts a shotgun into his hands. With a boisterous crowd seeming to turn hostile some time into the incident, the officer remembers an old movie where the town sheriff fires a shotgun into the air and it causes the crowd to calm down.

The untrained officer fires the shotgun in his hands and the rifled slug travels away at an angle and strikes and kills a woman in a second-story apartment down the block. If a supervisor does not give specific information about the functions and limitations of an assignment, there could be a failure to direct. If the supervisor does not adequately supervise the officer once he is performing in the assignment, there may be a failure to supervise.

If an officer is known to have, for example, been accused repeatedly of using excessive force against citizens, yet the responsible supervisor(s) fail to take action or actively discourage any in-depth examination of the officer's behavior, there may be grounds for negligent failure to discipline. And subsequently if there are findings that the officer did improperly use force on multiple occasions and no training, counseling, discipline or termination occurs, the agency may be liable for negligent retention of the officer. The mix of these theories of supervisory liability applies in some instances to the agency, sometimes to the supervisor(s), and sometimes to both. Further, a court may find the negligence as *gross* or *simple*, based on whether the negligence is deemed deliberately indifferent or that it was not exercised with great care, respectively.

Immunity

As noted earlier, and following the case of *Pierson v. Ray* (1967), within the scope of their jobs government employees at each level have a certain degree of immunity from lawsuits. It is generally necessary that employees are acting within the scope of their employment and are adhering to rules and guidelines established by their employer. *Absolute immunity* to damages, though not equitable relief, is enjoyed by judges, legislators, parole board members, and prosecutors. The practice is important so that these officials can perform their work with a reasonable degree of confidence that the inherent errors that may occur would not stifle their ability to do the work. It is certainly thought that such officials would be inordinately preoccupied with addressing lawsuits if they were allowed. *Qualified immunity* protects individual employees to the degree that the employee does not violate a "clearly established statutory or constitutional rights of which a reasonable person would have known" (*Harlow v. Fitzgerald*, 1982). Suits do go forward against federal as well as state and local agents and agencies when sued under Section 1983 (*Owen v. City of Independence*, 1980). The term and concept of qualified immunity has evolved over time but "operates to protect officers from the sometimes hazy border between excessive and acceptable force" (*Saucier v. Katz*, 2001).

If determining the appropriateness under the law seems challenging to observers, the Supreme Court's view of the "hazy border" between clearly excessive and clearly constitutional behavior in *Katz* (2001) provided an evaluation mechanism. If a violation *could* exist under *Garner* and *Graham*, the court would move to a second step of determining if qualified immunity was available to an officer. Excessive force claims are most frequently filed in federal court but may be filed as a tort action in state court for some claims, such as battery, unlawful arrest, or wrongful death.

State Law

For much of the country's history, state law was the primary source of legal authority on matters of force usage by local and state law enforcement officers. The federal laws discussed in the preceding section had not yet been fashioned or arrived at through case law interpretation. As such, the U.S. Constitution was largely viewed as silent on such issues. When the Supreme Court began to apply the Fourth Amendment's reasonableness standard to the use of force it clearly established such usage as "seizures" within the Amendment's meaning. Still, as noted above, not all states use a strict *Garner* interpretation to outline use of force criteria.

GOING GLOBAL

In British policing, authority is said to flow from the concept of "policing by consent." According to a Home Office release (2012), the principles are agreed to through general consent of the populace instead of state authority. The nine principles guiding officers in the U.K. since 1829 are:

1. To prevent crime and disorder, as an alternative to their repression by military force and severity of legal punishment.
2. To recognise always that the power of the police to fulfil their functions and duties is dependent on public approval of their existence, actions and behaviour and on their ability to secure and maintain public respect.
3. To recognise always that to secure and maintain the respect and approval of the public means also the securing of the willing co-operation of the public in the task of securing observance of laws.
4. To recognise always that the extent to which the co-operation of the public can be secured diminishes proportionately the necessity of the use of physical force and compulsion for achieving police objectives.
5. To seek and preserve public favour, not by pandering to public opinion; but by constantly demonstrating absolutely impartial service to law, in complete independence of policy, and without regard to the justice or injustice of the substance of individual laws, by ready offering of individual service and friendship to all members of the public without regard to their wealth or social standing, by ready exercise of courtesy and friendly good humour; and by ready offering of individual sacrifice in protecting and preserving life.
6. To use physical force only when the exercise of persuasion, advice and warning is found to be insufficient to obtain public co-operation to an extent necessary to secure observance of law or to restore order, and to use only the minimum degree of physical force which is necessary on any particular occasion for achieving a police objective.
7. To maintain at all times a relationship with the public that gives reality to the historic tradition that the police are the public and that the public are the police, the police being only members of the public who are paid to give full time attention to duties which are incumbent on every citizen in the interests of community welfare and existence.
8. To recognise always the need for strict adherence to police-executive functions, and to refrain from even seeming to usurp the powers of the judiciary of avenging individuals or the State, and of authoritatively judging guilt and punishing the guilty.
9. To recognise always that the test of police efficiency is the absence of crime and disorder, and not the visible evidence of police action in dealing with them.

(FOI release: Definition of policing by consent, 10 December 2012. Home Office)

Consent Decrees

The federal government through the Violent Crime Control and Law Enforcement Act (VCCLEA) of 1994 provided a tool to the civil rights division of the Department of Justice that allowed the division to begin civil proceedings against departments whose use of force rose to the level of a **pattern or practice** of constitutional deprivations for citizens. Primarily, such investigations by the Department of Justice arise from such excessive force issues or from ineffectively addressing the patterns and trends of misconduct by agency members. Consent decrees resulting from investigations and reviews of an agency's policies and practices by the federal government do not have the authority of law, but may have significant impact on those policies. Many observers suggest that the current administration in Washington may de-emphasize investigating or monitoring state or local agencies accused of having a pattern or practice of policing that fails to meet Constitutional muster (Alpert, McLean, and Wolfe, 2017). Before the enactment of the Violent Crime Control and Law Enforcement Act (VCCLEA), in 1980, Congress passed the Civil Rights of Institutionalized Persons Act (CRIPA). This legislation could be seen as the culmination of the preceding decade of revelations and litigation regarding conditions of confinement for America's incarcerated citizens.

In addition to consent decrees, the Department of Justice will more commonly work with an agency either through a memorandum of agreement, or a technical assistance agreement that draws upon federal assistance to address deficiencies. Each of the three mechanisms requires monitoring and reporting to ensure that goals are met to address the practices or shortages that gave rise to the investigation. Liability for criminal justice agencies emanates from a variety of actions, and a great deal of case law is established as a result of the litigation from police and corrections practices and policies.

WHAT-WHY: *EXAMPLE SUMMARY FROM A CONSENT DECREE MONITOR REPORT OF THE INVESTIGATION OF THE NEW ORLEANS POLICE DEPARTMENT*

On May 15, 2010, we opened an investigation of the New Orleans Police Department (NOPD) pursuant to the Violent Crime Control and Law Enforcement Act of 1994, the Omnibus Crime Control and Safe Streets Act of 1968 and Title VI of the Civil Rights Act of 1964. Following a comprehensive investigation, on March 17, 2011, we announced our findings. We found that the NOPD has engaged in patterns of misconduct that violate the Constitution and federal law, including a pattern or practice of excessive force, and of illegal stops, searches, and arrests. We found also a pattern or practice of gender discrimination in the Department's under-enforcement and under-investigation of violence against women. We further found strong indications of discriminatory policing based on racial, ethnic, and LGBT bias, as well as a failure to provide critical police services to language minority communities. On July 24, 2012, we reached a settlement resolving our investigation and asked the Court to make our settlement an order enforceable by the Court. On January 11, 2013, the Court approved the agreement.

(USDOJ, Civil Rights Division, retrieved from https://www.justice.gov/
crt/consent-decree-monitor-reports)

Summary

The use of force by criminal justice employees carries consequences, some of which may entail liability, legal challenges or actions. Force is constrained, as is officer discretion, by a variety of factors, not the least of which is law. State laws, federal law, and case law all provide direction and guidance on various aspects of force usage. The Supreme Court has developed over time various ways to evaluate the use of force including through the 4th, 8th, and 14th Amendments to the U. S. Constitution. Though the criminal charging of an officer is a rare occurrence, lawsuits initiated by citizens frequently seek monetary recompense for purported harms resulting from the actions of officers and agencies. Sometimes the federal government itself will seek to encourage reform of an agency through investigations and consent decrees or other mechanisms entered into between the U.S. Department of Justice and a state or local government or agency.

Much of what law enforcement officers, corrections officers, probation officers, and others do on a daily basis can find its way into a criminal or civil courtroom or proceeding. Certain legislative immunities have been established in recognition of the inherent challenges that exist in performing such jobs, as well as those of the judiciary, prosecutors, and parole boards. Supervisors and agencies may also be held liable if appropriate training has not been provided to officers or officers are hired when they shouldn't be, entrusted with equipment that they are not qualified to use, are not adequately supervised or monitored, or are retained when they should be released.

We conclude this chapter considering the effect of law and litigation on agency policies and procedures. We turn next to a consideration of force policies. What to do – risk management, role of risk manager, general counsel, training section, administration. This includes the need to seek input and buy-in as part of the policy implementation process.

KEY TERMS

Federalism
Supremacy clause
Section 1983 claims
Liability
Consent decree
Supervisory negligence
Immunity
Objective reasonableness

Discussion Questions

1.   What role does case law play in guiding the use of force in criminal justice?
2.   How do laws reduce the potential for excessive use of force?
3.   What are the policy implications of case law?
4.   Describe and discuss the effects of law on training of public safety personnel.
5.   Why should researchers study trends in laws that address the use of force?

TRY THIS

Go to the web page of the Special Litigation Section of the Civil Rights Division of the U.S. Department of Justice. Examine one or more cases and discuss what you learn about the process.

References

Alpert, G. P., McLean, K., and Wolfe, S. (2017). Consent decrees: an approach to police accountability and reform. *Police Quarterly*, 1–11.

Lee, H. and Vaughn, M. S. (2010). Organizational factors that contribute to police deadly force liability. *Journal of Criminal Justice*, 38(2), 193–206.

Ross, D. (2013). *Civil liability in criminal justice.* 7th ed. Waltham, MA: Anderson Publishing.

Cases Cited

Bivens v. Six Unknown Named Agents of the Federal Bureau of Narcotics, 403 U.S. 388 (1971)

Brosseau v. Haugen (2004)

Canton v. Harris, 489 U.S. 378, 388 (1989)

Estelle v. Gamble (1976)

Graham v. Connor, 490 U.S. 386 (1989)

Harlow v. Fitzgerald, 457 U.S. 800 (1982)

Hudson v. McMillian (1992)

Johnson v. Glick, 481 (1973)

Malley v. Briggs (1986)

Monell v. Department of Social Services of the City of New York, 436 U.S. 658 (1978)

Monroe v. Pape, 365 U. S. 167 (1961)

Owen v. City of Independence, 445 U.S. 622 (1980)

Pierson v. Ray, 386 U.S. 547 (1967)

Saucier v. Katz, 533 U.S. 194 (2001)

Scott v. Harris (2007)

Tennessee v. Garner, 471 U.S. 1 (1985)

Whitley v. Albers, 475 U.S. 312 (1986)

3

THE CONSTRUCTION AND CONTENT OF FORCE POLICIES

CHAPTER OUTLINE

Introduction
Components of use of force policy
Toward a model policy on the use of force
Use of force continuum
Use of force reporting
Investigating use of force by personnel
Summary
Features: What-Why, Going Global, Research Results
Key Terms
Discussion Questions
Try This
References

STUDENT LEARNING OUTCOMES

- Students will be able to explain factors that influence policy development.
- Students will be able to describe the components of a model policy on the use of force.
- Students will be able to explain the role of reporting in force monitoring.
- Students will be able to critique use of force policy.
- Students will be able to explain the steps to investigating use of force.

Introduction

As discussed in the prior chapter, statutory law and case law provide the broad parameters for policies addressing, among other things, the use of force by public safety personnel. Law alone, however, is not sufficient as many departments struggle with the Supreme Court's admonition to use "objectively reasonable" force. Agency level policies give greater direction and usually narrower definition to concepts, procedures, and requirements regarding the use of force by members of those agencies (Terrill and Paoline, 2017). Policy matters. When it comes to the critical domain of force usage, policy must be clear, complete, and current. These features also make policy *helpful*. This means well-constructed policy can assist agency members and citizens alike in understanding the guidelines for how and when to use force, as well as the authority and trust the public puts into the hands of police in a free society. Terrill and Paoline (2017) explained, "There is perhaps no greater example of the influence that organizational policy can have on police behavior than that of lethal force" (p. 193). They extend that to all issues of force and policy, saying "officers working within the most restrictive policy framework used force less readily than officers who operated within more permissive policy environments" (p. 193).

In this examination of policies regarding less lethal force, Terrill and Paoline note that while lethal force has received much attention, less lethal force policies have not (2016). We have already established that judgments about use of force by officers are influenced by knowledge of underlying causes of resistive behavior or crime commission. Additionally, there is no one best way to handle all circumstances any more than there is one always effective technique for physically controlling someone. Wilson (1968) noted in regard to policy that "the possibility of deciding in a particular instance that the police behaved wrongly does not mean that one can formulate a meaningful policy for how the police should behave in all cases" (p. 278). In fact no single individual or agency can lay claim to originating a consensus model policy on the use of force. Sir Robert Peel, considered the father of Western policing, and his leaders of the London Metropolitan Police stated in their 1829 "9 Policing Principles" that

> To use physical force only when the exercise of persuasion, advice and warning is found to be insufficient to obtain public cooperation to an extent necessary to secure observance of law or to restore order, and to use only the minimum degree of physical force which is necessary on any particular occasion for achieving a police objective.
>
> *(U.K. Home Office, 2012)*

With the professionalization of criminal justice agencies over the last century, have come better and more thorough written guidelines within those agencies. Researchers and practitioners sought to locate the one best way to perform functions in the style of such 20th century management luminaries as Frederick Taylor and Max Weber. And while few professionals trained in making force options ascribe to the view that there is one best way to accomplish most objectives requiring such use in law enforcement, there are guiding principles that can be encapsulated in policies. The principles are arrived at through aspirational and political agenda that (ideally) are empirically supported as effective means of addressing problems sought by or thrust upon criminal justice agencies. Meta-analyses of different policy areas confirm that effective programs and policies can be identified (Makarios and Pratt, 2012). There have been problems in achieving a consistently productive dialogue between criminal justice practitioners and researchers that leads to policy products born of both worlds (Rosenbaum, 2010). But with the recent rhetoric and attempts at evidence-based or intelligence-led policies (see for example Telep, 2016; Weisburd and Neyroud, 2014) it is hoped that the two groups have grown more comfortable with being in the same room together. The differences of perspective and language between researchers and criminal justice policy-makers and practitioners are not unique to public safety (Davis, 2010).

As an empirical matter, the use of force by law enforcement is considered infrequent (U.S. Department of Justice, 1999; Bayley and Garofalo, 1989; BJS, 2015; Hickman, Piquero, and Garner, 2008). Figures from the corrections environment are not readily accessible, but we will operate for the time being on an assumption of somewhat similar rates of use, even given a locked environment. Force remains a singularly important focus of public and practitioner attention because of its potential for harm and attendant concerns such as government accountability and legitimacy. While Bittner (1970) considered the use of force central to police, we can point to the umbrella use of discretion as perhaps the quintessential aspect of identity for U.S. police officers. Use of force certainly remains the most consequential embodiment of this discretion and is appropriately guided by law and administrative policy.

Even after the advent of written policies to direct the core functions of public safety agencies, directives were often intentionally brief with the possible aim of limiting liability through not tying officers to overly-detailed procedures. Court decisions have generally indicated a need for thorough policies and procedures that show diligence in providing guidance to public safety employees. Policy, along with training and supervision, is an important internal mechanism to control the use of force (Lersch and Mieczkowski, 2005). No policy can cover every potential variation of functions but they must be sufficient if they are to match the practices of employees and provide an adequate level of reduced liability for both employees and the agency.

Agency policy and officer practices are something of a two-way street. Practice should be consistent with policy guidelines and those policies should reflect the actual circumstances officers face. Policy designed in this way can reduce liability exposure for officers and agencies and increase protection for citizens. Mears (2010) correctly observes that these are important benefits for agency administrators when officers understand policy. Policies must be routinely reviewed and updated to reflect changes in the law and society, as well as the latest and most effective tactics. Consistent review of business practices, including by criminal justice agencies, has been a mainstay of private companies but has increasingly become the norm in public organizations (Mader, 2002). Clarity and thorough coverage of the major aspects of the use of force is critical (Gordon, 2003). While the writing of any policy or procedure must be thorough, thought must be given to the method of dissemination, accompanying training, evaluation of knowledge acquisition and a feedback mechanism for employees to seek clarification or provide feedback on the next iteration of policy.

Normative models of force policies have generally been brief and suggest the major components that should appear in a comprehensive policy. The International Association of Chiefs of Police (IACP) published its first Model Policy on Use of Force in 1989. Since that time, the landscape of force options has expanded. The Model Policy offered by the IACP has been updated a half a dozen times but remains around two pages in length. A use of force concepts and issues paper has accompanied each revision of the IACP Policy (2006). The brevity of the IACP model is not an indication that actual agency policies should be short. Rather, as noted, the model collects a brief description of the sections either found in numerous agency policies or that are judged to be important for a use of force policy. It would be an outdated view to conclude that fewer specific statements lead to fewer areas for critique or smaller exposure as the basis for legal action against an agency. An organization's policies provide general guidance and not the specific response to every conceivable situation that employees might encounter. Procedural manuals, training bulletins, and lesson plans, are intended to provide more detailed direction while the overarching policy often makes a statement of principles. With that said, policies are needed to form the basis of reasonable and legally effective responses. These policies must be robust to achieve fewer liability claims or lawsuits and thus serve the organization and the public.

The concepts and issues paper that accompanied the 2006 revision of IACP's Use of Force Model Policy, states in part:

> In constructing an agency policy on the use of force … a strong argument can be made to keep a use-of-force policy as short and simple as possible. It is essential that officers have a complete understanding and recall knowledge of their agency policy on this critical issue. But the longer and more complex the policy the less likely that this is possible. A use-of-force policy can and should be concise and incorporate only the essential principles to adequately guide officer decision making.
>
> *(IACP, 2006, p. 1)*

Hough and Tatum (2012) added: "While an effective policy should be succinct, it should not sacrifice thorough coverage of the following components: policy statement, report requirements, definitions, a process to review the use of force policy annually, criteria for providing medical aid, a force continuum, and training" (p. 21). The policy, for example, should not simply list *Tennessee v. Garner* and *Graham v. Conner* and admonish employees to act reasonably. Indeed, agencies have wide variation in their policies on force and how they direct officers to think about force levels and force decision-making (Terrill, Paoline, and Ingram, 2011).

An agency need not reinvent the policy and procedure wheel. It is common for departments to contact similar organizations and ask for input and current policies to inform their own policy development (Farber, 2007). In the pursuit of state or national accreditation, it is certainly common to contact accredited departments and ask for help, advice, and information on existing policies of the accredited agencies. The standards of an accrediting body likewise present major topic areas that agencies are expected to have developed policies and procedures on. Some academic research has examined policies across multiple agencies to determine if they contain similar topic sections (Terrill et al., 2011; Hough and Tatum, 2012). While similarity of topics was found, consistency of apparent importance of those topics, as reflected in volume of writing, has not always been found.

Policy and training must be aligned. Policies and procedures must give practical guidance to officers. Law, court decisions, and policy should be used as the foundation in building training for department employees. Reiteration of policy and current legal decisions should be incorporated in the periodic in-service training provided to officers. Initial employee training as well as annual refresher trainings are the appropriate location for such policy discussions, since the basic officer academy is often regional and not agency-specific, and therefore unable to give recruit officers specific guidance on how individual agencies direct different functions to be accomplished. Each state has some form of a standards and training commission that sets out the curriculum for training law-enforcement and correctional officers, though the decentralized nature of American criminal justice results in diverse training and certification procedures (Morrison, 2010). County and state probation agencies and juvenile justice agencies will also include policies on the use of force in their entry-level and in-service training initiatives.

Policies must be clear, adequately comprehensive, reflect current law, and ideally lead to positive outcomes. An important and obvious component of positive policy outcomes is less injuries to citizens and officers when following policy (White, 2001). In addition, sound policies will somewhat predictably lead to fewer lawsuits or public dissatisfaction. This last point may be impacted by past or prevailing views of an agency in its community, even if policy and practices have evolved or improved.

Toward a Model Policy on the Use of Force

Organizations such as the Police Executive Research Forum (PERF) and the International Association of Chiefs of Police (IACP), as well as the International Law Enforcement Education and Training Association (ILEETA) and others, have conducted research and summarized best and most frequent practices within the field and addressed many areas of agency operation. For many years the IACP has published model policies addressing a wide range of law enforcement issues. These model policies are intentionally somewhat brief and enumerate the significant areas that a policy on a particular topic should address. State accreditation associations and national ones such as the American Correctional Association (ACA) and the Commission on Accreditation for Law Enforcement Agencies, Inc., (CALEA), publish standards that specify what policies an agency should have at a minimum, but not the content of those policies. Accrediting bodies typically specify what matters should be addressed in policy but not how an individual agency accomplishes the task.

Policy also develops from a grounded approach, taking shape based on the real world experiences of public safety personnel, trainers, scientists, and others. Famously paraphrased is the notion that, "If the map doesn't match the ground, ignore the map." In other words, if an officer faced with the imminent need to utilize force has available only policy or procedure that will not accommodate or effectively manage the threat he confronts, he must do something else. This may literally be an imperative if the officer has utilized the policy guidelines and procedural methods available and is facing harm or the failure of his lawful duty.

Whatever the source of policies, as in law, officers must be aware of policies and understand the mandates and guidance prescribed. Most contemporary agencies develop policies to address myriad aspects of agency operations and to provide guidance and set expectations for individual employees. The policies compiled are accessible in manuals available not just on a bookshelf but increasingly with the typing of a few keys from an officer's mobile car computer or wireless device. Agency members are required to acknowledge receipt and understanding of policies and to participate in annual training and information sessions reaffirming agency values, mission, and resources. Annual review of policies is the norm resulting from the accreditation movement, in addition to point-in-time updates brought about by an extraordinary event.

WHAT-WHY

What is evidence-based policy? There are certainly ample examples of policies labelled as such across many disciplines. If there is credible and robust examination or evaluation of an issue that follows the scientific method, someone may put it forward as supporting one position or another on that thing. Adherents of policy analysis may rankle at all this newfangled discussion of evidence-based policy as nothing more than old wine in new bottles. They will point rightfully to the last 30 to 50 years as policy analysis became a field in its own right, separate and apart from public administration (itself not particularly old) or the study of politics, with us since the time of the Greeks. The disciplines of both public policy and public administration concern themselves greatly with how problems are nominated in the process by which "solutions" are arrived at. Birkland (2016) provides a solid starting point by listing these attributes of public policy:

- Policy is made in response to some sort of problem that requires attention.
- Policy is made on the "public's" behalf.
- Policy is oriented toward a goal or desired state, such as the solution of a problem.
- Policy is ultimately made by governments, even if the ideas come from outside government or through the interaction of government and nongovernmental actors.
- Policy is interpreted and implemented by public and private actors who have different interpretations of problems, solutions, and their own motivations.
- Policy is what the government chooses to do or *not* to do.

(p. 8)

The reality that trained managers and analysts must embrace is that value weighting and the ultimate selection of a policy alternative by a policymaker may be determined more by a political climate than a compelling compilation of facts and "evidence." In respect of that we turn to a pithy observation by Pawson (2006): "Evidence based policy is much like all trysts, in which hope springs eternal and often outweighs expectancy, and for which the future is uncertain as we wait to know whether the partnership will flower or pass as an infatuation."

(p. 1)

While it is unlikely that policymakers will return to a state of disregard of all research regarding criminal justice policies in general or force policies in particular, it seems responsible to remind that policy decisions rarely rest solely on cold hard facts and that "the fundamental goal of the social sciences ... was a different project than the policy makers had in mind."

(Moore, 2002, p. 33)

Policies across the more than 20,000 public criminal justice organizations in the U.S. are not consistent. There is no central authority to mandate verbiage or even the organization or format of policies, let alone data collection (Shane, 2016). When it comes to force usage, one agency may prohibit or restrict vehicle pursuits, while the adjacent jurisdiction may have a less restrictive policy. One state might teach recruits a force continuum during basic academy training only to have the recruits find that when they are hired by a specific department and come under that organization's policy manual, that the force continuum is somewhat different. Still, the officer should be able to articulate the structure of his agency's continuum if one is in use as well as the reasoning for having a force continuum (Rogers, 2001).

Researchers, training efforts, plaintiffs, and advocacy groups all have a keen interest in the state of policy relative to the contemporary practices of the field. One private group offers a website that claims to present their "analysis" of 91 of the 100 largest police departments' use of force policies.

There is no attestation that the policies in their database are current, though they note which were acquired only after Freedom of Information Act (FOIA) requests. Such organizations, while not neutral, may gather useful information for critical examination. Unfortunately, rhetoric or conclusions not supported by the available documents or subject to rigorous analysis may be less than helpful.

Law enforcement agencies are bureaucracies. The term bureaucracy is not used here as a pejorative, rather it is used as merely descriptive. Government agencies tasked with law enforcement must develop policies and protocols to ensure consistent, constitutional, and effective approaches to their functions. While rulebooks can grow in volume to remarkable proportions, values statements and frequent reinforcement of agency and leadership support of principled actions provide an overarching logic for members to embrace. No employee can cite chapter and verse of each and every policy of his agency, yet she should have a clear understanding of expected behavior. In the past, agencies may have opted for intentionally brief policies with the idea of allowing maximum flexibility for employees or, cynically, perhaps believing the fewer rules that are written the less the agency may be held to. An absence of policy is in some ways its own policy through failure to address important organizational responsibilities or functions.

Agency policy and training, and officer performance must recognize the immediacy issue often present in a potential use of force situation. Observers from different perspectives have long-held concerns of possible hesitant action by officers ostensibly the result of the officer involuntarily pausing to contemplate legal or policy constraints (Petrowski, 2002; Bostain, 2006). While little empirical evidence currently supports this hesitancy hypothesis, it is not difficult to picture increased risk at an event when confusion may exist, not with policy selection, but between two or more officers working to control one or more persons in an evolving situation. Noted criminal justice ethicist Edwin J. Delattre (1996) observed, "Once in a situation, two officers should not be at cross purposes, at least not until the immediate danger is addressed. If disagreement is unavoidable, so be it, but not during risk of violence" (p. 56).

Use of Force Continuum

The social turmoil in America during the 1960s brought many changes. More comprehensive and centralized reporting of crimes revealed increases in violent offenses against citizens. Training methods in law enforcement were becoming more organized and the techniques and tactics officers were instructed in benefited from the application of teaching and training methods. One component of the more effective training in force options was the incorporation of force continuums (Williams, 2002; Peters, Peters, and Brave, 2006). The graphic depiction of such continuums was by largely linear models that presented increasingly painful or potentially injurious options for officers to employ.

In the half century that has passed since the broad awakening of rights movements across the country, tensions between groups and between government and these groups have resulted in the insertion of law enforcement officers at the various points of social friction. It was and continues to be appropriate to search for methods of controlling individuals that hold the least potential for inadvertent injury. As force methods changed and options expanded, the force continuums used to illustrate and explain the methods and options were required to change as well. This expansion from fists, truncheons, and pistols, led some observers to assert that officers might face widespread and

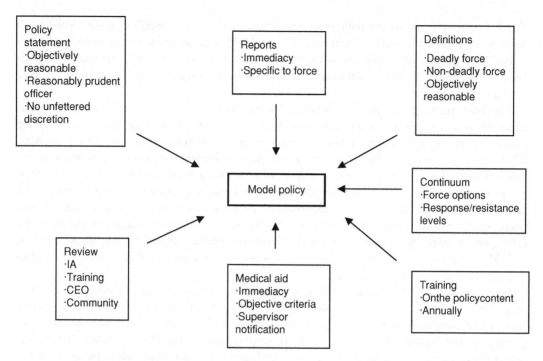

FIGURE 3.1 Components of Model Use of Force Policy
Source: Hough and Tatum (2012).

dangerous uncertainty of what option to use at the moment when force usage was needed (Petrowski, 2002). The models intended to help explain decision-making during attempts to control people encompassed representations of "stairs, pyramids, tables, and ladders" (Williams, 2002, p. 14), or circular depictions of factors and options (Fridell, 2005).

Policy must be incorporated into training curricula for the use of force. Criminal justice training has moved to include more problem-based and scenario-style training to present corrections and law enforcement officers with experiential learning that includes assessing threats and responses in a dynamic environment (Hundersmarck, Vanderkooi, and Vasicek, 2016). Using graphic aids, reading assignments on relevant law and human behavior, and scenarios to practice and master skills, trainers work to equip recruits and in-service officers with the tools to effectively face control-and-restraint encounters. The use of a continuum or model is understood by not just trainers, but by risk managers, agency administrators, and counsels general, as helpful in explaining the complexities of force.

It is simplistic to assert that a model of how something works or of its component parts may induce so much confusion as to render someone incapable of making a timely decision in a moment of threat. Yet this is essentially the stance of a number of force trainers and observers. It seems a strange idea, even to the point of stretching credulity, that in teaching a policy area of such importance, one should not utilize models and conceptual frameworks. A use of force continuum is not a one-dimensional view of a mechanically designed and implemented process. Law enforcement and correctional officers as well as private employees with duties to maintain security are all aware that physical control attempts do not always proceed in a smooth interaction with the person quickly and politely deferring to authority. Those who officers try to control may punch and kick and gouge and fall to the ground in a heap with the officer struggling to keep hold of the individual and achieve a purchase to apply handcuffs. Very often the officer is placed in a reactionary posture by the suspect (Alpert and Dunham, 2004; Williams, 2002). Trying to get out from behind the curve of action and reaction may certainly not occur in a straight line series of exact and incremental steps. Bostain (2006) points out the inherent weakness of models such as a use of force continuum and asserts that the result is officer confusion over what to do. Any such framework or model of action steps to accomplish a physical or intellectual task faces the same challenge without rendering the model pointless or worse, counterproductive.

Something of a debate remains within the force training community over the use of continuums to illustrate and reinforce available selections to use in controlling and responding to resistance versus adherence to the vague standard of "objective reasonableness" established by the Supreme Court case of *Graham v. Connor* (1989). This argument is not merely semantical, as trainers and officers work to maintain a common understanding of just what an officer can do and when. As with virtually every other policy area in public safety, there is no universal set of force option definitions or decision-making in the United States. The "totality of the circumstances" on the ground is conceptually what each officer must understand as she reacts and responds to threat circumstances, and as she articulates in formal documentation those circumstances after the fact.

Grossi (2006) points out that the use of force continuum is appropriately used to explain the involved concepts to the community as well as to members of a jury. In regards to juries, officers must be capable of explaining that the "force decision was the most reasonable one, based on the threat you were facing" (Grossi, 2006, para. 4). He goes on to emphasize that "framework ... when they have to justify and articulate their force applications" (2006, para. 5), and this is certainly true when explaining a force encounter from beginning to end and in a way that allows jurors to understand how officers are trained to respond. In a study reported by Ross (2013), trends in police litigation were examined in selected cities for the period 2004–2010. While the study looked at only a dozen or so cities, the costs of litigation ran from a couple of million dollars to hundreds of millions of dollars. These figures cover more than just payments made to plaintiffs in use of force cases, but serve to illustrate the price tag attached to some of the tasks carried out by officers. It is important that a jury understand use of force cases. One of the best ways to facilitate this understanding is through the use of a matrix or model that allows the officer, trainer, or expert to focus attention on specific components of force decision-making.

A segment of force trainers have expressed concerns that officers in general may have the perception that a continuum imposes force applied in an up and down, one-dimensional way and where this may occur they believe there is a risk of "a state of doubt in the mind of the officer who then becomes worried not only about being injured but also about being disciplined or sued ..." (Williams, 2002, p. 16). That we often use the terms escalation and de-escalation does not imply an inherent weakness of a continuum approach or that trainees and officers are not fully aware that various force options and dynamics may occur cyclically within even one encounter. An officer completing defensive tactics training in an academy and subsequently working to control another person during a street arrest or correctional restraint understands the complexity of the process.

The Move away from Use of Force Continuums in Policies

The opinions expressed in court cases vary as to aspects of the appropriateness of use of force by employees within the criminal justice system. There is perhaps a disconnect between the court decisions and commentary about force usage and the expectations of some that such opinions relieve the need of legislators and criminal justice policy makers to create clear policies. Indeed, some feel that court opinions are sufficient to essentially adopt as agency policy (Peters et al., 2006). In the *Graham v. Connor* (1989) decision, the Supreme Court created an important set of parameters for the use of force (Petrowski, 2002). In this case, "the Court established that excessive force claims arising out of arrests, investigatory stops, or other seizures … are properly analyzed under the Fourth Amendment's objective reasonableness standard" (Ross, 2002, p. 300). The Court noted that there is no "precise and mechanical application possible for this test of reasonableness" (Ross, 2002, p. 300; see also Hall, 1997; Williams, 2002; Klinger and Brunson, 2009). While there is no commentary that the Court intended to write policy for agencies across the country, it did list criteria that should be seen to impact an officer's force decision: "severity of the crime, whether the suspect poses an immediate threat to the officer or others, and whether the suspect is actively resisting arrest or attempting to evade arrest by flight" (Ross, 2002, p. 300).

The standard of objective reasonableness established in *Graham v. Connor* has remained intact. Peters et al. (2006) asserted that "unless state law is more restrictive," the ruling in *Graham* is "the only standard that need appear in an agency's use-of-force policy regarding seizures of free people" (Peters et al., 2006, p. 8). Further, Peters et al. (2006) asserted that the presence of a continuum in agency policy or training exposes the agency to criticism or even liability if an officer is identified as having violated policy even if not the Supreme Court's reasonableness standard. The media-informed perception of the community may also be negative without a complete understanding of the semantics or legal ramifications.

The opinion of some that the reasonableness standard is sufficient in and of itself seems based at least in part on the idea that a continuum signals the mechanical application of a use of force method (Petrowski, 2002). Petrowski asserts that the use of a continuum can result in hesitation in the face of threat. More extensive research on the general hesitancy to use force against other humans (Grossman, 1995) puts this contention in need of empirical support. While such research results may come, decades of studies have examined the complexity and range of factors that have been shown to impact force decision-making. Competent, comprehensive use of force training should work to improve skills including threat assessment while mitigating any factors that increase officer or citizen risk.

Alpert and Smith (1994) pointed out that the standard of "reasonableness" may not be sufficient. The definition of "appropriately reasonable" is elusive, even to court interpretation (Ross, 2002). Struggling with a suitable definition or even "knowing it when you see it," is likely to continue for courts, agencies, researchers, police practice experts, media, and the public. Lay-citizens form their views based largely on media exposure (including stylized television dramas) and have neither the training background nor sufficient contextual insights to conduct analysis of a 10-second video. Citizens, with prior criminal justice system experience or not (Pickett, Mancini, Mears, and Gertz, 2015), can understand the dynamics of force situations and the reasonable officer standard through explanations and illustrations including use of force continuums or models. Just as Alpert and Smith (1994) labelled the reasonable officer standard vague, they also noted that the views of officers themselves and the public may differ based in part on not sharing a common set of experiences.

RESEARCH RESULTS

Agencies struggle to assess officer conduct using the reasonable officer standard and various other internal policies (Klinger and Brunson, 2009). Research that examines the components of force policies across agencies highlights the inconsistency of definitions and the varying use of court interpretations and continuums (Hough and Tatum, 2012). This also increases the challenge of defining *excessive* force, and agencies must avoid the urge to "reduce these critical issues to overly simple rules of application" (Hall, 1997, p. 32). This is one of the reasons that the Police Executive Research Forum (PERF) stated in its 2016 "Guiding Principles" that, "Departments should adopt policies that hold themselves to a higher standard than the legal requirements of *Graham v. Connor*" (p. 2). Doing so, however, may self-impose liability complications from officers acting within the law but in apparent contradiction to overly restrictive policy.

Use of Force Reporting

Somewhat of a maxim in many professions and disciplines is that "If it wasn't written it didn't happen." This expresses the importance and need to document relevant and important activities of medical personnel, safety inspectors, criminal justice officers, and many others. For reasons of appropriate public record-keeping, supervision and monitoring, training considerations, accreditation requirements (for those participating), liability, public transparency, media requests, and more, criminal justice agencies should require documenting force usage by policy. Most agencies incorporate such reporting as a matter of contemporary criminal justice business (Hough and Tatum, 2012).

A number of agency report forms include a section to indicate, via a force continuum matrix, subject resistance levels and officer response levels (Hough and Tatum, 2012). Officers know that a force encounter may take a roller-coaster ride of actions, reactions, and efforts as the subject experiences the emotions and realization of being restrained. How then to correctly document those multiple force levels becomes a matter of policy and training (Terrill, 2003). Some agencies also include an anatomical chart or figure to indicate injuries either to the subject or an officer. As soon as practical after a use of force, officers should report any known or suspected injuries to medical personnel. EMS and fire department personnel often respond to the scene of a violent incident or arrest with apparent injuries. All available information regarding possible injuries or medical factors should be communicated to these personnel. Such information should also be conveyed to booking personnel when a prisoner is delivered and transitions to the status of an inmate. Many if not most county jails require that a patrol officer delivering an individual claiming injury or apparently injured have that individual cleared by a local hospital before they will accept them for processing.

Investigating Use of Force by Personnel

The policy of each individual agency will dictate which incidents officers are required to write about. Once again, the lack of uniformity across agencies in the United States results in various types of reporting, including in the area of use of force. While handcuffing a compliant arrestee may not require a report in one agency, the adjacent jurisdiction may mandate that even a routine arrest with no claimed injuries must be recorded on a departmental use of force form. Qualitatively, the inmate who has to be pulled out of a cell versus the one who comes out swinging will both generate a use of force report, though the circumstances create an important difference in how the force is used, *even if both are appropriate*. This may illustrate a misguided notion that some agencies may have of lowering force incidents by reclassifying or simply not recording some acts (even authorized ones) for the sake of numbers (Wittrup, 2016).

The forms and reports generated from incidents that involved force usage are stored at each agency. The agency may use the reports in criminal prosecutions, to monitor and enhance training efforts, to bolster public transparency and accountability, and to assist supervisors and managers in assessing personnel performance. If a pattern of force usage is identified regarding either an officer or perhaps a geographic area or temporality, it may assist the department in various ways. Early Intervention (EI) or Early Warning (EW) monitoring and systems are the natural offshoot of data-driven approaches in public or private organizations. And again, there is no aggregation of data at the national or even state level regarding the use of force by criminal justice system employees (Shane, 2016). The collection and interpretation of information is critical for any department to know what it is doing and how efficiently or effectively (ideally both). EI begins from establishing thresholds or tolerances for categories of activity (outputs), feedback such as complaints or accolades (inputs), and training or corrective processes such as supervisory counseling, training or discipline. Refinement of these types of processes is ongoing (Ceriale, 2016; Shjarback, 2015) and agencies are cautioned against taking a simplistic approach to "counting" reports (Bazley, Mieczkowski, and Lersch, 2009) or considering a citizen complaint without taking into account the various other factors of officer assignment and experience. If it is determined that an officer has used force in a way not within policy or that shows the potential to move outside of policy without a training effort, the department can assign the officer remedial training. Additionally, officer action may warrant formal counseling or discipline, and this may be determined through an administrative investigation which reviews available reports of an incident in addition to interviews and examination of any relevant physical evidence.

In addition to investigating the use of force conducted proactively by an agency or as the result of document review and supervisory monitoring, a department should have a clear, accessible, and robust program to encourage citizens to report improper employee behavior, including the use of force. While this will be augmented by the rapidly developing use of body-worn cameras (BWCs) (Ariel, Farrar, and Sutherland, 2015), it should not be assumed that such use will immediately deter bad behavior or fully explain any partially depicted event.

GOING GLOBAL

Adherence to evidence-based policy efforts is neither confined to the U.S. nor to a particular discipline. Policing in the United Kingdom has long been of concern to citizens. In an ongoing effort to improve policing in England and Wales, the National Policing Improvement Agency (NPIA) was created in 2008 (though dissolved in 2012) and sought to enhance practices and outcomes through a reliance on empirical evidence of best practices. While not facing the volume of distinct law enforcement agencies that populate the American landscape, the NPIA sought to coordinate the efforts of several distinct bureaucratic structures to improve coordination, training, and a common emphasis of policing programs.

Embracing scientific and technological innovation has not always or automatically included examining day-to-day police practices to find consensus on what is most effective.

(Neyroud, 2009)

Summary

Policies flow from law and are operationalized further by procedures, training, and the realities of the environments where they are implemented. Linking evidence and research results to those policies is challenging but important work as criminal justice agencies strive to address, at least to the extent they can, the problems that reside at the intersection of human behavior and law. Each police, corrections, probation, or juvenile justice agency creates its own policies regarding operations, including the use of force. While it is unsurprising that the vast majority of these policies address many similar issues, it is also to be expected that differences exist. Virtually any policy in any organization is impacted by the influence that supervisors have in modelling behavior and monitoring practices (Lim and Lee, 2015).

Different governmental, research, and professional organizations have designed and recommended use of force policies. Some include utilizing a use of force continuum to help explain force dynamics and subject and officer actions and responses. Virtually all agencies require reporting in the instance of a serious force incident, and the actions of officers are subject to review and investigation internally as well as external to the department. Such policies must include a component for citizens to register complaints regarding the actions of employees. A national database on the use of *all* force is a long way off, if indeed it will ever exist practically (Alpert, 2016; Klinger, Rosenfeld, Isom, and Deckard, 2016), but greater local efforts are appropriate given the decentralized U.S. system. Research continues in an attempt to link empirical evidence to policy and practice in the area of force usage.

KEY TERMS

Model policy
PERF
IACP
ILEETA
Use of force continuum
Early warning/early intervention
Evidence-based
Objectively reasonable

Discussion Questions

1. Describe how agency policy influences the use of force by officers.
2. What difference is there between policy and law as it applies to force?

3. Discuss the components of a model policy on the use of force.
4. What role does the force continuum play in designing policy?

TRY THIS

Examine several law enforcement and correctional agency websites. Try to locate the use of force policy. List and discuss the sections or components that you found within the policy. After that locate and examine PERF's "Guiding Principles on the Use of Force." How do they compare?

References

Alpert, G. P. (2016). Toward a national database of officer-involved shootings: a long and winding road. *Criminology and Public Policy*, 15, 237–242.

Alpert, G. P. and Dunham, R. G. (2004). *Understanding police use of force: officers, suspects, and reciprocity*. New York: Cambridge University Press.

Alpert, G. and Smith, W. (1994). How reasonable is the reasonable man? Police and excessive force. *Journal of Criminal Law and Criminology*, 85, pp. 481–501.

Ariel, B., Farrar, W., and Sutherland, A. (2015). The effect of police body-worn cameras on use of force and citizens' complaints against the police: a randomized controlled trial. *Journal of Quantitative Criminology*, 31(3), 509–535. doi:10.1007/s10940-014-9236-3

Bayley, D. H. and Garafalo, J. (1989). The management of violence by police officers. *Criminology*, 27, 1–23.

Bazley, T., Mieczkowski, T., and Lersch, K. (2009). Early intervention program criteria: evaluating officer use of force. *Justice Quarterly*, 26(1), 107–124.

Birkland, T. A. (2016) *An introduction to the policy process: theories, concepts, and models of public policymaking*. 4th ed. New York: Routledge .

Bittner, E. (1970). *The functions of the police in modern society*. Washington, DC: National Institute of Mental Health.

Bostain, J. (2006). Use of force: are continuums still necessary?, *FLETC Journal* (Fall), 33–37.

BJS (Bureau of Justice Statistics) (2015). *Police use of nonfatal force, 2002–2011* (NCJ-249216). Washington, DC: Government Printing Office. Retrieved from https://www.bjs.gov/index.cfm?ty=pbdetail&iid=5456

Ceriale, Matthew A. (2016). Early intervention systems: an evaluative review of their history and use. Honors in the Major Theses, Paper 32. Ph.D. thesis, University of Central Florida.

Davis, R. C. (2010). A new approach in Dallas. *Police Practice and Research: An International Journal*, 11(2), 129–131. doi:10.1080/15614261003593104

Delattre, E. J. (1996). *Character and cops*. 3rd ed. Washington, DC: American Enterprise Institute.

Farber, B. J. (2007). Civil liability for use of tasers, stunguns, and other electronic control devices – Part I: 4th Amendment claims for excessive force. *AELE Monthly Law Journal*, 101, 101–109.

Fridell, L. (2005). Improving use-of-force policy, policy enforcement, and training. In L. Fridell and J. Ederheimer (Eds.), *Chief concerns: exploring the challenges of police use of force*. Washington, DC: Police Executive Research Forum, pp. 21–55.

Gordon, K. (2003). Teaching use of force. *Law Enforcement Executive Forum*, 3(2), pp. 103–110.

Grossi, D. (2006). Setting the record straight on force continuums. *The Police Marksman*, 31(January-February), 57–58.

Grossman, D. (1995). *On killing: the psychological cost of learning to kill in war and society*. New York: Little, Brown.

Hall, J. (1997). Police use of nondeadly force to arrest. *FBI Law Enforcement Bulletin*, 66(10), 27–32.

Hickman, M., Piquero, A., and Garner, J. (2008). Toward a national estimate of police use of nonlethal force. *Criminology and Public Policy*, 7, 563–604.

Hough, R. M. and Tatum, K. M. (2012). An examination of Florida policies on force continuums. *Policing: An International Journal of Police Strategies and Management*, 35, 39–54.

Hundersmarck, S. F., Vanderkooi, G., and Vasicek, M. (2016). Police use of force: transitioning policy into practice. *Police Forum*, 26(3), 3–8.

IACP (International Association of Chiefs of Police). (2006). *Use of force concepts and issues paper*. Washington, DC: IACP National Law Enforcement Policy Center.

Klinger, D. and Brunson, R. (2009). Police officer's perceptual distortions during lethal force situations: informing the reasonableness standard. *Criminology and Public Policy*, 8, 117–140.

Klinger, D., Rosenfeld, R., Isom, D., and Deckard, M. (2016). Race, crime, and the micro-ecology of deadly force. *Criminology and Public Policy*, 15(1), 193–222. doi:10.1111/1745-9133.12174

Lersch, K. M. and Mieczkowski, T. (2005). Violent police behavior: past, present, and future research directions. *Aggression and Violent Behaviour*, 10, 552–568.

Lim, H. and Lee, H. (2015). The effects of supervisor education and training on police use of force. *Criminal Justice Studies, 28*(4), 444–463. doi:10.1080/1478601X.2015.1077831

Mader, D. P. (2002). Design for Six Sigma. *Quality Progress*, 35(7), 82–86.

Makarios, M. and Pratt, T. (2012). The effectiveness of policies and programs that attempt to reduce firearm violence: a meta-analysis. *Crime and Delinquency*, 58(2), 222–244.

Mears, D. P. (2010). *American criminal justice policy: an evaluation approach to accountability and effectiveness*. New York: Cambridge University Press.

Moore, M. H. (2002). The limits of social science in guiding policy. *Criminology and Public Policy*, 2(1), 33–42.

Morrison, G. B. (2010). Deadly force in the United States. In J. B. Kuhns and J. Knutsson (Eds.), *Police use of force: a global perspective*. Santa Barbara, CA: Praeger, pp. 132–140.

Neyroud, P. (2009). Squaring the circles: research, evidence, policy-making, and police improvement in England and Wales. *Police Practice and Research*, 10(5/6), 437–449. doi:10.1080/15614260903378418

Pawson, R. (2006). *Evidence-based policy: a realist perspective*. London: Sage.

Peters, J., Peters, J.Jr., and Brave, M. (2006). Force continuums: three questions. *The Police Chief*, 73(1). Available at: www.iacp.org (accessed 26 May 2009).

Petrowski, T. (2002). Use-of-force policies and training: a reasoned approach. *FBI Law Enforcement Bulletin*, 71(10), 25–32.

Pickett, J. T., Mancini, C., Mears, D. P., and Gertz, M. (2015). Public (mis)understanding of crime policy: the effects of criminal justice experience and media reliance. *Criminal Justice Policy Review*, 26(5). doi:10.1177/0887403414526228

PERF (Police Executive Research Forum). (2016). *Use of force: taking policing to a higher standard, 30 guiding principles*. Washington, DC: Author.

Rogers, D. (2001). Use of force: agencies need to have a continuum and officers need to be able to articulate it. *Law Enforcement Technology*, 28(3): 82.

Rosenbaum, D. P. (2010). Police research: merging the policy and action research traditions. *Police Practice and Research: An International Journal*, 11(2), 144–149. doi:10.1080/15614261003593203

Ross, D. (2002). An assessment of Graham v. Connor, ten years later. *Policing: An International Journal of Police Strategies and Management*, 25, 294–318.

Ross, D. (2013). *Civil liability in criminal justice*. 7th ed. Waltham, MA: Anderson Publishing.

Shane, J. M. (2016). Improving police use of force: a policy essay on national data collection. *Criminal Justice Policy Review*, 1–21. doi:10.1177/0887403416662504

Shjarback, J. A. (2015). Emerging early intervention systems: an agency-specific pre-post comparison of formal citizen complaints of use of force. *Policing: A Journal of Policy and Practice*, 9(4), 314–325. doi:10.1093/police/pav006

Telep, C. W. (2016). Expanding the scope of evidence-based policing. *Criminology and Public Policy*, 15(1), 243–252. doi:10.1111/1745-9133.12188

Terrill, W. (2003). Police use of force and suspect resistance: the micro process of the police–suspect encounter. *Police Quarterly*, 6(1), 51–83.

Terrill, W. and Paoline, E. A. (2017). Police use of lethal force: does administrative policy matter? *Justice Quarterly*, 34(2), 193–216.

Terrill, W., Paoline, E., and Ingram, J. (2011). *Final technical report draft: assessing police use of force policy and outcomes.* Unpublished report submitted to U.S Department of Justice. Retrieved August 4, 2017 from https://www.ncjrs.gov/pdffiles1/nij/grants/237794.pdf

U.K. Home Office. (2012). *Definition of policing by consent.* December 10. London: HMSO.

U.S. Department of Justice, Office of Justice Programs. (1999). *Police use of excessive force – use of force by the police: overview of national and local data.* Washington, DC.

Weisburd, D. and Neyroud, P. (2014). Police science: toward a new paradigm. *Journal of Current Issues in Crime, Law and Law Enforcement*, 7(2), 227–246.

White, M. D. (2001). Controlling police decisions to use deadly force: reexamining the importance of administrative policy. *Crime and Delinquency*, 47, 131–151.

Williams, G. (2002). Force continuums: a liability to law enforcement? *FBI Law Enforcement Bulletin* (June), 14–19.

Wilson, J. Q. (1968). *Varieties of police behavior.* Cambridge, MA: Harvard University Press.

Wittrup, B. (2016). Improving use-of-force outcomes. *Corrections Today*, 78(6), 40.

Cases Cited

Graham v. Conner, 490 U.S. 386 (1989)

Tennessee v. Garner, 471 U.S. 1 (1985)

4

THE USE OF LESS LETHAL FORCE

STUDENT LEARNING OUTCOMES

- Students will be able to list and discuss factors affecting the use of force decision.
- Students will be able to describe the less lethal options available to officers.
- Students will be able to explain the role of technology in controlling people.
- Students will be able to discuss the techniques of tactical communication.
- Students will be able to explain the methods of defensive tactics.

Introduction

Law enforcement and correctional officers, and few others, at times must employ the use of force. Officers may be defending themselves or others, attempting an arrest or detention, or trying to overcome resistance or stop an escape. It is fair to say that varied circumstances can lead to varied force methods or devices used to control or restrain individuals. A person facing arrest poses a known potential for resistance. Yet many other individuals who were not the focus of an officer's enforcement effort may suddenly insert themselves or be brought unwillingly into a situation of being restrained.

How officers make decisions to use force, which option(s) the officer selects or reacts with, and subsequent evaluations of the officer's actions given the specific circumstances known to the officer are important topics for officers, agencies, citizens, and researchers. Among the sometimes near instantaneous decision components in a perceived threat event is what force option to react or respond with. A semantic debate of questionable consequence is the terminology choice of *non-* or *less*-lethal. Jason Bourne and James Bond show us that most objects can be used to kill a person but most public safety tools are not intended for that. In an article addressing the use of such options by the military, Kaurin (2010) put it this way: "These weapons are not intended to kill, permanently injure or maim; any effects are intended to be temporary, minor, and reversible" (p. 102).

An officer is imbued with the authority of society, designated to the government by its citizens. The authority allows the officer to conduct investigations and, in certain instances, take away a person's freedom. The laws and "rules" for exercising this immense authority are codified in law, prescribed in agency policies and procedures, reviewed by courts, commented on by media representatives, and supported and critiqued by citizens. The restraint of freedom ranges from brief detention to inquire after a person's activities if that person is believed to be involved in a crime, to taking the life of someone who poses an immediate threat of severe harm to another person or the officer.

The ability of law enforcement officers to wield the various tools of governmental authority is granted and ultimately judged or evaluated by the public. The legitimacy of this grant of authority is inextricably bound to the concept of accountability. Law enforcement organizations construct policies and procedures that guide the decision-making of their officers but also as a way to ensure this accountability. The ability of citizens to review the policies of their police agencies and indeed the reports regarding specific incidents and events is a critical component of the overall accountability mechanism that allows the public to have confidence in the department (President's Task Force on 21st Century Policing, 2015). Improper actions by law enforcement officials diminish the perception of legitimacy by citizens. There are many actions that can negatively impact the view of our local law enforcement agencies but the misuse of force against a fellow citizen is surely high on the list. In his seminal work on "street-level bureaucracy," Michael Lipsky (1980, 2010) devotes a great deal of time to the challenge of "holding workers to agency objectives" (p. 162). One of the challenges that Lipsky notes is adequate monitoring of employees by managers when the managers are dependent upon information from those very workers. This challenge exists in organizations of public service including law enforcement, social services, and education. Within policing organizations of contemporary society the limitations of worker information are mitigated through the use of formal reporting, supervisory observations and review, media scrutiny, potential court action, and the openness of records typical in such agencies. Of concern would be not the most routine functions of law enforcement officers, but more likely the infrequent but consequential and sometimes dramatic employment of force.

The jobs of law enforcement and corrections are hazardous. Skolnick and Fyfe (1993) said, "Certainly, force is sometimes appropriate – that's why cops carry batons and guns. Police should not be labeled 'brutal' simply because they employ forceful measures" (p. 10). Many police officers are killed in traffic-related circumstances based in part on the number of hours driving in a year and the necessity to be outside of the car near traffic. But people also assault and kill officers. While some observers oddly equate the overall number of people killed by police with officers being killed, the intention of those who murder society's peace-keepers is not the same as the lawful use of force by law enforcement. Fridell, Faggiani, Taylor, Brito and Kubu (2009) examined the impact of agency factors on violence against the police and noted that the National Institute for Occupational Safety and Health (NIOSH) (1996) list of ten risk factors for workplace assault include at least seven applicable to law enforcement officers:

> contact with the public, having a mobile work place, working with unstable or volatile people, working alone or in small numbers, working late at night or during early morning hours, working in high-crime areas, and working in community-based settings.
>
> *(p. 542)*

Some force is used to an extent not in keeping with need, policy, or perhaps law. Many people use the terms excessive force and police brutality synonymously. It is not mere semantics to draw a distinction between these two concepts; they are different. If, when opening a jar of pickles, your grip on the glass is too tight and the force with which you twist the lid is greater than necessary, the jar may shatter and the contents may spill out upon the ground. You perhaps misjudged the resistance of the lid or the rigidity of the container, but you certainly did not mean to cause damage in accessing the condiment. In this analogy, excessive force may result from incorrect or disproportional physical force or technique absent an intention to cause harm to a person or do something not authorized by law or policy. If we follow this metaphor to its culinary conclusion, had you taken the jar and thrown it on the ground we might approximate police brutality given that it was your *intention* to break the container.

It is important to note that the use of force is not a frequent occurrence. In addition to most use of force being infrequent (Hickman, Piquero, and Garner, 2008), most involves low level forms (National Institute of Justice, 1999; Garner, Buchanan, Schade, and Hepburn, 1996; IACP, 2012; PERF, 2016; Terrill, 2003). These low level forms of force "are minimal, with officers using their hands, arms or bodies to push or pull against a suspect to gain control" (NIJ, 2011a). A brief struggle to handcuff a person who does not comply may involve little in the way of physical force. But even the detention or arrest of a person to be searched or for a minor law violation can rapidly escalate to a violent attempt to resist or escape and result in harm or death to an officer. Over time, great effort has been spent in the design of devices to assist officers in overcoming resistance. No single device, technology, substance, or physical technique has proven completely effective in all cases. At times officers are disarmed by individuals and the very devices intended to help control the situation are used against them.

Trained techniques and devices may assist officers in carrying out the function of controlling a person. Applying physical techniques and employing various devices will not always occur without unintended consequences. The courts have recognized that 20/20 hindsight is not the vantage point for judging the appropriateness of selecting one tool over another or using one physical technique instead of a different one. There are always *different* choices that can be made; the issue is whether the actual choice was objectively reasonable (Terrill, 2009). Less lethal devices used in the civilian environment range from just a tactical choice and application to a strategic choice that, when feasible, may reduce negative outcomes on multiple levels. The U.S. military has often been called to perform peace-keeping duties and this too requires the ability to use something other than lethal force (Donaldson, 2015). While we consider this in greater detail elsewhere in the book it is important to emphasize that the inventory of options presented in this chapter does not imply a hierarchy or relative weighting.

Tactical Communications

The discussion over how much the use of words, tone, and body language are implicated as a use of force topic is not settled (Terrill and Mastrofski, 2002; Alpert and Dunham, 1999; Klinger, 1995). The sheer volume of verbal direction, including coercive commands, cannot be overlooked in considering use of force and how to train officers. While verbal de-escalation methods have been emphasized, verbal and nonverbal communication skills permeate all aspects of an officer's interactions with citizens, suspects, and inmates. This reality suggests communication absent physical technique as a central component of a 360-degree force options model.

As discussed elsewhere in the book, a psychological approach based on the individual characteristics of an officer would properly incorporate assessment of his verbal abilities. As with many skills and techniques, this can be developed in officers. The long popular "Verbal Judo" (Thompson, 1994) is but one example of a program developed and marketed to offer tips and techniques to facilitate interactions with the public. Interpersonal communication skills have long been a component of academy curricula. Understanding the components within a communications model and the different factors that influence the overall communications process is important if one wants to achieve an effective level of skill in communications. There is no shortage of research on communication between and among people. Various researchers and observers have proposed different frameworks or emphasized specific techniques, yet each is built upon the platform of a sender, a receiver, a message, and the medium used to convey the message.

The human officer is equipped with the exquisite learning machine known as the brain. This allows the officer to absorb and process information, to learn over time based on experiences, and to utilize language and non-verbals to convey information to others. It is not the case that simply by virtue of being able to verbalize from a young age and then spend portions of every day of life speaking to others that a person becomes a master of communication. Learning, practice, insights and reflection are all parts of how a person consciously improves his or her ability to receive and convey information, including directing others. How effectively an individual officer is able to control some situations and influence individuals, while not solely dependent on the officer, can certainly be influenced in most tasks by an officer's mindset and approach. Basic recruit academy training as well as in-service blocks of instruction on interpersonal communications reinforces for the officer those skills used in effective communications as well as the advantages of gaining compliance without the use of more forceful measures than language and body posture.

As part of their Critical Issues in Policing series, in 2016 the Police Executive Research Forum (PERF) launched a new conceptualization of a law enforcement communications model, 'Integrating Communications Assessment and Tactics' (ICAT). PERF subtitled this training as a guide for defusing critical incidents. Observations by the organization's executive director Chuck Wexler note that officer safety and the safety of people police encounter is directly connected to police–community relationships (PERF, 2016). The ICAT training guide is intended by PERF to be utilized with another recent publication by the organization, *Guiding Principles on Use of Force* (2016). A premise of the training is that officers need more training and better quality training. Further, that the situation in which officers specifically face a person behaving erratically but possessing no firearm presents challenges that have often had a negative outcome. Administrators certainly hope to avoid loss of life or injury, and to enhance the abilities of their officers to respond in various ways to do that.

Rory Miller and Lawrence Kane in their book *Scaling Force* (2012) referred to the presence of an officer as "skillfully doing nothing." The implication is that while physical force other than perhaps a guiding touch is not used at this stage of an interaction, the officer still has the ability to influence the behavior of the subject. How does this come about? Each of us has had many opportunities in life to interact with someone who presented themselves as competent, powerful, domineering, wise, or in other ways that induced or compelled compliance. In the positive sense of this apparent ability, a person may give direction to others, calm a situation, or provide comfort seemingly through their mere presence. We may refer to "military bearing" or "command presence" as manifestations of this apparent competence.

Law enforcement academy instruction emphasizes command presence as an important way to gain the cooperation or compliance of citizens. Though police officers in the U.K. rarely carry firearms, even American officers who possess them rarely use their presence as something to gain the compliance of the citizen in an average encounter. No – it is through presence and words that almost every interaction is conducted and resolved. How an officer looks, how she sounds, and how she carries herself are important parts of communicating on the job. Clearly the words and behavior of the officer matter as well. If officers present themselves well in uniform and are well-groomed they may still be less than effective if their behavior is unprofessional in any way. The interplay of an officer giving direction and a person disregarding or resisting that direction may be implicated in a subsequent use of force (Alpert and Dunham, 1999). An individual who fails to follow the ostensibly lawful directions of a law enforcement officer presents a tangible warning sign of further resistance and potentially a threat to safety. And when a suspect uses force it has been consistently found to impact subsequent use of force by police (Leinfelt, 2005; Garner, Schade, Hepburn, and Buchanan, 1995).

The verbal aspect of communication cannot be divorced from the non-verbal in the world of officers interacting with people on the street or in a correctional setting; it's simply part of the process. Still, verbalizing a request, instruction, or command has bits and pieces that officers should work to grasp – their own and the subject's. The speed or rate a person speaks can convey information in different ways. If you have ever practiced a presentation or speech you have experienced this. Likewise, the volume at which someone speaks may be intended to simply gain attention, or keep attention through variance (Micklo, 2012). Without varying the pitch or tone of your voice, it may be difficult to convey much emotion. And while an officer may control his voice with the intention of calming a situation (see for example Knowlton and Larkin, 2006), he may be perceived as uncaring or detached. An officer must learn to be consciously aware of these factors in the voices of others as well as when changes occur which can signal the change in emotion that may precipitate resistance. Officers enter most encounters trying to talk to subjects. It is important for officers to recognize the point at which communication tactics are failing and so turn to other options for safety (Wolf, Mesloh, Henych, and Thompson, 2009).

Defensive Tactics

Whether attempting to control and restrain a person or responding to assault, the use of various physical techniques has a long history. From the Greek *pankration* to Chinese *shuai jiao*, early civilizations developed systems of fighting that combined balance displacement, holds, and strikes as the forerunners of today's martial arts, military close-quarters combat methods, and defensive tactics and control techniques for officers.

It is not semantics to refer to most control techniques as defensive tactics. When a citizen drives by a traffic stop or observes on a television show multiple officers struggling with an individual, he can misinterpret what he sees as "ganging up" on a person. Trying to control a resisting or assaulting person's limbs without causing injury is a different proposition to striking the person into submission or incapacitation. Multiple officers are often more effective (when they are available) to accomplish an arrest or restraint with less chance of anyone being seriously injured.

The importance of teaching effective physical control methods would seem self-evident. The goal of such defensive tactics training is to equip an entry level officer with the skills to defend him- or herself and bring resistant individuals under control, preferably without harm to either person. This is ambitious indeed, with officers generally constrained to techniques aimed at restraining the hands and arms of a resistant subject, while that subject may feel no compunction about using any available method and as much ferocity as is required to defeat the arrest attempt or outright assault the officer.

Part of the training of law enforcement and correctional officers is to conduct threat assessments of situations and people. This involves gauging the abilities and intent of people whom the officer encounters, whether on the street or in a cell block. One aspect of threat assessment is the verbal communication with the subject that may provide clues to the person's intention in conjunction with observed physical behavior. Some situations, such as an impending arrest or a forced cell move, heighten an officer's awareness that resistance may lead to force usage. Many other circumstances can give rise to what was an uncertain or even unlikely need for force that arose as an incident progressed. The various situational factors and types of subject resistance correspond to appropriate and hopefully effective force. How physical techniques are taught and practiced with peers by necessity avoids the intensity or intention to harm one another. All those who train in physical control skills work toward effective employment of the skills in what will be unpredictable conditions with a subject or subjects acting, reacting, and intent on not being controlled.

Foundational to safe officer interactions are the concepts of body movement and positioning. An officer is constantly reminded during training sessions to maintain balance and consider ways to unbalance a person struggling against restraint. Recruits are taught the interview stance, a positioning of the body to be prepared in case the person suddenly attacks the officer. Added to the stance is awareness and adjustments in relative positioning to the subject, in order that position and distance work to the officer's advantage until the time comes to approach someone to restrain them. The concept of a "reactionary gap" is taught as a minimum distance to keep between an officer and a subject, a distance that is sufficient to thwart an initial attempt to strike or kick the officer.

Officers learn pressure point techniques to use "pain compliance" to induce a subject to stop resisting. Various arm holds and locks called "transporters" can be effective in many situations to stop a person's resistance or at least control some of their movement. These holds are also intended to aid the application of restraint devices such as handcuffs. Along with the use of restraint devices comes the need to search an arrestee. There should never be an assumption that a person who may have his hands or even his ankles restrained by some device is not still dangerous or is unable to strike or use his body. Recruits learn blocking techniques to try to absorb or redirect sudden attack. Knowing that action precedes reaction reminds officers that they may not be completely successful in avoiding being struck by someone. Striking techniques using the officer's hands or feet can be used to both redirect a subject's attention while the officer works to gain control, and to gain compliance through pain.

Some fights will end up on the ground. A subject may tackle or trip an officer, an officer may tackle or trip a subject, or both may lose their balance during a struggle and fall. Recruits are taught ways to fall so as to minimize the risk of injury. Also, specific take down methods dating back to antiquity are taught to gain the advantage over the fighting or resisting person. Grappling with another person can tire an officer quite rapidly, and this increases the danger of an event ending badly. Any number of people have had exposure to ground-fighting techniques that may result in an officer being taken down, and increased uncertainty about the outcome of a fight that places all of the officer's tools within easy reach of the subject. Speed, effectiveness, and acting within both policy and law, are prerequisites to a use of force event having a successful outcome. These circumstances surrounding the force usage must be thoroughly documented by the officer involved.

Batons

We imagine early humans using a club made of a tree limb offensively or defensively: possibly a less than effective weapon against large carnivores, but handy against a fellow *homo sapiens*. Variations in armed conflict saw wood augmented with spear tips for piercing or blades for slicing people, or even the legs of horses in battle. Historically, the truncheon of the early British constable was iconic and has remained an available tool since the early 1800s. More contemporary use of batons and similar tools provides the option of an impact weapon or in some circumstances a leverage device for defense, countering an attack, and overcoming resistance. The use of a baton provides something of a distance advantage over bare hands alone as well as the multiplier effect of physics as the device gains momentum through the swing before it makes contact with the intended target. As with comparable body mechanics in a variety of sports, the person using the baton must combine body mechanics with speed to impart kinetic energy to the body part targeted. Striking an area of the body (typically large muscle groups) can cause pain to someone whose physical sensations are not overly impeded by intoxication, emotion, or physiological resistance based on another factor.

The modern baton is worn in a holder on the officer's utility belt. Compact expandable metal batons such as those manufactured by ASP fit into a shortened holder. This overcomes the problem in years past of an officer quickly exiting a patrol car and leaving the longer baton in a holder or on the seat of the car. Smaller weapons in the baton family include yawaras, kubotons, and more dated devices such as the sap or blackjack. These compact rods are concealable and easier to carry for an officer in plainclothes. As with a piece of defensive equipment, the officer must be trained in its use and the agency should have a written policy addressing its possession or use. Such devices are obviously only effective at close range and with varied results. Most would be used to strike a nerve bundle or muscle group, or apply steady, concentrated pressure on an available pressure point to gain compliance through pain.

WHAT-WHY: *TOOL OR TROUBLE?*

Nunchukas were popularized in American culture through the movies of Bruce Lee. The small town of Anderson, California seems as likely or unlikely a place as any to try out the use of nunchuckas as a defensive tactics tool for their police department. The nunchuka is two pieces of wood connected by a cord and they are often seen as an offensive weapon used to strike, much like their ancestor, thought by many to be the rice thresher. While the device can be manipulated to produce pain on a joint or pressure point, the challenge of adequate training hours devoted to becoming proficient with such techniques deems it a questionable substitute for the expandable baton or other tools.

(Keating 2016)

Electronic Control Devices

Electrical current induces muscle contraction and can motivate human action or cessation of action when combined with commands in a situation of officers seeking control over an individual. Introduction of such electro-muscular disruption has been accomplished through the development of a number of tools over many years. Variously known as electronic control devices (ECDs), electronic control weapons (ECWs), or conducted energy devices (CEDs), the tools are used with the hope of reducing officer and subject injuries (Lin and Jones, 2010; Smith, Kaminski, Rojek, Alpert, and Mathis, 2007) and avoiding the use of more injurious options including deadly force (Ferdik, Kaminski, Cooney, and Sevigny, 2014; NIJ, 2011b).

In 2010, the IACP published "Electronic Control Weapons." In this model policy, the IACP defined an ECW this way: "A weapon that uses electricity to override voluntary motor responses, or apply pain in order to gain compliance or overcome resistance" (p. 1). With a near-ubiquitous presence of CED's in law enforcement agencies, and significant numbers of correctional facilities issuing pepper spray to some or all officers or supervisors, less lethal technologies offer the potential for reduced injuries to subjects and officers.

> Unlike a professional hockey fight where a player would be severely sanctioned for using his stick instead of his fist, an officer is expected and trained to deploy weapons such as a baton, pepper spray, or Taser to counter an offender determined to fight an officer. Use of these technologies is certainly considered a justified, reasonable, and appropriate use of force by an officer sworn to uphold the law and maintain public safety, and is an important action to minimize injury to both officers and suspects.
>
> *(IACP/COPS, 2012)*

While guidelines and recommendations have been promulgated by some groups and individual researchers (Alpert and Dunham, 2010; PERF and U.S. Department of Justice, 2011), each agency makes its own determination of where to include the CED within it policies and training (Thomas, Collins, and Lovrich, 2011). That public service providers including police struggle with the challenges of a mentally disturbed person who is violent, offers explanation why TASER use was seen as twice as likely to be used over oleoresin capsicum (OC) (Brandl and Stroshine, 2015).

CEDs have been generally judged to be effective in bringing people under control or stopping or deterring them long enough to be controlled (Crow and Adrion, 2011; Paoline, Terrill, and Ingram, 2012). Like every less lethal option, the devices are not a panacea. And like every device, they may be used at the wrong time, in the wrong way, or to no effect. In the case of *Bryan v. McPherson* (2009), TASER usage on a motorist was held to be excessive force when the agitated but arguably non-attacking man was shot with TASER, causing him to fall down and receive significant facial injury. It is important that agencies inform the public about appropriate device usage, the effectiveness of the CEDs, and what the known medical risks or factors are (Ready, White, and Fisher, 2008). The IACP in their model policy on ECWs also notes that personnel should summon EMTs if any of a number of things occurs to signal the possibility of an injury (2010). There is some observation that *Bryan* may also be of note to corrections when considering whether a force option is used maliciously and to cause harm (Ninth Circuit's Police Taser Decision not Landmark Described by Media, but Still Raises Points of Interest for Corrections, 2010).

Pepper Spray and Chemical Sprays

Throughout the history of warfare people have harnessed irritating substances to gain a battlefield advantage. Historically, 3,000-year-old accounts exist of Chinese use of irritants (and poisons), burning sulfur employed by the forces of different societies to irritate or temporarily blind enemies, and the development and weaponization of various poisonous agents in modern warfare. For law enforcement and corrections the intention is to disrupt and disperse groups or to impair an individual while taking him into custody.

The modern formulation of capsicum or pepper spray uses capsaicin taken from peppers. The oleoresin capsicum (OC) is generally separated by grinding the pepper and using an organic solvent which leaves a sticky oleoresin. The substance is suspended in water using an emulsifier and then placed into a pressurized container, sometimes with additional agents, to disperse in a stream, a cone pattern, or as foam. There are large canisters of spray for crowd or prison-yard dispersal, pepper balls that vaporize to a mist on contact, and weapon-propelled canisters to deliver at some distance. Each delivery method has situational applications.

The effects on individuals, bears, dogs, and other creatures, include inflammation of eyes and nasal passages causing an inability to see and difficulty in breathing. Officers are generally required to undergo exposure to the spray as part of their certification to use the product. This is so that they do not panic when they feel partial effects themselves when someone has deployed OC. Also, it provides an opportunity for empathy: to understand that using the OC does cause pain or discomfort, and the importance of assisting a subject in cleaning off the residue after control is achieved. Indeed, Ross (2005) noted, in his review of multiple use of force studies, a reduction in baton use as pepper spray use increased. The effect of using CEWs has also brought less use of lethal and less lethal force as noted above.

OC has been gauged as effective over the past 20 years and in a number of studies (Adang, Kaminski, Howell, and Mensink, 2006; Kaminski, Edwards, and Johnson, 1999; Morabito and Doerner, 1997). It has also been noted by researchers (though already known by many officers) that OC was least effective on people who were most resistant (Brandl and Stroshine, 2015) or under the influence of alcohol or narcotics (Kaminski and Edwards, 1997) and that further force was likely to be used in these cases.

K-9

History is also replete with examples of the use of animals in warfare, hunting, and for security. The Greeks, Romans, Babylonians and others all used various but generally large breeds of canine for defensive and offensive purposes. Whether for fighting, carrying communications, or as mascots, dogs have filled many roles. In modern law enforcement and corrections, the trained canine is used in tracking wanted individuals who have escaped or fled, the search for dead bodies or living missing persons, as deterrent and security at facilities or events, searching for drugs, explosives, or evidence of arson, and to locate places where suspects have hidden.

Many of the larger canine breeds have the jaw strength and dentition to be effective offensively and defensively in addition to their primary role in detection, tracking, or deterrence. In contemporary society the issue of using dogs to attack and bite a suspect has been a subject of some debate (Mesloh, 2006, 2015). A component of the controversy over canine use comes in claims of overuse against African Americans during arrest or open air events. A research article from 1961 stated the following:

> From the survey it appears that the public has fully accepted the canine corps. There were only three complaints reported, one not described and the other two stemming from the feeling among Negroes that dogs are used in their areas disproportionately to the need for them. It is probably true that dogs are used in Negro areas more than in white areas, but they are assigned according to the crime rate of an area, not to the color of the people living in it.
>
> *(Handy, Harrington, and Pittman, 1961)*

Historically, armies armored some dogs for battle; modern law enforcement often outfits the canine with ballistic armor protection and may equip some with cameras. In an age when technology is used ever-increasingly, the use of electronics to monitor canine health and performance has led to calls for sensitive devices to track the biometrics of animals (Keller, 2016). In contemporary times, the use of canines to augment officers remains a useful option to reduce harm to officers as well as exploit a dog's abilities such as sniffing and tracking. The selection and training of canines and officers is key (IACP, 2015).

Restraints

The use of restraints is considered by some departments as a use of force. Where this is the case, there is the potential for misunderstanding or misconstruing the use of force when comparing agencies. The practice of handcuffing those arrested is near-universal, and this can obscure the distinction between "real" use of force and those merely handcuffed per policy and accepted safety procedures. Though an officer may simply place handcuffs on a compliant arrestee for the duration of a squad car ride to jail, she may be required to write a use of force report, or at least include the use of handcuffs in her arrest report. This type of documentation is important and also reflects the fact that handcuff usage as a use of force can be judged excessive (Civil Liability for the Use of Handcuffs, 2008). Restraints also include waist chains for the transportation of some inmates to court or to a different facility from where they are housed, especially if they are deemed a high security risk. Ankle cuffs or shackles are utilized to deter a person from running away, again at court or during transport.

Particularly violent persons have been restrained through the use of both handcuffs and a leg hobble connected behind their back making them unable to stand. This has been referred to as a "hog-tie" position and has been criticized by some for its use during arrest-related or in-custody death cases. This is not to say that the hobble was a cause of a death. A person in such a state of agitation that officers decide to restrain him using a hobble, may die because of the condition or circumstances that brought him to the attention of police. Officers should adjust positioning of the subject as needed, monitor his behavior, and document all steps taken during the arrest incident and information gained from others about the person's behavior prior to being restrained if possible.

Documenting and Investigating Force

Regardless of the force option selected, it is important to document the usage, compile all reports, review them for policy and training implications, and follow up through administrative action. The more force used or the greater an injury, the more documentation and greater the level of detail generally called for. An application of a CED may cause little damage past a small barb laceration, but if the stunned subject falls against a hard object and sustains an injury, a complete recounting of the incident is in order. In the IACP/COPS 2012 document *Emerging Use of Force Issues: Balancing Public and Officer Safety*, a symposium group to discuss use of force made a recommendation, among others, to:

> Review current use of force reporting policies in the context of both state and national models, and update or revise those policies as appropriate or needed. Proactively use that data to conduct annual use of force reviews that can influence policy and training enhancement.
>
> *(p. 29)*

The various issues of data collection and analysis are of concern in all uses of force, lethal and less lethal. In assessing the types and trends of force and working to identify excessive force, data quality is as much a concern as in many areas of the criminal justice system. It is questionable whether the currently decentralized and inconsistent collection methods are sufficient to provide a valid basis to analyze the state of the field (Hickman and Poore, 2016). When the bulk of information known to the public regarding use of force comes from media, it is important for agencies to work to educate, through various news outlets, about appropriate use of force options and how these are monitored.

External Oversight

Reporting of force usage is available generally to any citizen, media outlet, attorney, court or other that seeks to review specific reports. The discussion of consent decrees, memoranda of agreement, and technical assistance initiated by the U.S. Department of Justice's Civil Rights Division is one approach to external action. In addition, a number of communities and agencies have review boards in place to examine the use of force and other activities of their local law enforcement agency. This may be in conjunction with a consent decree or other action, or through local efforts alone. Given the large numbers of public safety agencies in the United States it would be accurate to say that only a small fraction utilizes formal citizen oversight boards or mechanisms. An external review board is an arrangement often arrived at following a history of problems in the pattern of force use by agency members. Citizen oversight tends to focus on use of force be a law enforcement agency, yet the backdrop of community conditions and tensions is often deserving of attention.

The much publicized deadly use of force against a black man by an officer of the Ferguson, Missouri Police Department, was ruled self-defense, but long-simmering questions exist both about the treatment of citizens by local law enforcement, and about the way historic inequity stirs so much emotion in communities across the country. Sances and You (2017) note in a recent study of patterns of municipal fines, that blacks are disproportionately impacted by a practice of using "exploitative revenue sources." Examining data from over 9,000 cities, the researchers illuminate a connection between proportion of black citizens and the use of fines as a significant source of government revenue. This may implicate the police as an instrument of a potentially biased practice, much as slave patrol in the 1800s. But the *policy* is that of the locally elected representatives, not the police.

As we focus in the book on the use of force by employees of our criminal justice system, we must remember that individual officer actions often reflect the practices of the field and that in turn many of these practices derive from the policies of lawmakers and elected decision-makers who may create law and policy from a frame of national views or priorities. It is generally beyond the purview of a line-level officer, or even an administrator within a criminal justice agency, to recognize, let alone change, possible paradigms potentially informed by social conflict more than consensus theory operating in the background of society.

GOING GLOBAL

Amid talk of increased terror attacks and threats and increased gang crime, police in the U.K. are being surveyed to gauge their view about whether they should carry firearms. Strong views are held for and against increasing numbers of firearms officers, even as government sources chronicle the reduced numbers of those equipped, according to a July, 2017 *Guardian* newspaper article. The last such survey took place in 2006. Estimates are that just 5 percent of police in England and Wales carry firearms and doing so is voluntary and comes with extensive training. If an officer is designated an Authorized Firearms Officer (AFO), he or she is available for assignment to what is referred to as firearms operations. These are incidents where officers are authorized in advance to carry firearms. At the twelve months ending March 2016, 14,753 such operations were recorded, with only seven incidents in which a gun was actually fired (National Police Chiefs Council and Home Office).

Summary

That there are less lethal options available to resolve certain incidents and fill certain force needs is good and important. And while it is not always feasible to use a less-lethal option or even to mechanically run through a list to determine the "least" forceful option, training and technology have given modern officers and agencies improvements over decades past. Examination of the circumstances in which officers use force has been extensive and mixed. Resisting arrest, apparent intoxication, as well as patrol encounters in a crime-prone area are among several factors correlated with increased incidence of force employment.

As new items are added to the repertoire of criminal justice personnel they understandably go through a shake-down phase as agencies and individual officers determine in real-world settings how and when they can be used to best advantage. With pepper spray and CEWs, for example, there was a predictable upswing in usage as the tools proved effective in halting resistance. These devices brought reductions in the use of more potentially harmful options as well as lowering the numbers of subjects and officers injured.

Physical techniques remain standard in controlling movement, resistance or assault by subjects, and officers must be trained to effect an arrest or restraint in the most appropriate manner. The human officer fulfills many duties and tasks; very few of these involve using force against another human. Given this fact, it is unrealistic to assume, even as important as the use of force is, that the human officer will be a master of restraining all manner of people without injury or error. Agencies create policy and training and provide supervision to ensure that employees have adequate tools and guidance to perform at an acceptable level and with the proper intent to carry out their duties lawfully.

KEY TERMS

Less lethal force options
Chemical restraint
Conducted energy device (CED)
Defensive tactics
Oleoresin capsicum

Discussion Questions

1. What factors impact the use of force decision?
2. How can technology affect use of force outcomes?
3. Why is defensive tactics training important? How much should officers receive?
4. Describe and discuss the less lethal options available to officers.
5. What role do tactical communications play in reducing the need to use force?

TRY THIS

Research governmental websites and credible sources for information about pepper spray. What new information did you learn about its use and effects?

References

Adang, O. M. J., Kaminski, R. J., Howell, M. Q., and Mensink, J. (2006). Assessing the performance of pepper spray in use-of-force encounters: the Dutch experience. *Policing: An International Journal of Police Strategies and Management*, 29, 282–305.

Alpert, G. P. and Dunham, R. G. (1999). *The force factor: measuring police use of force relative to suspect resistance.* Washington, DC: Police Executive Research Forum.

Alpert, G. and Dunham, R. (2010). Policy and training recommendations related to police use of CEDs: Overview of findings from a comprehensive national study. *Police Quarterly*, 13(3), 235–259.

Brandl, S. G. and Stroshine, M. S. (2015). Oleoresin capsicum spray and TASERs: a comparison of factors predicting use and effectiveness. *Criminal Justice Policy Review*, 27, 1–28. doi:0887403415578732

Bryan v. McPherson, 630 F.3d 805 (2009).

Civil liability for the use of handcuffs: part I – handcuffs as excessive force. *AELE Monthly Law Journal*, 10 (2008), 101–109. www.aele.org/law/2008LROCT/2008-10MLJ101.pdf

Crow, M. S. and Adrion, B. (2011). Focal concerns and police use of force: examining factors associated with TASER use. *Police Quarterly*, 14, 366–387.

Donaldson, P. (2015). On the cusp of something with much promise but level of uncertainty. *Military Technology*, 39(11), 57–59.

Ferdik, F. V., Kaminski, R. J., Cooney, M. D., and Sevigny, E. L. (2014). The influence of agency policies on conducted energy device use and police use of lethal force. *Police Quarterly*, 17(4), 328–358.

Fridell, L., Faggiani, D., Taylor, B., Brito, C. S., and Kubu, B. (2009). The impact of agency context, policies, and practices on violence against police. *Journal of Criminal Justice*, 37(6), 542–552.

Garner, J., Schade, T., Hepburn, H., and Buchanan, J. (1995). Measuring the continuum of force used by and against the police. *Criminal Justice Review* 20(2): 146–168.

Garner, J., Buchanan, J., Schade, T., and Hepburn, J. (1996). Understanding the use of force by and against the police. National Institute of Justice, Research in Brief, November. Washington, DC: United States Department of Justice, National Institute of Justice.

Handy, W. F., Harrington, M., and Pittman, D. J. (1961). The K-9 Corps: the use of dogs in police work. *Journal of Criminal Law, Criminology and Police Science*, 52(3), 328–337.

Hickman, M. J., Piquero, A. R., and Garner, J. H. (2008). Toward a national estimate of police use of nonlethal force. *Criminology and Public Policy*, 7(4), 563–604. doi:10.1111/j.1745-9133.2008.00528.x

Hickman, M. J. and Poore, J. E. (2016). National data on citizen complaints about police use of force: data quality concerns and the potential misuse of statistical evidence to address police agency conduct. *Criminal Justice Policy Review*, 27(5), 455–479.

International Association of Chiefs of Police. (2010). *Electronic control weapons, model policy.* Alexandria, VA: Author.

International Association of Chiefs of Police. (2012). *Emerging use of force issues: balancing public and officer safety.* Alexandria, VA: Author.

International Association of Chiefs of Police. (2015). *Patrol canines: concepts and issues paper.* Washington, DC: IACP National Law Enforcement Policy Center.

Kaminski, R. and Edwards, S. (1997). Assessing the incapacitative effects of pepper spray during resistive encounters with the police. *Policing*, 22(1), 7–29.

Kaminski, R. J., Edwards, S. M., and Johnson, J. W. (1999). Assessing the incapacitative effects of pepper spray during resistive encounters with the police. *Policing: An International Journal of Police Strategies and Management*, 22, 7–29.

Kaurin, P. (2010). With fear and trembling: an ethical framework for non-lethal weapons. *Journal of Military Ethics*, 9(1), 100–114.

Keating, M. (2016). Calling Bruce Lee: will more police acquire nunchucks? (with related video). *American City and County Exclusive Insight*, 1.

Keller, J. (2016). DHS needs rugged dog-wearable electronics to monitor health of trained canines. *Military and Aerospace Electronics*, 27(8), 26.

Klinger, D. (1995). The micro-structure of nonlethal force: baseline data from an observational study. *Criminal Justice Review*, 20, 169–186.

Knowlton, G.E. and Larkin, K.T. (2006). The influence of voice volume, pitch, and speech rate on progressive relaxation training: application of methods from speech. Pathology and Audiology. *Applied Psychophysiology Biofeedback*, 31(2), 173–185. doi:10.1007/s10484-006-9014-6

Leinfelt, F. H. (2005). Predicting use of non-lethal force in a mid-size police department: a longitudinal analysis of the influence of subject and situational variables. *The Police Journal*, 78, 285–300.

Lin, Y. and Jones, T. (2010). Electronic control devices and use of force outcomes: incidence and severity of use of force, and frequency of injuries to arrestees and police officers. *Policing: An International Journal of Police Strategies and Management*, 33(1), 152–178.

Lipsky, M. (1980). *Street-level bureaucracy: dilemmas of the individual in public services*. New York: Russell Sage Foundation.

Lipsky, M. (2010). *Street-level bureaucracy: dilemmas of the individual in public service*. New York: Russell Sage Foundation.

Mesloh, C. (2006). Barks or bites? the impact of training on police canine force outcomes. *Police Practice and Research*, 7(4), 323–335. doi:10.1080/15614260600919670

Mesloh, C. (2015). An examination of police canine use of force in the State of Florida. Ph.D. dissertation, University of Central Florida.

Micklo, Erin (2012). Performing poetry: managing tone, pitch, volume and rate. *Understanding Poetry*. Paper 3. http://digitalcommons.imsa.edu/poetry/3

Miller, R. and Kane, L. A. (2012) *Scaling force*. Wolfeboro, NH: YMAA Publication Center.

Morabito, E. V. and Doerner, W. G. (1997). Police use of less-than-lethal force: oleoresin capsicum (OC) spray. *Policing: An International Journal of Police Strategies and Management*, 20, 680–697.

National Institute of Justice. (1999). *Use of force by police: overview of national and local data*. DOJ Publication no. NCJ 176330. Washington, DC: U.S. Department of Justice, Office of Justice Programs, National Institute of Justice.

National Institute of Justice. (2011a). *Police use of force, tasers and other less-lethal weapons*. DOJ Publication no. NCJ 232215. Washington, DC: U.S. Department of Justice, Office of Justice Programs, National Institute of Justice.

National Institute of Justice. (2011b). *NIJ special report: study of deaths following electro-muscular disruption*. DOJ Publication no. NCJ 233432. Washington, DC: US Department of Justice.

National Institute for Occupational Safety and Health. (1996). *Violence in the workplace: risk factors and prevention strategies* (Current Intelligence Bulletin 57). Washington, DC: U.S. Department of Health and Human Services.

Ninth Circuit's police taser decision not landmark described by media, but still raises points of interest for corrections. (2010). *Correctional Law Reporter*, 21(6), 81–96.

PaolineE. A. and Terrill, W. (2007). Police education, experience, and the use of force. *Criminal Justice Behavior*, 34(2): 179–196.

Paoline, E. A., Terrill, W. and Ingram, J. R. (2012). Police use of force and officer injuries: comparing conducted energy devices (CEDs) to hands- and weapon-based tactics. *Police Quarterly*, 15(2), 115–136.

Police Executive Research Forum.(2016). *Integrating communications, assessment, and tactics*. Critical Issues in Policing series. Washington, DC: Police Executive Research Forum.

Police Executive Research Forum.(2016). *Use of force: taking police to a higher standard. 30 guiding principles*. Critical Issues in Policing series. Washington, DC: Police Executive Research Forum.

Police Executive Research Forum andU.S. Department of Justice. (2011). *2011 electronic control weapon guidelines*. DOJ Publication no. e021111339. Washington, DC: Office of Community Oriented Policing Services.

Ready, J., White, M.D., and Fisher, C. (2008). Shock value: a comparative analysis of news reports and official police records on TASER deployments. *Policing*, 31(1), 148–170.

Ross, D. (2005). A content analysis of the emerging trends in the use of non-lethal force research in policing. *Law Enforcement Executive Forum*, 5(1), 121–148.

Sances, M. W. and You, H. Y. (2017). Who pays for government? descriptive representation and exploitative revenue sources. *Journal of Politics*, 79(3), 1090–1094.

Skolnick, J. and Fyfe, J. J. (1993). *Above the law: police and the excessive use of force*. New York: Free Press.

Smith, M.R., Kaminski, R.J., Rojek, J., Alpert, G.P., and Mathis, J. (2007). The impact of conducted energy devices and other types of force on officer and suspect injuries. *Policing*, 30(3), 423–446.

Terrill, W. (2003). Police use of force and suspect resistance: the micro process of the police–suspect encounter. *Police Quarterly*, 6(1), 51–83.

Terrill, W. (2009). The elusive nature of reasonableness. *Criminology and Public Policy*, 8(1), 163–172.

Terrill, W., Leinfelt, F. H., and Kwak, D. (2008). Examining police use of force: a smaller agency perspective. *Policing*, 31(1), 57–76.

Terrill, W. and Mastrofski, S. (2002). Situational and officer based determinants of police coercion. *Justice Quarterly*, 19, 215–248.

Terrill, W. and Paoline, E. A. (2017). Police use of less lethal force: does administrative policy matter? *Justice Quarterly*, 34(2), 193–216.

The President's Task Force on 21st Century Policing. (2015). *Final report*. Washington, DC: U.S. Department of Justice.

Thomas, K., Collins, P., and Lovrich, N. (2011). An analysis of written conductive energy device policies: are municipal policing agencies meeting PERF recommendations? *Criminal Justice Policy Review*, 23(4), 399–426.

Thompson, G. J. (1994). *Verbal judo*. Jacksonville, FL: Institute of Police Technology and Management.

Wolf, R., Mesloh, C., Henych, M., and Thompson, L. F. (2009). Police use of force and the cumulative force factor. *Policing*, 32(4), 739–757. doi:10.1108/13639510911000795

5

THE USE OF LETHAL FORCE

STUDENT LEARNING OUTCOMES

- Students will be able to describe common characteristics of lethal force situations.
- Students will be able to describe the correlation between firearm prevalence and firearm death.
- Students will be able to explain the impact of *Tennessee v. Garner* on police use of lethal force in the United States.
- Students will be able to discuss the process of investigating the use of lethal force by officers.
- Students will be able to explain the dynamic of perceiving lethal threat.

Introduction

A representative definition from Florida law that is consistent among the states says that "the term 'deadly force' means force that is likely to cause death or great bodily harm ..." (FSS 776.06, 2017). It is clear that the use of deadly force by an officer is the most consequential action he can take. One or more people may be seriously injured or killed in the event. Trauma will likely follow for numerous people. An intense investigation with potential agency or legal ramifications will occur. Does all of this go through the mind of an officer in the seconds preceding a use of deadly force? This thought is debated, surveyed, studied, and parsed. While officers know that being involved in a deadly force encounter may occur in their career, they cannot know the emotions associated with such an event unless it actually occurs.

Deadly force employed by law enforcement officers is generally confined to instances in which an officer perceives he or another person is at risk of death or serious injury, or where a person who has committed a violent crime or will commit another violent crime is fleeing arrest. In considering the use of deadly force, one matter frequently taught to law enforcement and to civilians is whether a threatening individual had *ability, opportunity,* and presented *jeopardy* (Ayoob, 2014). If the threat appears to have the physical capability or power from a weapon of causing death or serious injury this is *ability*. The *opportunity* refers to whether the threat can carry out his assault right now. Typically this is referred to as "imminent opportunity." In other words, the attack does not need to have begun. There is not a constitutional requirement that officers wait for an attack they reasonably perceive to be imminent. This last point is tied to what Ayoob calls jeopardy. Some observers refer to intent or motive, but how does anyone know another person's intent unless it is spoken? Jeopardy can be perceived through various cues, including physical and verbal.

Some assert that the Supreme Court has "failed" to provide "meaningful guidance" on the use of deadly force (see for example Gross, 2016). It is recognized that misdemeanors, or even non-violent felonies, are unlikely to involve the use of lethal force when apprehending the offender unless the added element of the perceived danger of serious injury is present. At the founding of the country, most felonies were violent crimes and were punishable by death. Arresting someone was likely done with few if any tools including a firearm. American officers began carrying firearms when departments were started in various large cities in the mid-1800s. The Model Penal Code (MPC), in section 3.07. Use of Force in Law Enforcement, specifies that the force be used when making or assisting in the arrest of a person and the force be "immediately necessary." Outlined in section 2 (b), deadly force is not justified unless:

i   the arrest is for a felony; and
ii   the person effecting the arrest is authorized to act as a peace officer or is assisting a person whom he believes to be authorized to act as a peace officer; and
iii the actor believes that the force employed creates no substantial risk of injury to innocent persons; and
iv   the actor believes that

1.   the crime for which the arrest is made involved conduct including the use or threatened use of deadly force; or
2.   there is a substantial risk that the person to be arrested will cause death or serious bodily harm if his apprehension is delayed.
3.   Use of Force to Prevent Escape from Custody. The use of force to prevent the escape of an arrested person from custody is justifiable when the force could justifiably have been employed

to effect the arrest under which the person is in custody, except that a guard or other person authorized to act as a peace officer is justified in using any force, including deadly force, which he believes to be immediately necessary to prevent the escape of a person from a jail, prison, or other institution for the detention of persons charged with or convicted of a crime.

There is no question that the use of deadly force by an officer is a serious matter. But how frequently does this happen? News coverage of such events is understandably quick to arrive and late to leave. The public's fascination is mixed with outrage at a possible misjudgment by an officer, sympathy for everyone involved including the officer, curiosity about how the event came about and transpired, and myriad other emotions and views. The FBI (2016) reports that with more than 321 million people in the country, 63 million contacts occurred between individuals and law enforcement. Within those encounters some 13 million arrests occurred, with an estimated 882,000 instances of use of *some* level of force. This works out to about 1.4 percent of the 63 million contacts. Most of the force usages are considered low level. About 1,000 uses of force per year in the United States result in a fatality. Approximately 60 percent of those 1,000 cases each year involved subjects armed with guns. Yet even the former director of the FBI, James Comey, lamented the lack of centralized and accurate data on police use of lethal force, calling it "ridiculous" and "embarrassing" (Davis and Lowery, 2015).

In some ways, these statistics illustrate the same perception that many drivers have when they marvel at the fact there are not more traffic crashes. Drivers are taught the basics of navigating a large, heavy piece of metal at speed among other similar devices. Experience generally improves decision-making and reactions. Success is important because failure can have significant consequences. The officer is similarly trained in the basics of defensive tactics and weapons usage. Experience likewise can enhance judgment and improve performance. Use of force measures, and firearms in particular, are necessary at times and will depend for success on various factors, some of which are outside the control of the officer. The literature does not show us a large scale study of instances when officers *could have* used deadly force and chose not to. Some commentary about this reality has been made (Klinger, 2004; Morrison, 2010; Terrill, 2016), as well as the observation that some instances of *not* shooting have resulted in the officer being harmed or killed (Patrick and Hall, 2017). Some question even the drawing of a firearm by police, although Skolnick and Fyfe (1993) point out that a "reasonable expectation" of life-threatening circumstances may lead to drawing a weapon. They go on to say that "the difference between drawing a gun and firing it is as big as the difference between showing the fleet and using it to launch an invasion" (p. 41). Data gathering must continue to expand to capture information on all events in which officers or subjects fired a weapon, how many times anyone involved fired, and what and whether anyone or anything was struck by a bullet. In addition, to be useful in evaluating such events, a comprehensive examination of circumstances should be generated.

This seemingly obvious assertion on data to be gathered has remained largely aspirational (Koper, 2016). Each of the thousands of law enforcement agencies in the U.S. is responsible for gathering crime statistics in its jurisdiction. States tabulate crimes as well as increases and decreases year-to-year to discern trends. A small cross-section of crimes is reported to the federal government with limited characteristics or information about those crimes. The Uniform Crime Report (UCR) of the FBI, first created in the 1920s by the International Association of Chiefs of Police, groups the data into

Part I and Part II crime categories. Part I includes murder, and non-negligent manslaughter, forcible rape, robbery, aggravated assault, burglary, larceny, arson and motor vehicle theft. Part II crimes comprise a somewhat larger collection of less serious crimes. The gathering of crime data is separate from the information the FBI compiles each year in the Law Enforcement Officers Killed and Assaulted (LEOKA) summary. One of the many consequences of not having consistent nationwide data on police use of lethal force is the difficulty in explaining the who, when, where, and why of these events.

For many years, the FBI has hoped for and worked toward more comprehensive data gathering on crimes reported, in a system known as the National Incident-Based Reporting System, or NIBRS. As of June 2012, 32 states had some level of reporting to the newer data system. This represents only around 29 percent of the nation's population and 27 percent of its crime. Small agencies often lack the staff to compile the data in the format required by the system and upload that information. Other agencies and states have chosen not to participate for other reasons and have no formal plan to do so (JRSA, 2017). Many states are also resistant to bearing the unfunded costs associated with such expanded data gathering and processing. White (2016) counters this with the observation, among several important ones, that the infrequency of the use of deadly force and the lengthy existence of the FBI's UCR infrastructure belie the claimed inability to report. Many point to the incompleteness and unreliability of the various and non-integrated databases (Williams, Bowman, and Jung, 2016; Zimring and Arsiniega, 2015).

As explored in Chapter 1, the use of force in a contemporary liberal democratic society is constrained as well as compelled by the framework and definition of that society. The use of deadly force by law enforcement officers was originally based in the common law (and to some extent still is) as discussed earlier in this book. Now, each state has enacted statutes to govern use of force by law enforcement. Under English common law, felony crimes were punishable by death, which resulted in the justification to use deadly force to halt someone fleeing from such crimes. Contemporary U.S. society finds the use of deadly force acceptable under the law if an officer perceives that she or another person faces the imminent threat of serious injury. It should be noted that there are differences among many countries as to how and against whom deadly force may be used by the police.

Fyfe said this in 1982 about the use of deadly force by police:

> The use of force at its most extreme is the use of deadly force which, with rare exception, can be described as a decision of a police officer to point a service revolver at another human being and fire it. This is the most momentous decision a human being can make – to take another life. Limiting such decisions to those instances when the use of force is absolutely necessary is one of the most important goals for the police agency. This is so, not only to reduce death and injury, but also to diminish the often woeful impact that police woundings and killings have on citizens' perception of the fairness and decency of police agencies.
>
> *(Foreword)*

The differences in how the use of deadly force is viewed and permitted are also reflected within the U.S. The use of deadly force to halt any felon from fleeing came to an end with the Supreme Court case of *Tennessee v. Garner* (1985) (Fyfe, 1988). Two Memphis police officers responded to a nighttime call of a prowler at a residence. The officers arrived to discover what they believed was a teen running from a burglary and attempting to climb over a fence. After one of the officers warned the young man, Edward Garner, to halt, Garner continued to climb a fence to escape. The officer shot Garner, who died a short time later. While the *Garner* decision had a significant impact on the laws of many states and the policies of many agencies, it did not carry the power of law to dictate how each state would address the use of force by its state and local law enforcement officers. As noted by Flanders and Welling in their 2015 article reviewing the status of the common law pertaining to the use of force even after *Garner*, states "still have the authority to dictate under what circumstances police could justifiably use deadly force, and so avoid punishment under state law" (p. 110).

"It is not better that all felony suspects die than that they escape. Where the suspect poses no immediate threat to others, the harm resulting from failing to apprehend him does not justify the use of deadly force to do so. It is no doubt unfortunate when a suspect who is in sight escapes, but the fact that the police arrive a little late or are a little slower afoot does not always justify killing the suspect."

(Tennessee v. Garner, 471 U.S. 1 (1985))

Officers Killing and Being Killed

Deadly force is used at times by criminal justice personnel. On many of these occasions the person is not incapacitated or even hurt by the attempt to use such force. But some people are killed by officers in various circumstances, and some officers die each year as the result of a felonious assault. Movies and television would have us believe that most deadly force incidents were clear cut and easily resolved in the mind of the involved officer.

As with most data in the criminal justice system, accuracy and completeness are problematic. There is no mandatory mechanism for the reporting of force usage, not even deadly force usage. While the Uniform Crime Report (UCR) of the FBI gathers information on a select few crimes to compile a fairly accurate tally of reported crime each year, even that is subject to a variety of weaknesses and inaccuracies. The National Violent Death Reporting System (NVDRS) is another mechanism for gathering data on certain deaths. The death of individuals is serious, and while one hopes for a high degree of accuracy in gathering information about the circumstances, the task remains decentralized and less than perfectly recorded (DeGue, Fowler, and Calkins, 2016).

Public and political pressure as well as research requests and a desire by agencies to improve methods, will all likely result in continued improvement in tracking data about lethal force usage. Regardless, individual incidents often receive a great deal of attention from the media. The manner in which media report such occurrences, especially in the early stages of examination or in the immediate aftermath of the incident, can have an impact on initial public reactions as well as influence views (Donovan and Klahm, 2015; Hough and Tatum, 2015). Each use of lethal force is unique in its circumstances. One study conducted in the Office of the Chief Medical Examiner in New York City (Gill and Pasquale-Styles, 2009), highlighted an aspect of frequent encounters that is not often heard in setting the context for a news story. Gill examined 42 gunshot death cases that occurred in a 4-year period in New York City and noted that 78 percent had ethanol or drugs of abuse in their system and that 90 percent of the decedents were armed at the time of the shootings (p. 185). Again, each case in each community is singular, yet journalists have more of an opportunity than researchers in contemporary technological America to provide contextual information for the public.

Race and the Use of Deadly Force

Similar to the simplistic notion that engaging in acts likely to cause someone else's death is straightforward and with few psychic consequences, the racial disparity seen in deaths attributed to public safety personnel is fodder for those with a narrow view of research or reality. There is significant research to support the historic mistreatment of African Americans (and others) along economic and social lines. There is also little dispute that over the course of law enforcement's development in the U.S. that police in many locations have been used as an instrument of suppression, were poorly trained if at all, and did not uniformly seek out the best and the brightest. What has more nuance, is the contemporary picture of the modern officer and agency in America.

The 1985 decision in *Tennessee v. Garner* established one of the parameters of deadly force usage, the application of the 4th Amendment's admonition against unreasonable seizures in analyzing the legality of such force. Criticism and debate in the United States over the use of lethal force by law enforcement has largely arisen from highly publicized cases where African American males have been shot and killed by white officers. There is a tendency for such shooting incidents to be subsumed under a general label of police shootings. As with most generalizations, this presents an inaccurate picture to laypersons that all force interactions between law enforcement and minority men are alike. Statistics do point out the disproportionate number of African Americans (largely males) who are killed by police. Research has also generally shown that when controlling for other situational factors, the role of race is not statistically significant (Jetelina, Jennings, Bishopp, Piquero, and Gonzalez, 2017; Lott, and Moody, 2017; Klinger, Rosenfeld, Isom, and Deckard, 2015). The *Washington Post* newspaper began a large project in 2015 attempting to chronicle instances of people shot and killed by police. In 2015 they compiled a list "based on news reports, public records, Internet databases and original reporting." The number used by the *Post* was 991 people. The *Post's* compilation tabulates 949 as male, 772 armed with a deadly weapon, 55 more with a vehicle, and another 43 with toy weapons. There were 254 who showed signs of mental illness, though the other 737 were listed as "no or unknown" on that point. Most killed were between the ages of 18 and 44 at 685 total. The *Post* listing noted 730 persons in an "attack in progress" under the category of threat level. For those people whose race was known, 495 were white, 258 were black, 172 Hispanic, 38 were classified other, and 28 unknown. The 26 percent black is disproportionate to their roughly 13 percent of the population. The total number of individuals killed arrived at by the *Post* for 2016 was 963. By the end of 2017, law enforcement officers had killed 987 individuals according to the *Post*.

The U.S. Census Bureau (2016) estimates that 13.3 percent of the population is black, with somewhat less than half that figure being males. The percentage of black inmates in jails, and state and federal prisons is approximately 40 percent. More than 50 percent of arrests for homicide are of blacks. High school graduation rates overall have been increasing, including those for minority students. In 2015, the Schott Foundation for Public Education reported the rates for black males, Latinos, and white males, at 59, 65, and 80, respectively. And, according to the Pew Research Center (2016), even with narrowing gaps in earning, blacks in the U.S. still earned just 75 percent as much as whites in median earnings. These quick, and admittedly partial, statistics illustrate that the country has a long way to go on addressing equity issues and their root causes. With that said, law enforcement officers face circumstances where they make decisions based on the perception of threat to the officer or others at the moment the officer uses force.

Harvard economist Roland Fryer undertook a study to examine racial differences in police use of force through analysis of two public datasets and the construction of two additional datasets. In a July, 2016 working paper, Fryer identified that non-lethal force usage was 50 percent more likely to be experienced by blacks and Hispanics during law enforcement interactions. In this well-constructed analysis, the disparity in the non-lethal force experience of minorities could not be fully explained even with controls. For lethal force, Fryer's work found "no racial differences in either the raw data or when contextual factors [were] taken into account" (p. 1).

Michael Brown was shot on August 9, 2014, in the town of Ferguson, Missouri by an officer responding to a report of a robbery at a nearby store. Brown had just stolen several packs of cigarillos and used physical force against the clerk who tried to stop the theft, legally turning it into a robbery. Officer Darren Wilson responded to the call of "stealing in progress" and located Brown and a friend walking down the street near the store. When Officer Wilson tried to get out of his squad car, the door was blocked at which point Brown reached inside the police vehicle and struck and grabbed the officer. When Officer Wilson drew his firearm as the only weapon he could access from his seated position, Michael Brown grabbed the gun, trying to take control of it. This is part of the account of Officer Wilson. There was nothing to discredit this account based on the extensive forensic evidence gathered.

After receiving a wound to his right hand, Brown ran from the car, but returned toward Officer Wilson who was attempting to pursue him. Officer Wilson, who stated his fear for his own well-being, shot Michael Brown. When Brown fell to the ground, Officer Wilson stopped firing. The approximately 2-minute encounter between Michael Brown and Officer Darren Wilson would bring out frustration and emotion as well as violence and civil unrest far beyond the town of Ferguson.

The FBI and the Criminal Section of the Department of Civil Rights Division of the U.S. Attorney's Office conducted a criminal investigation into the shooting of the unarmed man to determine if federal law was violated. The investigation was extensive and thorough, gathering forensic and physical evidence as well as interviews of more than 100 individuals who claimed knowledge of the incident.

Following this exhaustive investigation, the Department of Civil Rights determined that the officer, Darren Wilson, did not act in a way that violated federal criminal civil rights statutes. The sum total of the investigation looked to whether under 18 U.S.C. 242, deadly force usage by Officer Wilson was "objectively unreasonable." Measured against the Supreme Court's definition, the finding was that Wilson's actions could not be concluded to be "objectively unreasonable."

(Memorandum 2015: Department of Justice Report Regarding the Criminal Investigation into the Shooting Death of Michael Brown)

> ### GOING GLOBAL: *AUTHORISED FIREARMS OFFICER (AFO)*
>
> The police in the United Kingdom are not typically armed with firearms. The Association of Chief Police Officers (ACPO) of England, Wales and Northern Ireland subscribes to the *Manual of Guidance on the Police Use of Firearms* which addresses selection of both weapons and officers to carry them. A relatively small percentage of officers (about 5 percent as of 2017) in the U.K. are trained and authorized to carry firearms in what are termed police firearms operations. Such "operations" refer to incidents where a firearm was approved to be present, even if not used. In fact, in the year ending March 2015, out of a total of 14,666 police firearms operations, there were just six incidents of actual firearm discharge.
>
> The specialist officer who volunteers, and is selected and trained, to carry firearms is termed an Authorised Firearms Officer (AFO). Numbers of such AFOs were on a downward trend from a high point in 2010 of nearly 7,000, to 5,647 in March 2015. In January 2016, the chief of the Metropolitan Police in London committed to training at least 600 more officers to carry firearms and be available for response in London.

Firearms

In the U.S. "culture of the gun," the presence of so many firearms increases the likelihood of their misuse as much as more cars on the highway increases the risk of traffic crashes. Handguns are designed to kill people. It is inevitable that some will use the weapon to do just that. Various estimates place the numbers of guns per 100 of the population at between 90 and 100, perhaps more. By comparison, guns in the United Kingdom are estimated at 4–7 per 100 members of the public. The U.K. has strict gun ownership laws. Only around 5 percent of police are trained and armed with firearms.

The use of firearms as a tool in American law enforcement began in the early 1800s, roughly coinciding with the advent of police departments in larger, urban towns and cities. The carrying of firearms by U.S. police (as well as the wearing of a distinctive uniform) grew over time. In many 19th century communities, the carrying of firearms by police was voluntary and adoption was sporadic until the 20th century when it became the norm in the United States. And while U.S. police departments were approximating much of the British innovation led by Robert Peel, police constables in the U.K. remained without firearms until relatively recently – and still not universally within the U.K. with only about 5 percent of officers armed with guns. The formalization of law enforcement evolved through stages from community members organizing to safeguard their settlement or village against various threats, to appointed and paid individuals as the towns and responsibilities grew too big to be handled effectively by citizens volunteering their time. Today, while many agencies are quite small, almost all officers are trained and certified under the rule of their respective state or district and most departments pursue similar goals and perform common duties of enforcing the law and maintaining order through the general consent of the population.

Various tools and methods *may* cause the death of someone, but few such devices are designed to cause a lethal injury. Launching a small projectile at a velocity of possibly between 500 and 5,000 feet per second toward a person would be expected to result in injury or death if it strikes its intended target. The American public is exceptionally well armed vis-à-vis guns. With an estimated

300 million guns in the hands of citizens (Congressional Reference Service, 2015), and increasing manufacture and purchase of guns, it is not an unlikely proposition that most people can acquire such a weapon with a bit of effort – or very little effort. The ready access to firearms and their subsequent usage has impacts on society. A tangible aspect of the use of guns is the cost of treating those shot. In a study published by Stanford researchers in early 2017, an estimated cost to Americans for initial hospitalizations of people who were shot between 2006 and 2014 was more than $6.6 billion (Kohrman, 2017). Road rage on the highways of America, including the involvement of firearms, is on the rise. This spells more emotionally charged incidents where officers can face armed individuals already exhibiting anger.

These firearm-related considerations involve the context of contemporary society. This is the environment that officers work in every shift. Homicides for 2014 numbered 15,809 (U.S. Department of Health and Human Services, 2017). Of that number, 10,945, or 69 percent were firearm homicides. In the same year, the National Vital Statistics Reports (NVSR) reflected 35,594 deaths from firearms and that 63.7 percent of those deaths were classified as suicide. Guns are effective in killing people. Other weapons will do in a pinch, or if wielded with enough ferocity or frequency, but if you aim to end another person's life, a firearm is the weapon of choice. In the United States the rate of criminal homicide has declined gradually from what it was 20 years ago, to 4.5 per 100,000 in 2014; 2016 saw a rise to a rate of 5.3, but this remains below the rate of 7.4 for 1996 and is a 6 percent drop from 2007 when the rate was 5.7 (FBI, 2016). The lowest rate before 2014 was more than a half century ago when it was 4.6 per 100,000 in 1963.

The use of firearms by law enforcement officers and the number of lethal incidents has to be considered against the backdrop of an armed society. There are more firearms in the United States than there are adults to wield them. While these numbers are somewhat skewed by individuals who possess multiple firearms, there is little dispute that obtaining a firearm, either by lawful means or unlawfully, is not a challenging proposition in modern America. Officers, including probation and parole and security professionals, recognize that each interaction may reveal the presence of firearms in the immediate environment or possessed by the people the officers interact with. In addition, it is important to note that *every* law enforcement contact is an armed encounter in that the officer himself is armed. In a study of 791 fatal assaults on law enforcement officers in a 6-year period ending 2013, officers ambushed or spontaneously attacked were more likely than other types of assault to result in the officer being killed, and there was a two-fold likelihood of an assault being fatal when the suspect disarmed the officer (Crifasi, Pollack, and Webster, 2016). This fact is important when considering that many officers have been disarmed and then murdered with their own weapon. It is again important to note that the mantle of authority and the signifiers of the police role do not always protect the officer nor dissuade the individual intent on harming that officer.

Other Force Used to Lethal Effect

If an officer has perceived that the threat she faces is imminent and that she or someone else is in danger of serious injury, she may lawfully act. This action may take the form of deadly force. The employment of deadly force may or may not involve the use of a firearm. This largely depends on immediate reactionary or tactical considerations. If an officer has some type of object in her hands when the imminent threat of serious injury presents itself, the officer may strike the threat with whatever object that officer is holding. If the officer's perception was a reasonable one, then her actions will likely be evaluated as appropriate, within policy, and lawful. Such a reaction to immediate threat is one of the reasons that officers providing warning is not always feasible. The archaic notion of a warning shot makes that option even less desirable. A projectile fired must lodge somewhere. And while unintentionally injuring a bystander in this way is not criminal, it may cause the officer and agency difficulties in both civil liability and public sentiment.

Eric Garner, a resident of New York, died subsequent to his arrest by officers on suspicion of selling untaxed cigarettes. A grand jury that met for two months declined to indict the officer who, while trying to restrain Garner, placed his arm around Garner's neck area from behind. Garner, at 6' 3" and approximately 350 pounds, pulled away from Officer Daniel Pantaleo as the officer tried to place Garner's hand behind his back. While the medical examiner found no physical damage to Garner's windpipe or neck bones, the medical examiner concluded that Eric Garner's death resulted from compression of the neck and chest and being in a prone position while being restrained and that Garner also suffered from health issues including asthma, diabetes, and sleep apnea. These were reported by the medical examiner as contributing factors in Garner's death. While the NYPD investigation of officer actions has not concluded, the four EMTs and paramedics who responded to treat Garner were initially suspended pending investigation by medical authorities. Two returned to duty soon after, two did not.

Within the range of non-lethal devices previously discussed, many agencies equip their officers with batons, pepper spray or chemical spray, and conducted energy devices (CEDs) in some combination. These tools are not designed specifically to cause death and officers are not trained to use these devices to try and inflict death. Drawing a firearm can be an appropriate tactical decision in circumstances that may lead to a need to use deadly force. If the weapon is holstered when it may be needed, the officer may be at a deadly disadvantage in responding to a quickly developing threat. Physical control, or defensive tactics, techniques include joint manipulation, pain compliance, and strikes, but are similarly not conceived as lethal methods. Another method of control that may result in a death is a physical restraint where the controlling person places pressure on the neck and/or throat areas of the person they are trying to control.

Vehicles

Sometimes people flee from law enforcement. They may do this on foot or using some type of vehicle. We rarely see the foot chase on police reality shows. Car chases, on the other hand, may produce a recording of the chase captured by dashboard camera or in rare circumstances by helicopter footage. As with virtually all information on American law enforcement operations and actions, the decentralized and parochial nature of policing bars examination or analysis of comprehensive figures on pursuits or their outcomes (Schultz, Hudak, and Alpert, 2010). Nonetheless, sufficient knowledge of the often fatal result of pursuit dynamics has led a large number of U.S. police and highway patrol agencies to revise pursuit policies to be more restrictive than "Chase whoever runs from you."

The discussion of vehicle pursuits does not easily find a home in a chapter on lethal force, but it bears some discussion since, as with other techniques and devices, it *can* result in serious injuries or death. Innocent bystanders may be struck by the pursued or the pursuer; the pursued vehicle or the officers giving chase may collide with something and be injured or killed. An officer using techniques such as the originally named "Precision Immobilization Technique" or PIT maneuver, may combine with the physics of the encounter to result in a crash that kills or injures.

Pursuits happen because of minor traffic law violations, drunken decision-making, fear or avoidance of arrest, and occasionally a serious crime that has just occurred. There are several factors that agencies, officers, and supervisors should consider in guiding pursuit decision-making in advance through policy, and in the moment by the individual officer. The seriousness of the offense for which police pursue is consistently cited as an important factor in deciding to pursue or when to terminate a pursuit. The relative volume of vehicle and pedestrian traffic in the path of a pursuit, as well as weather and lighting conditions, are also immediately relevant in managing the event and making decisions. Officer training and vehicle safety technology are important considerations for the field (Scullin, 2014).

Technology has and will continue to play a role in pursuits. Police cruisers have, over the years, been equipped with powerful motors, traction and stability enhancements, and varying degrees of external identifying markings and visual and auditory alert systems. An officer may have available traffic spikes used to deflate tires of a fleeing vehicle if officers can determine the route someone fleeing apprehension will travel and safely deploy the device in time for the feeling vehicle. Safety is not assured during deployment and officers have been killed while attempting to use the devices. Discussion and some experimentation have taken place with electro-magnetic pulse technology to shut off a car's engine systems. An unresolved down-side is the reality that a contemporary automobile turned off becomes a large piece of metal uncontrolled in speed, steering, or braking, at risk of striking unintended objects and people. This largely fictionalized idea of a directed-energy device would also be challenged by an omni-directional effect on all vehicles with electronic systems.

The officer and the pursued driver are not on a closed track simply waiting on one to run out of gas. The vehicles are driven through various environments, urban, suburban, and rural, and in varying nighttime, dusk, or daylight conditions. The weather can play its part and the time of day may spell more or less traffic depending on the general location of the pursuit. Emergency vehicle operations driver training has included a mix of classroom, simulator, and "live" driving to develop the physical and cognitive skills needed by officers. Some aspects of the human actions and responses have been studied, such as attention and gaze duration (Crundall, Chapman, France, Geoffrey, and Phelps, 2005). As with the psycho-physiological response to threats such as a perceived firearm, a hazard introduced abruptly is likely to attract the driver's attention during a pursuit (Crundall, Underwood, and Chapman, 1999). Tunnel vision may come into play as the brain of the driver works to process the presentation of the unexpected item or condition, thus reducing available attention to keep track of the driver's visual periphery and simultaneously degrading reaction times. Experienced drivers may recover more quickly from the appearance of a potential hazard (Crundall, Underwood, and Chapman, 2002), but collisions can occur within moments. According to the non-profit organization Pursuit SAFETY (citing the IACP and the National Highway Traffic and Safety Administration), pursuit-related fatalities happen at a rate of approximately 1 per day in the U.S., up to one-third of pursuit-related fatalities are innocent bystanders, the vast majority of pursuits are for non-violent crimes, and 35–40 percent of pursuits end in a crash (www.pursuitsafety.

org). There is no knowing the skill level or sobriety of the pursued driver, or the performance and safety equipment of his vehicle.

A pursuit can end when an officer makes a decision to turn off the lights and siren and pull over to signal their quarry that the chase is off. There is some empirical support for the idea that the violator will then slow down, reducing the risk to all (Dunham, Alpert, Kenney, and Cromwell, 1998). Termination can also happen if one of the participants crashes, or if the person fleeing stops his vehicle. Of course, just as data collection is hampered by decentralized policing, the myriad municipal, county, and state agencies mean that pursuits often move through more than one jurisdiction as if a "bubble of policy" for one officer/agency is going to insulate it from a negative outcome. Training, technology, policy, and sometimes simply timing, all play a part in pursuit outcomes. In 2007, the United States Supreme Court held in *Scott v. Harris* (550 U.S. 372) that a "police officer's attempt to terminate a dangerous high-speed car chase that threatens the lives of innocent bystanders does not violate the Fourth Amendment, even when it places the fleeing motorist at risk of serious injury or death."

Officer-involved Shooting Investigations

As discussed at greater length in the chapter addressing force policies, the need to develop, implement, and routinely review a use of force policy is critical to protecting officers and the public and to avoid unnecessary liability or the erosion of public confidence in an agency. In the instant when deadly force is used, it may be seen as guided by law, policy, training, and experience.

But as noted by Squires and Kennison (2010),

> It is simply that when a finger pulls a trigger to send a bullet spinning towards a human target (where a decision made in seconds can have repercussions for years), it is not law, human rights or professional ethics, but physics and human biology, reactions, reflexes, skill, training and a fair measure of chance which determines what happens next.
>
> *(p. 3)*

An important aspect of the process of a lethal force incident is the investigation(s) that occur when it is over. Investigations will likely be of various types and overlap to some degree. Even non-lethal force usage will often involve a cursory "investigation" by a supervisor to determine whether an officer's actions were within department policy. Tying the investigation closely to the agency's policies is important to demonstrate accountability to the public and to model acceptable actions to officers who are influenced by clear and appropriately structured policy (Terrill, and Paoline, 2017; White, 2016). With shootings or other lethal force usage, this may include an investigation conducted by an outside entity to further ensure objectivity and transparency given the serious nature of such force usage. A department's internal affairs component or someone assigned to conduct administrative investigations may also perform an investigation of a shooting.

Depending on the circumstances of an officer-involved shooting incident, a criminal inquiry may be conducted to assemble facts and information to present to a grand jury or prosecutor's office. A further investigation can come in cases where there is a belief or allegation that an individual's civil rights were violated in the force incident. The officer-involved shooting may also give rise to a civil suit brought by an injured person or the family of someone who was killed as the result of police action. During the initial period after an officer-involved shooting, the officer is typically placed on administrative leave with pay while the department investigates the circumstances of the case to determine if the officer's actions were within policy. An agency's use of clear policy and thorough training should combine with engaged and knowledgeable supervisors to ensure successful implementation at the line level.

During the course of the post-shooting investigation, consideration must be given to the officer's psychological health and functioning. Implications for stress-related trauma including PTSD, and impacts on perceptions and memories of the event must be addressed (Engel and Smith, 2009).

July 6, 2016 marked the deadliest day for American law enforcement officers since 9/11. In Dallas, Texas a man ambushed and shot to death five officers and wounded seven other people. Less than two weeks later, three more officers were ambushed and murdered in Baton Rouge, Louisiana. Across the U.S. in 2016, more than 20 officers were shot and killed in ambushes.

A 48-year-old NYPD officer and mother of three, Miosotis Familia, was murdered while sitting in her police vehicle in the Bronx. A 34-year-old man with a pistol walked up to the vehicle and fired through the window, striking Officer Familia in the head and killing her. The killer ran off but was located by police and died after he turned his gun on officers and was shot by them.

The post-shooting investigation bears similarity to other investigations, albeit serious ones with more dimensions than most. In fact, many agencies have had a homicide detective conduct shooting investigations. It is important to immediately secure the scene of the event, gather evidence and interview all persons with knowledge of what occurred. Statements are taken while recognizing the rights of individuals including officers. Agency reviews are often effective mechanisms to gauge current training and policy and make recommendations for changes or enhancements. Rostker and others with the RAND Corporation (2008) examined the NYPD firearms training program and post-shooting investigation processes and recommended, among other things, expanded simulation and scenario training for recruit officers. As to shooting investigations, the RAND study recommended examining officer tactics as well as whether an officer's actions were in or out of policy. Pending liability in many shooting cases makes inclusion of tactics commentaries problematic for most agencies.

Summary

There is no interaction as consequential, while also being rare, as the employment of deadly force by an officer. While not entirely a case of "man bites dog," the volume of interactions between police and the public that are free of force usage, let alone deadly force, lead to a statistically small number of such unwanted outcomes. Yet each occurrence may involve someone dying and the aftermath of a death. Officers also fire guns and wound individuals and they shoot without striking their intended target.

The use of deadly force by officers has occurred throughout the history of policing in the United States. Controversy over some incidents is expected given the finality of the force usage, the emotions surrounding the death of a person, and the need to balance release of pertinent information with the necessity to conduct a thorough investigation before reaching conclusions regarding the legality of actions and the assessment of appropriate use of procedures. Laws, policies, and practices have changed since the founding of the country and the writing of the U.S. Constitution. These changes reflect, among other things, the views of how officers face potential deadly threats to themselves and the citizens they are sworn to protect. The punishment of death is rarely available for anyone convicted, even of murder, in the United States, and so the use of deadly force to stop even a suspected violent felon receives great scrutiny.

There is no factual debate that an "unarmed" person is not capable of killing another person. He can do so in a variety of ways including taking a weapon from the victim. Still, the uninformed public and the immediate and frequently inaccurate nature of social media, and hurried nature of news media sources, combine to stoke a fire of emotion before facts about circumstances and actions can be determined in a lethal force incident. Historic misuse of force in locations around the country predisposes many people to judge any such contemporary use of force as inappropriate before any inquiry takes place.

KEY TERMS

Deadly force
Lethal force
Defensive tactics

Discussion Questions

1. What circumstances may call for the use of lethal force?
2. Why are some techniques and technologies referred to as less lethal?
3. Discuss the role of investigations following an officer-involved shooting.
4. Why has the *Washington Post* newspaper taken it upon itself to chronicle lethal force incidents involving law enforcement officers?

TRY THIS

Examine several law enforcement agency websites. Try to locate the use of lethal force policy. List and discuss the factors that you found within the policy.

References

Ayoob, M. (2014). *Deadly force: understanding your right to self defense*. Iola, WI: Gun Digest Books.

Congressional Reference Service. (2012). *Report 7–5700, Gun Control Legislation, by William J. Krouse*. Washington, DC.

Crifasi, K. C., Pollack, K. M., and Webster, D. W. (2016). Assaults against U.S. law enforcement officers in the line-of-duty: situational context and predictors of lethality. *Injury Epidemiology*, 3(29). doi:10.1186/s40621-016-0094-3.

Crundall, D., Underwood, G., and Chapman, P. (1999). Driving experience and the functional field of view. *Perception*, 28, 1075–1087.

Crundall, D., Underwood, G., and Chapman, P. (2002). Attending to the peripheral world while driving. *Applied Cognitive Psychology*, 16, 459–475. doi:10.1002/acp.806

Crundall, D., Chapman, P., France, E., Geoffrey, U., and Phelps, N. (2005). What attracts attention during police pursuit driving? *Applied Cognitive Psychology*, 19(4), 409–420. doi:10.1002/acp.1067

Davis, A. C. and Lowery, W. (2015). FBI director calls lack of data on police shootings "ridiculous," "embarrassing." *Washington Post*. Retrieved from https://www.washingtonpost.com/national/fbi-director-calls-lack-of-data-on-policeshootings-ridiculous-embarrassing/2015/10/07/c0ebaf7a-6d16-11e5-b31cd80d62b53e28_story.html

DeGue, S., Fowler, K. A., and Calkins, C. (2016). Deaths due to use of lethal force by law enforcement: findings from the national violent death reporting system, 17 U.S. states, 2009–2012. *American Journal of Preventive Medicine*, 51(Supplement 3), S173–S187. doi:10.1016/j.amepre.2016. 08. 02doi:7

Donovan, K. M. and Klahm, C. F. (2015). The role of entertainment media in perceptions of police use of force. *Criminal Justice and Behavior*, 42(12), 1261–1281.

Dunham, R., Alpert, G.Kenney, D., and Cromwell, P. (1998). High speed pursuit: the offender's perspective. *Criminal Justice and Behavior*, 20, 30–45.

Engel, R. S. and Smith, M. R. (2009). Perceptual distortion and reasonableness during police shootings: law, legitimacy, and future research. *Criminology and Public Policy*, 8(1), 141–151.

Fatal force database. (2016). *Washington Post*. Retrieved from https://www.washingtonpost.com/graphics/national/police-shootings/

FBI (Federal Bureau of Investigation). (2016a). *Crime in the United States, 2015*. Clarksburg, WV: Author. Retrieved from https://ucr.fbi.gov/crime-in-the-u.s/2015/crime-in-the-u.s.-2015/tables/table-1

FBI (Federal Bureau of Investigation). (2016b) Table 1 – Crime in the United States, by volume and rate per 100,000 inhabitants, 1996–2015. Retrieved from: https://ucr.fbi.gov/crime-in-the-u.s/2015/crime-in-the-u.s.-2015/tables/table-1

Flanders, C., and Welling, J. (2016). Police use of deadly force: state statutes 30 years after Garner. *St. Louis University Public Law Review*, 35(1), 109–156.

Fryer, R. (2016). An empirical analysis of racial differences in police use of force. National Bureau of Economic Research. Available at www.nber.org/papers/w22399

FSS (Florida State Statute) 776.06 (2017). Deadly force by a law enforcement or correctional officer.

Fyfe, J. J. (1982). *Readings on police use of deadly force*. Washington, DC: Police Foundation.

Fyfe, J. J. (1988). Police use of deadly force: research and reform. *Justice Quarterly*, 5, 165–205.

Gill, J. and Pasquale-Styles, M. (2009). Firearm deaths by law enforcement. *Journal of Forensic Sciences*, 54, 185–188.

Gross, J. P. (2016). Judge, jury, and executioner: the excessive use of deadly force by police officers. *Texas Journal on Civil Liberties and Civil Rights*, 21(2), 155–181.

Hough, R. M. and Tatum, K. (2015). Murder investigation and media: mutual goals. *Law Enforcement Executive Forum*, 14(3), 71–85.

Jetelina, K. K., Jennings, W. G., Bishopp, S. A., Piquero, A. R., and Gonzalez, J. R. (2017). Dissecting the complexities of the relationship between police officer–civilian race/ethnicity dyads and less-than-lethal use of force. *American Journal of Public Health*, 107(7), 1164–1170. doi:10.2105/AJPH.2017.303807

JRSA (Justice Research and Statistics Association). (2017). *Status of NIBRS in the States*. Washington, DC: JRSA.

Klinger, D. (2004). *Into the kill zone: a cop's eye view of deadly force*. San Francisco, CA: Jossey-Bass.

Klinger, D., Rosenfeld, R., Isom, D., and Deckard, M. (2015). Race, crime, and the micro-ecology of deadly force. *Criminology and Public Policy*, 15(1), 193. doi:10.1111/1745-9133.12174

Kochanek, K. D. Murphy S. L.Xu J. Q., and Tejada-Vera B. (2016)*Deaths: final data for 2014*. National vital statistics reports, vol. 65 no. 4. Hyattsville, MD: National Center for Health Statistics.

Kohrman, M. (2017). The high cost of treating gun violence victims hits Southerners especially hard. *The Trace*, March 23.

Koper, C. S. (2016). Advancing research and accountability on police use of deadly force. *Criminology and Public Policy*, 15(1), 187–191. doi:10.1111/1745-9133.12192

Lott, J. R. and Moody, C. E. (2017). Do white police officers unfairly target black suspects? Accessed July 21. Available at: https://ssrn.com/abstract=2870189. Accessed August 16, 2017.

Memorandum (2015). *Department of Justice report regarding the criminal investigation into the shooting death of Michael Brown by Ferguson, Missouri Police Officer Darren Wilson*, March 4. Washington, DC.

Model Penal Code, Section 3.07: Use of Force in Law Enforcement

Morrison, G. B. (2010). Deadly force in the United States. In J. B. Kuhns and J. Knutsson (Eds.), *Police use of force: a global perspective*. Santa Barbara, CA: Praeger, pp. 132–140.

Patrick, U. W. and Hall, J. C. (2017). *In defense of self and others*. Durham, NC: Carolina Academic Press.

Pew Research Center (2016). Racial, gender wage gap persist in U.S. despite some progress. Retrieved from: www.pewresearch.org/fact-tank/2016/07/01/racial-gender-wage-gaps-persist-in-u-s-despite-some-progress/

Rostker, B. and Rand Center on Quality. (2008). *Evaluation of the New York City Police Department firearm training and firearm-discharge review process*. Santa Monica, CA: RAND Corporation.

Schultz, D. P., Hudak, E., and Alpert, G. P. (2010). Evidence-based decisions on police pursuits: the officer's perspective. *FBI Law Enforcement Bulletin*, 79(3), 1.

Schott Foundation for Public Education. (2015). *Black lives matter: the Schott 50 State Report on public education and black males*. Retrieved from: http://blackboysreport.org/national-summary/

Scullin, S. (2014). Kick pursuit training into overdrive. *Law Enforcement Technology*, 41(10), 8–16.

Skolnick, J. H. and Fyfe, J. J. (1993). *Above the law*. New York: The Free Press.

Squires, P. and Kennison, P. (2015). *Shooting to kill? Policing, firearms and armed response*. Chichester, UK: Wiley-Blackwell.

Terrill, W. (2016). Deadly force: to shoot or not to shoot. *Criminology and Public Policy*, 15(2), 491–496. doi:10.1111/1745-9133.12193

Terrill, W. and Paoline, E. A. (2017). Police use of less lethal force: does administrative policy matter? *Justice Quarterly*, 34(2), 193–216.

United States. (n.d.) *Criminal justice policy review*. Advance online publication. doi:10.1177/0887403416650927

U.S. Census Bureau. (2016). QuickFacts: population estimates, July 1, 2016. Retrieved from: https://www.census.gov/quickfacts/fact/table/US/PST045216

U.S. Department of Health and Human Services, CDC/National Center for Health Statistics (2017). Assault or homicide. https://www.cdc.gov/nchs/fastats/homicide.htm

White, M. D. (2016). Transactional encounters, crisis-driven reform, and the potential for a national police deadly force database. *Criminology and Public Policy*, 15(1), 223–235. doi:10.1111/1745-9133.12180

Williams, H. E., Bowman, S. W., and Jung, J. T. (2016). The limitations of government databases for analyzing fatal officer-involved shootings in the United States. *Criminal Justice Policy Review* (May). doi:10.1177/0887403416650927

Zimring, F. E. and Arsiniega, B. (2015). Trends in killing of and by police: a preliminary analysis. Commentaries. *Ohio State Journal of Criminal Law*, 13, 247–264.

Cases Cited

Tennessee v. Garner, 471 U.S. 1 (1985)

6

PHYSIOLOGICAL AND PSYCHOLOGICAL CONSIDERATIONS IN FORCE SITUATIONS

STUDENT LEARNING OUTCOMES

- Students will be able to distinguish between physiological and psychological factors involved in force situations.
- Students will be able to evaluate physical effects on the body during a force encounter.

- Students will be able to explain the role of training to prepare officers for psychological factors of force usage.
- Students will be able to explain inattention blindness.
- Students will be able to explain the potential effects on memory resulting from force events.

Introduction

It would be artificial or at least awkward, to keep physiological and psychological considerations completely separated. There is a cellular and cerebral flow back and forth in an interconnected dance of first waltz, then foxtrot, then salsa, ending in a promenade. In our waking hours, our senses are constantly receiving and reacting to inputs about our environment and anyone in it. We are considering the person we are facing or talking to as we position our body in anticipation of physical conflict or at least to signal our readiness to deal with it. The mind–body connection is, to say the least, complex. Our evolutionary past will be the backdrop for much of what we discuss about how we face perceived danger. Do we confront the threat (fight)? Do we move away as fast as possible (flight)? Do we work to reduce the threat to a neutral entity (adapt)?

If we perceive a threat or are responding to one, physiologically we shift into a different gear than the one we operate in under normal conditions. Our heart rate increases, blood pressure alters, vessels constrict to shunt blood to vital areas like a ship battening compartments against a storm, and there is an introduction of chemicals into the bloodstream in response to the increased heart rate. Respiration increases and vision may become distorted as physiology actually changes the functioning of the eye. Hearing may increase or decrease and perhaps focus on specific sounds more than or to the exclusion of others. Time and perceptual distortions may occur with implications in the moment as well as for memory and recall following a force event. Experts from many disciplines lend to our understanding of physical and psychological performance under stress, whether in sports, firefighting, military combat, or the street and cellblock encounters of officers.

Dave Grossman has written cogently on the experiences of killing and of combat (2009). Grossman, a retired Army Lieutenant Colonel and former Ranger, taught psychology at West Point, and he has researched and studied human aggression noting that most people have a phobic response to human aggression (Grossman and Christensen, 2008). Grossman's book *On Killing*, which was first published in 1995, has become required reading in many areas of the military and in law enforcement agencies around the country, and it provides knowledge and insights about violence as well as the psychological aftermath experienced by its participants as he notes how soldiers and law enforcement officers are typically not afforded the ability to avoid such circumstances (2009). With his continued research, lecturing, and collaboration with other experts, Grossman first published *On Combat* in 2004 and there have been a number of subsequent editions. In that book, and Grossman's other works, are some of the most often cited and thorough explanations of physiological and psychological concerns of people experiencing combat or violent encounters.

Grossman and Christensen (2008) address the many physiological and psychological aspects of survival stress and note that there may be a loss of the complex motor skills as the stress of facing a threat escalates and carries with it the heart rate into higher numbers that inversely diminish dexterity. A significant concern is the effect that sudden intense action can have not just on the body's function, but on decision-making responses as well as more "automatic" reactions. With physiological arousal comes the potential for diminished situational awareness, which may in turn impact use of force decision-making (Olson, 1998). While some things are turned over to auto-pilot, other functions remain under the direction of the conscious and deliberate mind. In understanding many aspects of the outcome of force usage it is important to keep in mind that this same body–brain whirlwind has caught up the actions of the person an officer faces. Asken, Grossman, and Christensen (2010) list the following as acute signs of stress:

> Stomach upset, increased heart rate, increased blood pressure, increased perspiration, increased respiration, sweaty palms, bowel/bladder urgency, muscle tightness, dizziness, visual changes, dry mouth/throat, fatigue, restlessness, concentration problems, word-finding problems, chest pain, tremors/shakes, decreased emotional control.
>
> *(p. 55)*

Training can help prepare officers to anticipate, recognize, and to some extent adapt to their physiological responses (Andersen, Pitel, Weerasinghe, and Papazoglou, 2016). Neither a policy nor a memo can eliminate these responses in the human officer. As expressed by Patrick and Hall (2017):

> The magnitude of the effects may fluctuate, but the occurrence and presence of the effects are unavoidable. They cannot be wished away nor ignored in any meaningful analysis of a deadly force incident. As with all other aspects of a deadly force confrontation, these elements must be recognized, assessed and judged from the perspective of a reasonable officer within the incident and not with the application of 20/20 hindsight.
>
> *(p. 175)*

When we consider the work settings in criminal justice it is also important to note that the officer cannot control the environment in most ways. We could imagine fewer chaotic events or undesirable outcomes if the officer could induce the "sterile cockpit" environment that aviation uses to prohibit "non-essential activities during critical phases of flight," or the analog to errors minimized during surgery by following a similar imposed expectation of behavior (Broom et al., 2011, p. 175).

Physiological

The body is the vehicle driven by our human agency. What we think or how we react is given over to the muscles to try and accomplish. But there are limitations to *how* we think as well as to how our bodies react, namely with imperfection to even the most perfectly formed thought direction.

Getting Excited over Excitement

The human autonomic nervous system is composed of the sympathetic nervous system (SNS) which rallies and directs bodily resources in the face of stressors including threat, and the parasympathetic nervous system (PNS) which provides regulation of those resources and attempts to bring the body back to stasis subsequent to the introduction of those stressors. Most people are familiar with the physical reactions from a startle response, a confrontation, or intense demands placed on the mind and body from stress. How the body reacts in response gives some insights into how we perform physically and how we think and perceive psychologically. Researchers examining the work of firefighters similarly use knowledge of the autonomic nervous system and the factors chronicled by

Grossman and others as they train firefighters (Brennan, 2009). As with law enforcement officers and soldiers, firefighters must be fully aware of the hazards and effects of stress in an emergency situation, knowing that disorientation when fighting a fire can lead to death.

The North Atlantic Treaty Organization (NATO) Advisory Group for Aerospace Research and Development (1989) noted in the preface to its Lecture Series 163, 'Human Performance Assessment Methods':

> The fighter has always been exposed to stress created by other men and by his physical and mental environment. Stressors usually exert a negative influence on performance, but may also have quite the opposite effect: we have all heard stories of heroic actions, performed under stress, that would be considered impossible under normal circumstances.
>
> Both the commander and the military doctor require knowledge of human response to stressors. The commander must be able to predict the fighting potential of his men; the doctor must be able to offer the appropriate treatment to those whose wellbeing is jeopardized by stress.
>
> *(p. iii)*

Not only do officers and other emergency service providers and soldiers need to understand the effects of stress, but those who supervise and care for them need to know as well.

This attention to stress is clearly an important one since acute or chronic stress is often a reality of working in criminal justice. The International Association of Chiefs of Police (IACP) has often addressed health and fitness issues of law enforcement officers. In one of the association's "Training Key" publications it lists the many health risks and benefits associated with physical fitness (IACP 2014) and, in regards to stress, notes:

> *Mental/Emotional Health.* Police officers are the guardians of society, providing assistance to those in distress and risking their lives in the process. However, this duty does not come without cost to the guardians themselves. Officers who are exposed to high levels of stress and trauma on a regular basis can become depressed and despondent. When this is combined with the stressors of everyday life, normal life difficulties, such as family finances or relationship challenges, can seem insurmountable.
>
> *(p. 4)*

Many Americans face high levels of stress and the short-term and potential long-term effects this causes (Everly and Lating, 2013; Understanding the stress response, 2011). People deal with the stress of life with varying types of coping mechanisms and varying results in terms of effectiveness. Police work, however, is seen as unusually stressful (McCraty and Atkinson, 2012). In fact, the acute situations sometimes encountered by officers when facing a perceived threat are also referred to as combat stress or survival stress. The physical arousal follows and is intertwined with the psychological arousal resulting from the perception of threat. Stress inoculation, or introducing increasing amounts of stress in a training environment, can help prepare emergency responders for the effects of stressful situations and boost confidence needed to face such situations (Foreman, 2013).

Researchers have also had success with initial efforts at relaxation training for military members prior to deployment to act as an inoculation and potentially lower rates of PTSD (Lewis et al.,

2015). Progressive muscle relaxation training has been shown to reduce stress, but also to free up working memory that is otherwise occupied by stress and anxiety (Hubbard and Blyler, 2016). And what if officers are not getting enough sleep? "Insufficient sleep and physical exhaustion is a key factor in predisposing you to be a stress casualty" (Grossman and Christensen, 2008, p. 27). Not all stress is debilitating or even bad. The effects of *eustress* have long been understood as helpful in getting "up" or prepared for a sporting event or to take a test. There is a tipping point or inverted-U principle (the Yerkes-Dodson Law) where decision-making under stress or physiological arousal is good – to a point. When the human has reached the point of maximal arousal, perceptual distortion and other factors begin to impact bodily functions and decision-making. There is also a psychological refraction time from the introduction of one stimulus to recognizing and responding to a second (Schmidt and Lee, 2014). Any boxer or officer who has been drawn in by a feint only to be struck by the actual intended blow understands the consequence. This can be said of military commanders down through the ages as well.

Tired of Being Tired

First, insufficient sleep is not good for anyone. Children and teens need it, adults need it. All in fairly agreed-upon amounts. Tiredness also reduces the ability to pay attention to your surroundings and to react to threats. Cognitive function declines quickly with sleep deprivation (Legault, Clement, Kenny, Hardcastle, and Keller, 2017), and there appears to be diminished ability to pay attention to or be alert (Fimm and Blankenheim, 2016). Many agencies have required periods of time between shifts (including if working a second job) for officers so that they may get needed sleep. The IACP in its training key on health and fitness cited a study from 2000 that showed the average law enforcement officer slept only 6.6 hours per day, and some got less than 5 hours (IACP, 2014). None of this is good for the officer on duty. Air traffic controllers, long-haul truckers, surgeons – these and several more are positioned to cause harm if sleep deprivation degrades their abilities or focus.

Following a survival stress event the body's parasympathetic nervous system directs that it is time to sleep and recharge. Grossman and Christensen (2008) chronicle observations from combat where officers had to keep troops awake after an action so they would not be caught totally unawares in a counter-attack. This concept has long been known to military forces:

> This is why the military always holds back a reserve. When the troops are suffering from the burden of exhaustion, and a fresh enemy unit attacks, the exhausted troops collapse like a house of cards.
>
> *(p. 16)*

Picture the officer who has fought to control and restrain a violent arrestee letting down her guard after the event only to be attacked by someone else who appears on the scene. The tidal surge and retreat cycle of combat is familiar to many combat-experienced military, but the intense struggle of an arrest can leave an officer at risk during the let-down period.

Health and Fitness

Take a moderately healthy and fit 22-year-old. Put him or her through an academy that incorporates some amount of physical activity over the course of the program, carried out by the way during "normal" waking hours for humans. The place of nighttime sleep in the circadian rhythm is fairly well maintained. Eating follows the schedule the person has likely had most of her life. Graduation day. The newly-minted officer heads off to years of rotating shifts in a correctional facility or squad car. Frequent sleep deficits may become the norm, diminishing the body's ability maintain an appropriate sleep/wake homeostasis. The sedentary time spent in a car or at a dorm desk. Eating at all hours and without the ready availability of late night healthy food options. The 32- and 42-year-old version of our officer may feel the effects of a physical erosion more pronounced than non-shift working members of society. Add to this regimen that unpredictable introduction of high-stress physical encounters which give way back to the routine of handling matters that do not involve fighting to control somebody.

Any number of people in non-public safety jobs follow recommended dietary and fitness guidelines and get proper sleep. Many in law enforcement and corrections strive to be healthy and fit as well, even with the challenges of shift work and sporadic high-stress events such as fighting someone unconcerned with their health or safety (Violanti, 2014). Heart attacks are more common for public safety personnel than the general population, occurring at a younger age, and over the entire 24-hour day, not just when on duty. Data from the 2011 IACP/BJA study of officer injuries revealed that "78.8 percent of the officers reporting injury were classified as overweight or obese by their Body Mass Index (BMI)" (IACP, 2014, p. 1). The same study noted fewer injuries among officers who "engaged in fitness training regimens" (p. 5). Many lifestyle factors of cardiovascular disease are controllable.

In a study of 4,500 deaths of police officers from 1994 to 2010, 441 sudden cardiac deaths were observed (Varvarigou, Farioli, Korre, Sato, Dahabreh, and Kales, 2014). Sudden cardiac deaths on duty were associated with restraints and altercations in 25 percent, or 108 of the cases; 88 or 20 percent during physical training; 53 or 12 percent while pursuing suspects, 8 percent during rescue and medical operations, and 23 percent or 101 during routine duties (p. 1). Too much exertion in a short time period can be a trigger for a cardiac event. This is contrasted with the importance of consistent exercise aimed at improving cardiovascular health. Intense emotions including anger have also been correlated to greater risk of heart disease and premature heart attacks (Chang, Ford, Meoni, Wang, and Klag, 2002). An angry response during an event may cause a stress reaction, present or mimicked in a violent attempt to control a fighting person who is trying to harm someone. The short-term psychological stress of an angry outburst has a higher risk of a cardiovascular event shortly afterward (Mostofsky, Penner, and Mittleman, 2014).

Psychological

As with physical health concerns, officers face challenges with psychological matters related to the job. The police psychological services section of the International Association of Chiefs of Police is a long-standing group that develops and disseminates information and guidelines for agency practices. The group is composed of psychologists and has issued guidelines, among others, addressing fitness for duty, officer-involved shooting, and peer support. The IACP stresses that officers need support following serious violent incidents such as deadly force encounters because of "the residual emotional, psychological, and behavioral effects often associated with … critical incidents" (IACP, 2014, p. 2).

Daily stressors in criminal justice can take their toll. Both corrections and law enforcement officers attribute some level of stress to the dangers of the job. Measuring work stress for officers is important as a means of better preparing them and supporting them. A great deal of literature has addressed the various stressors and how to appropriately measure them (Higgins, Tewksbury, and Denney, 2012a). Assaults on both sets of officers are not infrequent and this actual danger can cause a persistent stressor operating in the background of the officer's daily work life. "Understanding work stress among correctional officers is important because it provides insights into production and safety" (Higgins, Tewksbury, and Denney, 2012b, p. 395). While each officer may deal with stress somewhat differently, the reality of the risk inherent in the job results in some level of thought, even if only occasionally, about this particular job hazard. The preoccupation with the risk of force situations and the other stressors of an officer's work assignment can affect productivity and job satisfaction.

Any stress-inducing job should hold the opportunity for resilience training, and agencies should investigate how to provide this (Andersen and Gustafsberg, 2016). Organizations offer many points of stress for employees and, concomitantly, opportunities to mitigate stress through comprehensive health and well-being programs as well as following organizational approaches such as organizational or procedural justice (Greenberg, 2004; Lambert, Hogan, and Griffin, 2007). Post-traumatic stress disorder (PTSD) appears in the lives of many people as the result of chronic stress. Employee assistance programs (EAPs) have progressed in making counseling available to officers either voluntarily (and typically anonymously), or through the referral of a supervisor.

It is already clear that even in our brief coverage of these two very broad topics, that we cannot draw a bright line separating the physical from the psychological. Exertion introduces chemicals that can alter cognitive processes including decision making and memory. The stress already discussed relative to physiological responses has psychological impacts aligned with the acute arousal in a force usage situation. Armstrong, Clare, and Plecas (2014) used force simulations to gauge the effects of intensity on physical and emotional responses. The relevance of this broad set of concerns to the use of force in criminal justice is clear when we consider that many force incidents, involving fatal force or not, can happen "under conditions of fear, panic, and chaos" (Engel and Smith, 2009, p. 141).

There have been quite a few cognitive distortions noted by researchers that affect or are noticed by officers involved in shootings (Artwohl, 2008; Klinger and Brunson, 2009). The significant presence of various distortions has ramifications for officer training, post-event investigation, and potential court testimony. Klinger and Brunson (2009) found in their review of several previous studies (Artwohl and Christensen, 1997; Campbell, 1992; Nielsen, 1981; Solomon and Horn, 1986) and their own examination of 113 shooting incidents involving 80 different officers, that:

(1) Most often, officers experience at least two types of perceptual distortions during shooting incidents; (2) officers' perceptions (and distortions thereof) often change substantially over the course of shooting incidents; and (3) some specific distortions are more likely to occur in tandem with others, whereas some are less likely.

(p. 134)

Their results led them to conclude "that reasonable officers on the scene of police shootings are subject to experiencing substantial levels of perceptual distortions – both prior to pulling the trigger and as they fire" (p. 134). A summary table of the distortions officers reported experiencing prior to and during shooting listed a total of nine distortions among three categories; visual, auditory, and time. The visual distortion included tunnel vision, heightened visual detail, and both together;

auditory distortions included blunting or acuity, or both; and time distortions were the perception of time slowing, speeding up, or both types (Klinger and Brunson 2009, p. 127, table 1).

What We Should Remember about Memory

Recent research is shedding additional light on how stress and sleep loss may impact memory. Various studies have produced inconsistent findings on how memory is impacted when a stressor is introduced: prior to, during, or after encoding, as well as taking into account other contextual aspects of the event of interest (Shields, Sazma, McCullough, and Yonelinas, 2017). Recognition and recall memory are potentially affected by sleep loss (Chatburn, Kohler, Payne, and Drummond, 2017), and the combination of these two factors alone should be considered when agencies consider policies for interviewing officers following a lethal event. The restorative nature of sleep creates the ability to make memories, consolidate nascent ones, integrate them with existing memories, and more (Tononi and Cirelli, 2014).

The impact on psychological functioning, including memory, during and after an acute stress event such as a deadly force incident can be pronounced (Artwohl, 2002, 2008). This impact was also seen with the reaction of "fight or flight," as well as what have been termed "freeze" or "posture" responses in a recruit academy class asked to report their feelings and emotions (Broomé, 2011). Nieuwenhuys, Savelsbergh, and Oudejans (2012) found in a study of low- and high-anxiety simulation shooting exercises that appropriate decisions were impacted by the relative anxiety induced by the interactive scenarios. The effectiveness of simulations and scenarios is connected to the psychological fidelity of students suspending disbelief and feeling the reality of the training (FLETC, 2011).

If working memory capacity is reduced due to, for example, a number of sensory inputs occurring simultaneously, force decision making may be affected (Kleider, Parrot, and King, 2010). Efforts to improve resiliency may enhance sensory awareness, which holds the potential for improved use of force decisions (Kalish, Müller, and Tüscher, 2015). Recovery and remembrance is a concern when considering policy or best practice about how long to wait before interviewing officers after a shooting or serious incident. Sleep, rest, and memory consolidation have continued to receive research attention, with most studies recommending one or more sleep intervals prior to a formal interview.

Some Thoughts on Thinking

There are volumes and volumes written on how we think. Psychologists, sociologists, criminologists, organizational behaviorists: we all want our say. The list of commentators narrows just a bit, perhaps, when we move to the area of violent behavior stemming from our thoughts. And there are fewer still to assert how the human officer or the human combat soldier decides, acts, and processes force usage events. Decision making at the office is different than in a ditch with someone's arm wrapped around your neck or trying to get to your sidearm. The courts have recognized this in various decisions about not using 20/20 hindsight to evaluate the reasonableness of an officer's force decisions. With that tip of the hat to what could fill an entire degree program of study, here are a few relevant contributions.

In *Blink* (2005), noted journalist and author Malcolm Gladwell describes rapid cognition encapsulated in the concept of "thin-slicing." Gladwell says this is "the ability of our unconscious to find patterns in situations and behavior based on very narrow slices of experience" (p. 23). This "accelerated unconscious" evaluation of input based on our own prior experiences is a heuristic born of evolution that may have let our ancestors know that the look on the saber-tooth tiger's mug was hunger. Gladwell reminds readers of the importance of training and rehearsal to making good decisions in "high-stress conditions of rapid cognition" (p. 114). There is much in his writing that also lends support to many trainers who lecture on the ability to determine a great deal from facial expressions, even without the benefit of digital recording playback to discern "micro-expressions."

Daniel Kahneman, in his 2011 book *Thinking, Fast and Slow*, introduces us to what he calls System 1 and System 2. System 1 is "fast," unconscious, and arrives quickly at a decision based on our prior experience and our emotion. System 2 is "slow" and takes a more circumspect approach using logic and our conscious mind. There are insights within the writing about the bias to behavior we have hard-wired, which drives a great deal of decision making – arguably the type officers confront in many use of force situations. But Kahneman also warns that opportunity cost operates with thinking in the same way economists describe how we cannot go to the beach and to class at the same time (see also implications of Hick's Law in the discussion of mental chronometry below). System 2 takes more time, so maybe we don't use it as much as we should because we can be lazy thinkers. Shortcut decision-making practices may be comfortable and *efficient*, but they may not be *effective*, as they can be impacted by bias or misapplication to unique situations beyond the expertise or experience of the decision-maker.

Mistakes are more common when we face a stress decision that we have not previously faced. If a person is accustomed to similar stressful decision-making settings, a fast decision may suffice. Colonel John Boyd (USAF), a former fighter pilot and Pentagon consultant, described a decision cycle concept that is known to military commanders, and many public safety officers, as the OODA Loop (Coram, 2002). The acronym stands for Observation, Orientation, Decide, and Act. Gathering information during the observation period is multi-sensory for an officer (or fighter pilot) and can become more thorough and faster with increased experience. Putting the pieces together of what has crossed the threshold of our senses is the orientation period. The decision to act, and what action to take, follows and the person acts. It is the hope and practiced intention to accomplish all of these steps before your opponent does, thereby being "inside his loop." Physical reaction capabilities among people may be unevenly distributed, but the processing of information and the decision to act may herald the winner.

Another system known to many public safety practitioners and trainers is Cooper's Colors or the Gunsite (firearms academy) Color System, the awareness codification developed by the late Jeff Cooper (Fairburn, 2017). Cooper, a former Marine and renowned firearms instructor, conceptualized a simple hierarchy denoting levels of preparation officers find themselves in throughout the day. Situational awareness is all about how an officer remains alert to his environment. In Condition White the person is relaxed and essentially oblivious to tactical considerations around him. This is not where an officer ever wants to be while on duty. Condition Yellow still finds the officer relaxed but aware of things and people in an alert state but not anticipating an imminent attack. For most law enforcement families, this is why you see mom or dad pick the restaurant seat that gives them maximum visibility of the door and most of the dining area. The officer in Condition Orange has noted something of interest in the immediate vicinity and this person or situation draws his attention until he decides if it is a threat. An on-duty officer goes in and out of Condition Orange while on duty and positions herself for potential trouble while mentally planning a response.

If the person or thing of interest reveals itself as a threat, the officer moves mentally to Condition Red. An officer may draw her firearm at this point and move to a tactically advantageous position with a clearly identified threat or target.

In his 1997 book *The Gift of Fear*, Gavin de Becker talks at length about intuition and how it helps us interpret threats in our environment. Officers on the street or in a dormitory or recreation yard must be attuned to signals from other humans. Their level of sensitivity and grasp of surroundings must remain higher than that of other citizens – and almost constantly. It is clear that no one can remain vigilant at all times, or perhaps even completely vigilant for any length of time.

Inattentional Blindness

Laser focus is not our constant companion. There is a cost associated with a narrow and intense focus on one thing and not another. When we fail to notice items within our field of vision, this is called *inattentional blindness*. The cognitive load placed upon us as we look at a primary task or target can block even noticing other items or activity, typically when it is novel or unexpected, but this can also happen with expected items in our field of vision (the von Restorff effect). What we pay attention to can be remembered at greater volume if auditory and with increased detail if visual. With less attentional resources available during all manner of interactions, let alone the intensity and multiple parts of many force situations, important information and potential threats can be and are missed with regularity. Inattentional blindness is an important phenomenon for officers, supervisors, the court, and the public to understand.

There has been a great deal of study and research regarding distractions and how they can impact, for example, driving safety and how the perceptual load of driving can impact how people observe things in front of them (central load) or to the side (peripheral load) (Marciano and Yeshurun, 2015). In a similar vein, distractions in the operating room can result in adverse outcomes for patients (Sevdalis, Undre, McDermott, Giddie, Diner, and Smith, 2014). Law enforcement training manuals the world over address observational skills and factors affecting an officer's perception. The potential compromising of officer safety is ever present in failing to observe or accurately judge the movement and behavior of individuals the officer is interacting with or who may be on the periphery of an officer's activity.

Nexus

Mental Chronometry

The various physiological and psychological considerations discussed to this point are certainly important for officers to understand intellectually. It behooves trainers and administrators to be knowledgeable of these factors, and to incorporate information in both policy and training, and integrate them to provide effective guidance to officers, as well as to demonstrate that the agency recognizes the challenges present in use of force encounters. Prosecutors and courts should educate themselves in the dynamics and ramifications of physical and mental components of perceived threat and reaction and response. Beyond this is the practical impact that each or all of these factors may have in the moment when an officer has to react.

Mental chronometry involves gauging the time it takes to perceive and react to a stimulus. While recognition of the unavoidable time lag between action and reaction has been known for millennia, formal research is only a century or so old (Donders, 1969). In the high-stakes arena of threat assessment and decision-making in public safety (and military combat), it is important for officers to understand the dynamics of reaction time and work to shave the margins to improve safety outcomes. "The serialized nature of perceiving a threat, formulating a response, and enacting that response compounds reaction time within a context that is often chaotic" (Hough, 2017, p. 1).

The chaos or clutter of many settings for officers degrades reaction time even more. This reduction based on multiple sensory inputs and response options is referred to as Hick's Law (Hick, 1952; Schmidt and Lee, 2014). When potential risk is present, this increased delay to the already axiomatic reaction that follows action reality, can result in injury or death to an officer. Some research has indicated that experienced officers have greater efficiency relative to recruit officers in speed of threat identification and gaze control during firearms events (Vickers and Lewinski, 2012). This type of study has been performed to examine significance of eye movement, reaction time, and accuracy for the design of learning environments (Gegenfurtner, Lehtinen, and Säljö, 2011). Experience and training, therefore, may mitigate some errors, but reaction time deficits and misidentification or failure to identify a threat will persist with many officers.

It is desirable, to be sure, that an officer performs his absolute best in each and every encounter. While aspirational, it is not realistic to believe that he will. Defensive tactics instructors admonish recruits and officers to develop consistency in their tasks to improve outcomes. Search a person in the same pattern each time; approach a car or a subject on the street or an inmate in the same way each time. When you handcuff someone, double-lock the cuffs each and every time. The list goes on. This is not to be confused with treating things "routinely" that trainers rail against. In those circumstance there is danger when an officer falls into a rut where he is barely conscious of his movements or thoughts as he handles yet one more "false alarm" at a familiar bank building only to find a robbery in progress.

GOING GLOBAL

Workplace stress that continues unabated can certainly lead to burnout. Stress comes from the nature of the job, such as danger and dealing with hostile customers in policing and corrections, and from organizational factors including management (Kop and Euwema, 2001). The study by Kop and Euwema did not find the expected level of "emotional exhaustion" in the overall sample, but it did find a higher level in the observed officers who were more prone to forceful action toward civilians, as well as higher rates of "depersonalization" in those more accepting of force.

Among thousands of articles on burnout, dealing with demanding people reoccurs as a major factor. In a study from Zurich, Switzerland (Manzoni and Eisner, 2006), stress-related factors were not seen as correlated to the use of force, but an officer having been victimized does.

Family support was found as having potential to mitigate some level of stress before burnout in India, and given an increase in officer suicide and misconduct toward the public, work support has also been highlighted as important (Kumar and Kamalanabhan, 2017). Among patrol officers in Sweden, levels of social support were noted as contributing to the effects of stress, as well as the psychosocial work environment (Padyab, Backteman-Erlanson, and Brulin, 2016). On the point of support and agency efforts, a study of 681 German police officers (Ellrich and Baier,

2017) who had each been violently assaulted showed that "stress-protective features", such as preventive programs to address stress generally and make officers aware of issues that may arise because of stress from traumatic events, were effective.

Summary

We do not ask officers to be elite athletes, and it would not make sense to do so. Even being an elite athlete does not make a person competent in the ways of physical control and restraint. We also do not require that officers be mental health diagnosticians, therapists, members of the clergy, or possessing of in-depth knowledge in any of the myriad topical areas they are called upon to encounter during their shift as generalist police officer or corrections or security officer. Being physically prepared to face violence and subdue the person delivering it amounts to a very small portion of an officer's duties. We ask that he or she be a competent generalist in many, many areas. When facing the chaotic, tenuous, or unknown, officers learn to quickly try to control the scene. While people "not doing anything wrong" do not always understand or appreciate the forceful nature of what Blum (2000) called initiative-control methods, failure to engage in them can place the officer at increased risk.

Officers involved in a deadly force incident face many challenges. There will be organizational and external review of his actions that extend beyond a tactical debriefing to minute examination of all of the circumstances surrounding the event. The human officer is impacted psychologically by being in a position where in an instant it may have seemed absolutely necessary to take the life of another human. This reality, often thrust upon an officer in this way, will likely have ramifications for a long time to come. There will inevitably be second guessing, potential examination for criminal indictment, and a lawsuit alleging that whatever the officer did was incorrect, excessive, or motivated by bad intent.

The response of the body to stressors such as danger or fighting carries short- and long-term physical consequences. An officer may move on to any number of other activities immediately after engaging in a pursuit, tense search, or physical struggle. What may still be going on in the body and mind of that officer has likely not ended when the physical threat did. Caring for the officer is not solely the responsibility of that officer. Agencies and their governmental, insurance, health, and professional association partners should all be invested in the wellbeing of those who work to ensure society's wellbeing.

KEY TERMS

Physiological impacts of stress
Psychological impacts of stress
Inattention blindness
Mental chronometry
Post-traumatic stress disorder (PTSD)

Discussion Questions

1. Describe the concept of inattention blindness. How does understanding this help officers?
2. What do we know happens to bodily functions during a dangerous confrontation?

3. Explain post-traumatic stress and how law enforcement officers can be affected following violence.
4. What are the challenges faced by officers documenting an after action report?

TRY THIS

Go to www.smithsonianmag.com/videos/category/science/how-many-times-do-they-pass-the-ball/ and watch the video of basketball passing. Do this before reading the accompanying article. Discuss the implications for officers.

References

Andersen, J. P., and Gustafsberg, H. (2016). A training method to improve police use of force decision making: a randomized controlled trial. *SAGE Open*, 6(2), 1–13.

Andersen, J. P., Pitel, M., Weerasinghe, A., and Papazoglou, K. (2016). Highly realistic scenario based training simulates the psychophysiology of real world use of force encounters: implications for improved police officer performance. *Journal of Law Enforcement*, 5(4), 1–13.

Armstrong, J., Clare, J., and Plecas, D. (2014). Monitoring the impact of scenario-based use-of-force simulations on police heart rate: evaluating the Royal Canadian Mounted Police skills refresher program. *Western Criminology Review*, 15(1), 51–59.

Artwohl, A. (2002). Perceptual and memory distortion during officer-involved shootings. *FBI Law Enforcement Bulletin*, 71(10), 18.

Artwohl, A. (2008). Perceptual and memory distortion during officer-involved shootings (2008 update). AELE Lethal and Less Lethal Force Workshop, Las Vegas NV, November 12 2007. Chicago: AELE.

Artwohl, A. and Christensen, L. (1997). *Deadly force encounters*. Boulder, CO: Paladin Press.

Asken, M. J., Grossman, D., and Christensen, L. W. (2010). *Warrior mindset*. U.S.: Warrior Science Publications.

Blum, L. N. (2000). *Force under pressure: how cops live and why they die*. New York: Lantern.

Brennan, C. (2009). You want me to do what? The physiology and psychology of firefighting. *Fire Engineering*, 162(12), 45–54.

Broom, M., Capek, A., Carachi, P., Akeroyd, M., Hilditch, G., Broom, M. A., and Hilditch, G. (2011). Critical phase distractions in anaesthesia and the sterile cockpit concept. *Anaesthesia*, 66(3), 175–179.

Broomé, R. E. 2011. An empathetic psychological perspective of police deadly force training. *Journal of Phenomenological Psychology*, 42(2), 137–156.

Campbell, J. H. (1992). A comparative analysis of the effects of post-shooting trauma on the special agents of the Federal Bureau of Investigation. Unpublished Ph.D. dissertation, Department of Educational Administration, Michigan State University.

Chang, P. P., Ford, D. E., Meoni, L. A., Wang, N. Y., and Klag, M. J. (2002). Anger in young men and subsequent premature cardiovascular disease: the precursors study. *Archives of Internal Medicine*, 162(8), 901–906.

Chatburn, A., Kohler, M. J., Payne, J. D., and Drummond, S. A. (2017). The effects of sleep restriction and sleep deprivation in producing false memories. *Neurobiology of Learning and Memory*, 1 37, 107–113.

Coram, R. (2002). *Boyd: the fighter pilot who changed the art of war*. New York: Little, Brown.

De Becker, G. (1997). *The gift of fear*. Boston: Little, Brown.

Donders, F. C. (1969). On the speed of mental processes (W. G. Koster, Trans.). In W. G. Koster (Ed.), Attention and performance II, *Acta Psychologica*, 30, 412–431. (Original work published 1868).

Ellrich, K. and Baier, D. (2017). Post-traumatic stress symptoms in police officers following violent assaults. *Journal of Interpersonal Violence*, 32(3), 331–356.

Engel, R. S. and Smith, M. R. (2009). Perceptual distortion and reasonableness during police shootings: law, legitimacy, and future research. *Criminology and Public Policy*, 8(1), 141–151.

Everly, G. S. and Lating, J. M. (2013). *The anatomy and physiology of the human stress response: a clinical guide to the treatment of the human stress response.* New York: Springer.

Fairburn, R. (2017, July 21) Cooper's colors: A simple system for situational awareness. PoliceOne.com. Retrieved from: https://www.policeone.com/police-trainers/articles/2188253-Coopers-colors-A-simple-system-for-situational-awareness/

Fimm, B. and Blankenheim, A. (2016). Effect of sleep deprivation and low arousal on eye movements and spatial attention. *Neuropsychologia*, 92, 115–128.

Fletc (Federal Law Enforcement Training Center). (2011). *Stress and decision making.* Glynco, GA: Author.

Foreman, K. (2013). Facing the four-letter word: fear. *Kentucky Law Enforcement Magazine*, 12(4), 40.

Gegenfurtner, A., Lehtinen, E., and Säljö, R. (2011). Expertise differences in the comprehension of visualizations: a meta-analysis of eye-tracking research in professional domains. *Educational Psychology Review*, 23(4), 523–552.

Greenberg, J. (2004). Stress fairness to fare no stress: managing workplace stress by promoting organizational justice. *Organizational Dynamics*, 33(4), 352–365.

Grossman, D. (2009). *On killing: The psychological cost of learning to kill in war and society.* Revised ed. New York: Back Bay Books.

Grossman, D. and Christensen, L. W. (2008). *On combat: the psychology and physiology of deadly conflict in war and peace.* 3rd ed. U.S.A.: Warrior Science Publications.

Hick, W. E. (1952). On the rate of gain of information. *Quarterly Journal of Experimental Psychology*, 4, 11–26

Higgins, G. E., Tewksbury, R., and Denney, A. S. (2012a). Validating a measure of work stress for correctional staff: a structural equation modeling approach. *Criminal Justice Policy Review*, 24(3), 338–352.

Higgins, G. E., Tewksbury, R., and Denney, A. S. (2012b). Measuring work stress among correctional staff: a Rasch measurement approach. *Journal of Applied Measurement*, 13(4), 394–402.

Hough, R. (2017). Mental chronometry and officer training. *Law Enforcement Executive Forum*, 17(2).

Hubbard, K. K. and Blyler, D. (2016). Improving academic performance and working memory in health science graduate students using progressive muscle relaxation training. *American Journal of Occupational Therapy*, 70(6), 1–8.

IACP (International Association of Chiefs of Police). (2014) *Training key #685: Health and fitness: importance to law enforcement officers.* Alexandria, VA: IACP.

International Association of Chiefs of Police, Center for Officer Safety and Wellness and The Bureau of Justice Assistance (2014). *Reducing officer injuries: final report.* Alexandria, VA: IACP.

Kalisch, R., Müller, M. B., and Tüscher, O. (2015). A conceptual framework for the neurobiological study of resilience. *Behavioral and Brain Sciences*, 38, e92.

Kleider, H. M., Parrot, D. J., and King, T. Z. 2010. Shooting behaviour: how working memory and negative emotionality influence police officer shoot decisions. *Applied Cognitive Psychology*, 24(5), 707–717.

Klinger, D. A. and Brunson, R. K. (2009). Police officers' perceptual distortions during lethal force situations: informing the reasonableness standard. *Criminology and Public Policy*, 8, 117–140.

Kop, N. and Euwema, M. C. (2001). Occupational stress and the use of force by Dutch police officers. *Criminal Justice and Behavior*, 28(5), 631–652.

Kumar, V. and Kamalanabhan, T. (2017). Moderating role of work support in stressor-burnout relationship: an empirical investigation among police personnel in India. *Psychological Studies*, 62(1), 85–97.

Lambert, E. G., Hogan, N. L., and Griffin, M. L. (2007). The impact of distributive and procedural justice on correctional staff job stress, job satisfaction, and organizational commitment. *Journal of Criminal Justice*, 35(6), 644–656.

Legault, G., Clement, A., Kenny, G. P., Hardcastle, S., and Keller, N. (2017). Cognitive consequences of sleep deprivation, shiftwork, and heat exposure for underground miners. *Applied Ergonomics*, 58, 144–150.

Lewis, G. F., Hourani, L., Tueller, S., Kizakevich, P., Bryant, S., Weimer, B., and Strange, L. (2015). Relaxation training assisted by heart rate variability biofeedback: implication for a military predeployment stress inoculation protocol. *Psychophysiology*, 52(9), 1167–1174.

McCraty, R. and Atkinson, M. (2012). Resilience training program reduces physiological and psychological stress in police officers. *Global Advances in Health and Medicine*, 1, 44–66.

Manzoni, P. and Eisner, M. (2006). Violence between the police and the public: influences of work-related stress, job satisfaction, burnout, and situational factors. *Criminal Justice and Behavior*, 33(5), 613–645.

Marciano, H. and Yeshurun, Y. (2015). Perceptual load in different regions of the visual scene and its relevance for driving. *Human Factors*, 57(4), 701–716.

Mostofsky, E., Penner, E. A., and Mittleman, M. A. (2014).Outbursts of anger as a trigger of acute cardiovascular events: a systematic review and meta-analysis. *European Heart Journal*, 35(21), 1404–1410.

Nielsen, E. (1981). *Salt Lake City Police Department deadly force policy shooting and post shooting reactions*. Salt Lake City, UT: Salt Lake City Police Department.

Nieuwenhuys, A., Savelsbergh, G. J. P., and Oudejans, R. R. D. (2012). Shoot or don't shoot? Why police officers are more inclined to shoot when they are anxious. *Emotion*, 12(4), 827–833.

North Atlantic Treaty Organization (NATO) Advisory Group for Aerospace Research and Development. (1989). *Human performance assessment methods*. AGARD Lecture Series 163. Neuilly sur Seine, France: AGARD Aerospace Medical Panel and the Consultant and Exchange Programme.

Olson, D. T. (1998). Deadly force decision making. *FBI Law Enforce Bulletin*, 67, 1–9.

Padyab, M., Backteman-Erlanson, S., and Brulin, C. (2016). Burnout, coping, stress of conscience and psychosocial work environment among patrolling police officers. *Journal of Police and Criminal Psychology*, 31(4), 229–237.

Patrick, U. W. and Hall, J. C. (2017). *In defense of self and others: issues, facts and fallacies – the realities of law enforcement's use of deadly force*, 3rd ed. Durham, NC: Carolina Academic Press.

Schmidt, R. A. and Lee, T. D. (2014). *Motor learning and performance*. 5th ed. Champaign, IL: Human Kinetics.

Sevdalis, N., Undre, S., McDermott, J., Giddie, J., Diner, L., and Smith, G. (2014). Impact of intraoperative distractions on patient safety: a prospective descriptive study using validated instruments. *World Journal of Surgery*, 38, 751–758.

Shields, G. S., Sazma, M. A., McCullough, A. M., and Yonelinas, A. P. (2017). The effects of acute stress on episodic memory: a meta-analysis and integrative review. *Psychological Bulletin*, 143(6), 636–675.

Solomon, R. M. and Horn, J. H. (1986). Post-shooting traumatic reactions: a pilot study. In J. T. Reese and H. A. Goldstein (Eds.), *Psychological services for law enforcement officers*. Washington, DC: U.S. Government Printing Office.

Tononi, G. and Cirelli, C. (2014). Sleep and the price of plasticity: from synaptic and cellular homeostasis to memory consolidation and integration. *Neuron*, 81, 12–34.

Understanding the stress response. (2011). *Harvard Mental Health Letter*, 27(9), 4–5.

Varvarigou, V., Farioli, A., Korre, M., Sato, S., Dahabreh, I. J., and Kales, S. N. (2014). Law enforcement duties and sudden cardiac death among police officers in United States: case distribution study. *British Medical Journal*, 349, g6534.

Vickers, J. N. and Lewinski, W. (2012). Performing under pressure: gaze control, decision making and shooting performance of elite and rookie police officers. *Human Movement Science*, 31(1), 101–117.

Violanti, J. M. (2014). *Dying for the job: police work exposure and health*. Springfield, IL: Charles C. Thomas.

7

TRAINING TO USE FORCE

CHAPTER OUTLINE

Introduction
Use of force continuum and other models
Academy training
In-service training
Presence, verbalization, and the use of force-fulness
Scenario-based training
After the restraint
Summary
Features: What-Why, Going Global
Key Terms
Discussion Questions
Try This
References

STUDENT LEARNING OUTCOMES

- Students will be able to critique factors related to response or force continuums.
- Students will be able to describe the use of presence and verbalization by officers.
- Students will be able to explain the dynamics and benefits of scenario-based training.
- Students will be able to discuss the factors used to determine length of training for different topics in force.

Introduction

Accomplishing the goals of any organization, public or private, requires an understanding by all employees of what those goals are. Following this, members of an agency must be aware of their specific roles in accomplishing the goals. Once this is established, each person needs to know *how* to perform the tasks assigned to her. It is to this last point we now turn as we examine the current state of public safety training with a focus on force.

At the same time that we consider the effectiveness of training for specific duties, we must be conscious of how the function, in this case force usage, fits into the overall training effort for a correctional, probation, law enforcement officer or other officer. To be sure, the criminal justice system has evolved and become both more efficient and more effective in accomplishing a wide variety of tasks. This reflects the number and diversity of responsibilities that we have decided or defaulted for officers to do. For many decades now the police officer in Western democratic society has been viewed as a generalist. In the best sense of the term we expect officers to go out into the community and take on myriad calls for service and demands upon the state-vested authority to try and "fix things." But can police officers actually fix things? Can a corrections officer correct an inmate? Certainly a police officer can respond to a burglar alarm and investigate to determine if the offender is still present, has made off with the property of another citizen, or has been thwarted by the preventive devices that the private owner has put in place. We see modestly effective low level deterrence when an off duty uniformed officer is paid to park or stand outside the local movie theater on a Friday or Saturday night to impose a sense of orderliness and safety on the theatergoers. Corrections officers generally ensure inmates do not escape and, if available, facilitate program staff members to interact with offenders.

What about tasks of greater complexity or nuance? If an officer is called to a home, either by an occupant or neighbors, to investigate or intervene at an incident of intimate partner violence (IPV), how best should she proceed? The officer must investigate and ideally determine a primary aggressor in the incident. Most states would then favor the officer arresting the identified offender. This action may even act as part of a larger and longer strategy to "fix" the instant problem. But then again it may not. When a deputy sheriff or a police officer responds to a self-storage facility where 38 units have been burglarized over the weekend he may write out a series of reports and admonish the business owner to add alarms, cameras, and maybe a large dog. Increased patrol presence may be initiated for a short period of time to watch this barn door after the horses are gone. There are endless types and versions of calls and correctional program challenges that we could ruminate on regarding the ability of an officer to have a salubrious effect. In contemporary society, we now call the guards and jailers of the past "correctional officers." This is surely aspirational and important but there would be a lively debate regarding the role of the officer vis-à-vis inmate rehabilitation.

When it comes to discrete incidents of enforcement action we see a quantifiable measure. If the officer caught the burglar in the act an arrest would be made. If the officer assembled sufficient investigative information to charge a spouse batterer, an arrest would be made. If a corrections officer worked in concert with others, similar to the unit management approach initiated in the 1970s, and learned some time later that a released offender has become gainfully employed and turned from deviant responses to society's rules, a mark could be placed in the plus column. These are all countable actions. We like numbers. They give us a sense of permanence and accomplishment. This is probably why many researchers are drawn more to quantitative methods of analysis while criminal justice administrators and others live with the reality of a qualitative world and struggle to employ intelligence-led approaches.

But what of force usage? Identifying, perhaps in the blink of an eye, the need to use force in a given situation represents an instrumental response to an instant situation. The burglar produces a knife and violently resists the arresting officer. The batterer descends deeper into a self-righteous rage over interference with how he runs his family and strikes the officer squarely in the face. Attempts at controlled usage occur in the face of violent, often unpredictable, action by thinking humans with a capacity to harm or kill and with little regard to worsening what is likely an already bad situation. Training then becomes an infinitely branching set of heuristics that begins with making recruits and officers aware of the potential for force situations. After a period of intellectual indoctrination in the realities of resistance and outright violence, the recruit or officer must then begin to absorb training to become competent in physical control methods and the employment of various aids in restraining someone. The person being restrained likely does not wish to be controlled and thus may react or respond at any instant throughout the controlling or force-usage event, making it necessary for officers to make a high-stakes prediction, with potentially dire consequences for inaccurate prediction in either direction.

We return to a background issue regarding the role of officers; the use of force is statistically infrequent during the course of one's duties. And yet, this one task may hold the potential for the greatest impact on the officer and the individual that he or she deals with. If an officer fails to act, a situation may get further out of control. If an officer reacts with too much force an injury may occur that, while it may not be unlawful, is certainly undesirable. If an officer after restraining someone *punishes* the individual with an inappropriate application of a conducted energy device, a policy violation and a crime has likely been committed. This partly underscores the challenge that many people face in their jobs, of performing competently a task that they only perform infrequently. Mistakes are made, but the overwhelming majority of force uses are done within policy, law, and without long-term harmful consequences to anyone. If the training environment is paced appropriately, and subsequent on-the-job experiences accrue in an ideal fashion, the properly selected and average adult learner may acquire competence in the occasional use of low-level or moderate force. We put aside momentarily the individual fitness, predisposition, and discernment of each recruit on the training mat.

Most law enforcement officers never fire a gun at someone; corrections officers do not routinely engage in hand-to-hand techniques to disarm an inmate wielding a shiv; probation officers are not attacked on a daily basis as they go to the home or workplace of a probationer; and a bailiff in the courtroom rarely has to subdue an angry defendant. But within the approximately 10,000 days of the average officer's career, any of these scenarios may play out – and more than once. So preparation for this infrequent but important function of physically restraining an uncooperative (and possibly extremely violent) person is at once a priority and a challenge. If an agency presents and has officers participate in an acceptable program of updates to resistance response and force training it is fulfilling its responsibility to both the citizenry and the officers. The training must be aligned with agency policies, and supervisors must accept their role as guides and monitors to support officers and ensure compliance with guidelines. There is some evidence that "highly educated and trained supervisors moderate their subordinate officers' uses of higher levels of force" (Lim, Goodman, and Lee, 2015, p. 444).

Failure-to-train law suits highlight officer actions that reflect no, little, or inadequate training to perform those tasks. The plaintiff must show the training was inadequate, that the inadequate nature of the training resulted from the governmental entity's deliberate indifference, and that it caused or was closely related to the injury the plaintiff claims to have incurred. Training adequacy is often an area of litigation by plaintiffs. Training typically occurs first at the recruit academy. Most agencies then provide additional annual training for officers. Let's turn first to academy training.

Academy Training

The 1967 President's Commission on Law Enforcement and Administration of Justice thought it would be good if by 1982 all law enforcement officers could have a bachelor's degree. The report generated by the commission, titled *The Challenge of Crime in a Free Society*, spoke of the need for greater professionalization, attention to recruiting, improved management practices, and more training for police officers. The independent and non-centralized nature of American policing is but one factor that hindered that aspirational goal. Let's think for a moment about the difference between the concept of *training* and that of *education*. The training that occurs at the basic recruit academy is largely concerned with *how* tasks are completed; a vocational primer, if you will. In contrast, education at the college down the road is generally more about the *why* officers and agencies do what they do. It is simplistic to assert that there is not a good deal of cross-pollination between the two approaches, but it is helpful to let you think about this distinction as you consider the relative and synergistic benefits of each modality.

Students of police management know that August Vollmer is known as one of the most influential early proponents of the professionalization of law enforcement officers. Often referred to as the father of American law enforcement, Vollmer, in the early 1900s, was the first police chief to require officers to obtain a college degree. Vollmer himself taught at the University of California at Berkeley and in that role continued to influence those who would professionalize the field of policing. Vollmer's influence included teaching O.W. Wilson, who went on to found the first college police science program at what is now Wichita State University. There are now hundreds of programs offered in criminal justice, criminology and other fields that help educate students in the criminal justice system. Federal efforts such as the Law Enforcement Assistance Administration (LEAA) provided money for criminology research, and the Law Enforcement Education Program (LEAP) gave money to students to attend criminal justice classes in college.

National attention to the needs of professionalizing police agencies and educating people to study and contribute to the field ran alongside state and local efforts to improve criminal justice services through development of civil service exams, state training standards, and all-around better recruitment and selection practices. With the evolution of law enforcement and correctional officer training academies, came a general consensus on topics to include in the curriculum for basic training. The Bureau of Justice Statistics conducts a nationwide survey of academies that offer law enforcement training, which included some 664 in 2013. Eighty-nine percent, or 591, of the eligible academies responded to the 2013 Census of Law Enforcement Training Academies (CLETA).

The 2013 Census of Law Enforcement Training Academies (CLETA) indicated that from 2011 to 2013 an average of 45,000 entry-level recruits began training in academies around the U.S., with approximately 86 percent graduating. In most states graduation is followed by sitting for a state certification exam. If an individual achieves certification he or she generally applies to an agency with hopes of being employed. Some agencies are large enough to operate their own academy while adhering to the state-mandated curriculum of instruction. The 600+ academies were run in various ways emphasizing more or less of a military regimen and based in either an academic institution such as a college or technical school, or operated by municipal police, sheriffs' offices, state police or highway patrol, or state peace officer standards and training agencies (BJS, 2013).

For law enforcement basic recruit classes, the length was an average of 840 hours, some run eight hours per day and some in a combination of night and weekend classes. Academy topics include patrol operations, investigations, law, communications, and various types of service calls, critical incidents, and many others. Many academies and states refer to "high-liability" blocks of training as those including firearms, emergency vehicle operations, first responder (medical), and defensive tactics. The BJS survey reports that a combined average of 168 hours of training was devoted to "weapons, defensive tactics, the use of force, and nonlethal weapons" (State and Local Law Enforcement Training Academies, 2013, NCJ 249784, para. 6). As to use of force training, the survey reported:

> Mock scenarios were used in reality-based training to encourage recruits to practice critical decision making, execute standard operating procedures, and employ potentially life-saving tactics under realistic conditions. Almost all (99%) recruits received reality-based use-of-force training, and 74% of recruits received this type of training on the use of nonlethal weapons. Additionally, 9 in 10 recruits received training on firearm use at night, in reduced light, or under simulated stressful conditions.
>
> *(Bureau of Justice Statistics, State and Local Law Enforcement Training Academies, 2013)*

Physical techniques are taught in every law enforcement or corrections academy class. A well-meaning and relatively competent cadre of instructors likely were gathered in a task force or working committee under the auspices of a state body to opine on the collection of techniques that are sufficiently effective in controlling a person as to instruct recruit officers. But *where* did the collection of techniques originate? Intense experimentation? A misty mountain in the Himalayas? No single technique is effective on every person on every day and in every situation.

Learning to do something necessarily involves repetition. Typically this learning, even when guided and introduced piecemeal, involves trial and error during the iterative process of doing something over and over again until proficiency is achieved. In virtually all vocations, including those within the fields of criminal justice, training is structured, typically sequential, and evaluated against established standards. The use of force in criminal justice is taught in part through the use of various models. Repetition of techniques with other recruits is a staple of the defensive tactics curriculum. But simulations, scenario-based training and models such as problem-based learning (PBL) (Makin, 2016), can all be applied in different ways to task learning in force usage. These models depict and to some extent describe levels and modes of response and force available to officers, resistance and responses exhibited by subjects, and varying illustrations to guide this matrix of actions and (generally) reactions. A significant challenge faced by those in criminal justice is this last point about reacting.

It is axiomatic that reaction follows action. This has real weight in circumstances where the "action" is one person attempting to harm or escape from another person. The ramifications of this immutable action-precedes-reaction rule include the likelihood that someone intending harm to another person may do so before the victim has time to react. There are variously presented continuums that list these factors. A continuum is an illustration. This illustration is designed and intended to help teach concepts and reinforce knowledge of optional methods of responding to a perceived threat or in furtherance of a required duty (Hough and Tatum, 2012). This distinction deserves further explanation. Predicting threat is very often challenging for those who work in public safety. For the soldier entering a field of combat or a known hostile territory, the stakes are similarly high but the mindset of the soldier should or may be more attuned to a potential attack.

This is not to say that a soldier, law enforcement officer, corrections officer, or anyone similarly situated would not be vulnerable to the mental fatigue that comes with remaining constantly vigilant.

Different levels of awareness and observations of corresponding physiological and psychological arousal and effects have been studied at great length. We find research and practical experience gathered together in fields of medicine, human performance, sports, the martial arts, military science, and among trainers and educators in criminal justice use of force. Observational skills take time to develop and are specific to the functions of identifying and responding to threats. The development of physical skills also takes time. Biomechanists conduct qualitative and quantitative analysis of the movements of athletes and others, aiming to improve performance or rehabilitate after injury. Their work applies to the design and instruction of the physical skills taught to officers who only sporadically employ physical principles and methods as they work to control someone.

The amount of time necessary to become and remain proficient in physical techniques is a challenging proposition when one considers the time an officer spends using physical control (Buttle, 2007). Is this the case for all force usage skills? If you consider officer presence (command presence) and projection of authority in the continuum of control, the officer uses his skill sets daily, though not always with mindfulness. Quigley (2008) noted that many offenders size up an officer for fitness while judging whether or not they can "take them." The basic recruit academy training typically reserves a significant number of hours to train officers in the use of firearms. The use of conducted energy devices, pepper spray, batons, and physical defensive tactics takes up varying amounts of time, based primarily on state level dictates by an officer standards training commission.

As noted above and elsewhere in the book, it is surprising to many in the public, media, and even within the law enforcement community, that force usage events are relatively infrequent. Still, because of the safety and liability consequences inherent in the function, appropriate training efforts are demanded. Numerical frequency aside, and despite what some critics may claim, the work of officers remains dangerous. Each year the FBI compiles some of the voluntary reports of assaults on law enforcement officers. The 2015 statistics from the Bureau's law enforcement officer killed and assaulted (LEOKA) summary showed more than 50,000 reported assaults against on-duty officers. Of these, 79 percent involved "personal weapons," meaning hands, fists, feet and other personal weapons. Of this number, approximately 28 percent of officers sustained some type of injury.

The LEOKA data represents the experiences of agencies representing around 75 percent of the nation's population. The reports are voluntary and also only include reported assaults. It is often the case that officers do not report every shove they receive or errant elbow while they are struggling to arrest someone. The contacts are not always seen by the officer as warranting an additional charge for the arrestee, and are therefore not reported. Trainers know, and must teach officers, that the risk of assault or injury is always present. It is an ongoing effort to prepare officers for eventualities.

According to the Police Executive Research Forum (PERF), most use of force training includes a matrix for illustrating force options available to officers. There has been a semantics debate for some time over various forms of continuums or whether to use them, and differences exist in recruit curricula for use-of-force training. Still, most use-of-force training continuums depict subject resistance and officer response or force in either a circular or stair-step model or an objective reasonableness-based model.

PERF in its guide for Integrating Communication Assessment and Tactics (ICAT), states that firearms and defensive tactics training for recruit and in-service officers is "substantial" (PERF,

2016). The number of hours assigned by each state to physical defensive tactics skills would likely be seen by trainers as in need of an increase to impart the techniques specified in the state's standards curriculum and to ensure an appropriate level of proficiency for recruit officers. This same 2016 PERF study showed that as few as 50 hours may be spent in basic academy training on physical techniques aside from weapons. The study showed that for in-service training, 87 percent of agencies in the sample reported having *some* defensive tactics component. The hours assigned had a median of 5.5.

Florida Study

The Florida Department of Law Enforcement (FDLE) oversees the basic recruit academy curriculum for law enforcement and corrections through the Florida Criminal Justice Standards and Training Commission (CJSTC). FDLE surveyed a sample of law enforcement and correctional officers, as well as probation officers and defensive tactics instructors, in December 2016, seeking information about which defensive tactics (DT) techniques law enforcement, corrections, and correctional probation officers currently use and find effective. The survey sought officer and trainer views about whether the number of techniques taught in the recruit academy was sufficient or excessive, and how often officers continued defensive tactics training once they had graduated.

About 50 percent of some 2,200 responses indicated that the academy training was adequate. The general response also indicated that respondents felt confident in using the techniques. On other curriculum-related issues, 43 percent of instructors said there were situations when they wished they had better DT skills. Instructors of defensive tactics should be expected to have relevant insight about the training. Officers may also believe that certain tactics were effective, even if they were not performing them exactly the way they were taught.

Some of the other results of the survey included:

Ground fighting: Asked which type of tactic would have been most helpful, the greatest number of responses was in the category of ground fighting and grappling.

More realism: Significant numbers of all respondents noted that real-life simulation training could be improved. It's important to emphasize that this is a recurring theme within the training community as well as among those being trained.

What works: All four groups surveyed agreed in various percentages that the top five tactics taught in basic were takedowns, ground fighting/grappling, strike/blocks, restraint devices, and weapon defense/retention/disarming. Escorts and transporters, pain compliance, including pressure points in joint manipulation, stance/movement, and verbal communication rounded out the rest of the list.

Too little training: The largest percentage of responses indicated that agency in-service training occurred on an annual basis, but the vast majority of respondents agreed that it was too little. Calibre Press (2016), a well-known police training entity, conducted a sample survey and received responses that seem to support the Florida study.

In-service Training

Initial academy training for law enforcement, corrections, juvenile detention, and probation officers varies in length from state to state and focuses on basic skills. Most agencies follow the academy training with some form of field training where an officer is paired with a more experienced trainer (or several) to provide further and advanced training to the new officer. The training environment becomes the actual environment which can lead the trainee to qualitatively better insights and command of methods, but also allows for the unpredictability of real life and real people. The selection or default of a use of force response does not always align with the simplistic view of resistance and response presented by a continuum or admonition to use objectively reasonable methods.

There is a likelihood that in-service officers may struggle with reviewing the physical principles of defensive tactics, for example, as compared to the more concrete feedback of a specific score achieved in some firearms training. This does not mean that officers do not take seriously the need to review and refresh techniques and discuss what has or has not been effective in their experience. The in-service training also allows trainers to reinforce important concerns such as adherence to agency policies, proper report writing, and attention to any medical concerns following a force usage.

The shelf-life of basic skills learned and subsequently practiced infrequently, may be brief. Techniques and methods change to reflect new research or changes in law and policy. While the amount of training for each and every skill at the basic academy level may be less than the new officer would like, each class must come to an end and pass the recruit on to trainers in the field. The many circumstances on the street or in a locked facility add layers of experience, insight, and a repertoire of responses as officers encounter individuals, groups, and situations with varying degrees of complexity. The experiential depth that accrues also is representative of critical thinking under stress. This type of response/reaction to physical resistance can be approximated in the academy, but the emotions induced by the unknown outcome of a "real" fight have a different quality in the street or the cell. There is a role for intensity in training, but instilling fear in a training scenario is often more difficult to achieve.

Presence, Verbalization, and the Use of Force-fulness

As we consider the tools and methods available to officers, we first consider the actual physical presence of the officer. The concept of command presence is taught to new officers as projecting authority and decisiveness through physical appearance coupled with communicating clearly, effectively, and respectfully. The uniform, badge, and gun are all components of the avatar of authority in the minds of people in Western democracies. While an officer's bearing and appearance does not quell every disturbance, the tendency does exist for many people to acquiesce to the authority figure giving specific firm commands. Conversely, if an officer does not project alertness, competence, or confidence he may put himself at risk of assault (Pinizzotto and Davis, 1999). Assessing non-verbal behavior is a two-way street: the person an officer is dealing with and (hopefully) assessing is evaluating the officer at the same time. The FBI's research found that offenders who assaulted officers "paid very close attention to the officers' behaviors prior to assaulting them" (Pinizzotto, Davis, and Miller, 2000, p. 2).

The concepts of verbal and non-verbal behavior discussed in the chapter on less-lethal force are quite important to officers. Most people believe themselves to be competent if not exemplary communicators. How to influence hostile or uncooperative individuals to follow a direction, even to turn around and place their hands behind their backs, has variations but is the stock in trade of public safety professionals. Jim Glennon, co-owner and lead instructor for Calibre Press, a public safety training company, in his book *Arresting Communication*, talks at length about the importance of non-verbal communication: "practically all species on earth communicate with others of their kind, and all but man [sic] do it without using words" (2010, p. 148). Glennon also shares a profound insight that "the most important aspect of staying alive is not how big or tough you are, it is the way you communicate" (p. 191).

The stakes can be high when trying to communicate with someone in the grip of emotion, alcohol, drugs, or some unknown thought process. Skilled officers in both law enforcement and corrections develop effective techniques to defuse or deescalate many tense situations. Sometimes this involves talking and guiding a conversation. Sometimes the officer lets people vent. Sometimes this leads to people becoming even more upset. Many of the lessons learned by hostage negotiators can be applied to street or housing unit officers, but time is rarely the friend of the officer in an immediate situation.

Scenario training can facilitate a deeper understanding of non-verbal components of communication and the risks that commonly present in face-to-face contact with citizens and inmates. Every defensive tactics (DT) instructor teaches every recruit that as you close the distance with someone, the potential for someone to be physically injured increases. This principle is taught starting on the first day of DT training and continues until academy graduation. The study of kinesics, the body movements that convey information (see for example Birdwhistell, 1970), and proxemics or how we use space when communicating (Holoka, 1992), is in-depth and certainly relevant to every officer hoping to control a situation and preclude an assault or unnecessary violence.

GOING GLOBAL

A bit north of the U.S. and sharing a recognition of the British monarchy with the U.K., Canada confronts many of the same criminal justice system challenges as its southern neighbor and its cousin to the east. Canadian police and correctional training in general, and use of force training specifically, has kept pace with much of the U.S. and U.K. Canadian police have adopted much of the same simulation- and computer-based technologies used in the United States to train officers how to respond to scenarios they face in the field.

WHAT-WHY

Most agencies that certify officers to use pepper spray or a conducted energy device require an officer to undergo exposure to the effects of the tools. There is a variety of reasons to support the brief exposure in a controlled environment. An officer needs to know the degree to which a person may be affected by pepper spray or a brief surge of voltage. The insight is useful and important, but not to be taken as the only response a subject may have. Goal-directed people have been known to fight through the effects of pepper spray, or swipe aside the barbs of a CED. Additionally, a spray of OC may only partly envelope the intended target area of someone's face, and a CED contact may not be adequate to introduce the intended shock that induces brief muscle incapacitation.

The experience of being sprayed by OC or being stunned with a CED also provides an opportunity for empathy with subjects who may have such force used on them. The added practical effect of this is the ability to assure a court or jury that the officer did understand the discomfort the arrested individual experienced since they too have felt it.

Scenario-based Training

Training in various fields (e.g., aviation, medicine, social work) has made increasing use of scenario-based methods. Placing learners into different roles and "working through" the dynamics and challenges that arise can teach a certain level of adaptability while deepening experiential reserves that can be drawn on in real circumstances. The more student-centered scenario model is an example of the andragogy or adult learning model that emphasizes self-directed learning (Birzer, 2003). Long known in sports training is the data collection and feedback that videography provides (Branco, Branco, and Vencesbrito, 2016). Using video playback to point out technique errors or to reinforce coaching points can be a benefit to trainees as they learn by watching their own movements and those of fellow recruits.

Scenario-based teaching can also be effective in more closely simulating actual encounters than strict lecture pedagogy. Such simulations can heighten trainee arousal and show them the complications of interacting with live role models. Inducing stress responses in officers has been shown to be more effective in a scenario environment compared with the classroom setting (Andersen, Pitel, Weerasinghe, and Papazoglou, 2016; Armstrong, Clare, and Plecas, 2014). And stress responses can affect decision-making and the outcome of an encounter (Andersen and Gustafsberg, 2016). Reduction of stress after a high-stress call or situation is also likely amenable to stress reduction efforts to control breathing and heart rate (Andersen, Pitel, Weerasinghe, and Papazoglou, 2016). Teaching officers to be aware of stress responses and consideration of long-term consequences has been addressed by many academy programs and individual agencies (Artwohl and Christensen, 1997; Blum, 2000; IACP, 2014).

Firearms training remains emphasized by virtually all recruit programs around the country. This continues into an officer's career with annual training and often multiple qualifications throughout the year. Contemporary academy firearms training is typically one or a combination of three formats: "live-fire scenarios at a conventional range, role-playing with non-gun props or ones fitted to fire marking cartridges, or computer video-based simulations" (Morrison, 2010, p. 140). The integration of training modalities is useful as an officer works to improve accuracy in shot placement while improving accuracy in judgment as well (Lee, 2016). Pepper spray training as well as firearms training and qualifications often make use of physical activity prior to deploying the weapon. These raise heart rate and respiration in the officer or recruit and sensitize them to the difference from a static drill.

This same scenario-type approach can be used for other tasks such as foot pursuits, which are more common than firing a gun, and place an officer at risk of catching up to a person who has already shown they are desperate to elude the officer (McAllister, 2015). Once the trainee catches up to the offender it can be much like the dog who chased the car – now what? Trainers know that statistically the farther an officer is from a clear threat or an unknown threat, the safer he is (Young, 2016). If an officer has reduced options in such a situation or finds himself entangled with the suspect he can work through movements and techniques to try and gain the advantage and bring the person under control. Having force instructors work with recruits in an interactive way that allows the learner to adapt to changing elements in the scenario can assist the recruit in grasping and retaining the movements or techniques being taught (Staller, Bertram, and Körner, 2017).

After the Restraint

Subsequent to the use of force by an officer, an assessment of potential injury to everyone involved should be undertaken as soon as it is practical. Any pertinent information in this regard should be passed on to responding EMS or fire personnel and communicated to an emergency room if someone is transported to a hospital, to booking personnel if someone is taken straight to the local jail, or to medical personnel of a corrections facility if the action was inside. Policy will generally dictate specific protocol following CED deployment, which can include removing barbs from a subject's skin and monitoring him for any adverse reaction. Officers may go through the "decontamination" of someone after he has been pepper sprayed. This generally involves simply rinsing a person's face with water and exposing him to fresh air. Officers should document the actions taken to show they were mindful of potential medical concerns including their own actions and notifications to medical personnel or first responders.

To support a criminal charge of battery or resisting arrest, or to support a charge or rule violation in a jail or prison, the officer must adequately describe behavior that led to that charge. Use of force reporting is required by many agencies to be included on separate, specific report forms that capture typical aspects of the force encounter. The forms may have a check box section of subject resistance and officer response levels or actions that occurred, as well as a narrative section to articulate the subject's behavior and other relevant aspects of the setting. The officer's report will describe how the elements of specific crimes charged were met on the use of force report or in a general incident report, along with completing a probable cause affidavit necessary for the arrest if one was made.

A component of the training each recruit receives is instruction about assessing the "totality of the circumstances" in a use of force situation. The courts consider this as all the facts and circumstances known to the officer at the time along with his perceptions. The courts (and possibly a jury) use these factors to evaluate whether an officer's actions were objectively reasonable. An example listing of factors from the Florida Criminal Justice Standards and Training Commission follows:

> The totality of circumstances includes consideration of the subject's form of resistance, all reasonably perceived situational factors that may have an effect on the situation, and the response options available to the officer.
> Some situational factors may include the following:

- severity of the crime
- subject is an immediate threat
- subject's mental or psychiatric history, if known to the officer
- subject's violent history, if known to the officer
- subject's combative skills
- subject's access to weapons

- innocent bystanders who could be harmed
- number of subjects versus number of officers
- duration of confrontation
- subject's size, age, weight, and physical condition
- officer's size, age, weight, physical condition, and defensive tactics expertise
- environmental factors, such as physical terrain, weather conditions, etc.

(Florida Basic Recruit Training Program, High Liability, Volume 2, 2014,
by the Florida Department of Law Enforcement (FDLE))

Summary

Some of the takeaways from the ongoing effort to examine the defensive tactics curriculum include the need to reevaluate tactics and delivery methods in basic recruit training; the usefulness of tactics in real-world settings; the need to focus on gross motor skills techniques; consideration of more time to teach defensive tactics; and the importance of conducting workshops with instructors and officers to gain insights and information. Scenario training and continuous movement methods are promising approaches to improve outcomes. To the point about more time needed to teach defensive tactics, a practical response might be to focus on fewer techniques with more repetitions and scenarios.

In the future the discussion should be aimed at reminding everyone in the criminal justice community that while force usage is statistically infrequent, the potential for the use of force and injury to officers and arrestees is ever-present. Every state and each individual agency should examine the amount of time devoted to physical skills training as well as the selection of techniques and the practical focus of what officers are taught. Continued use of innovative approaches or those used successfully in other fields (such as scenarios, simulations, and PBL) holds great promise for deeper learning that can improve safety and outcomes.

KEY TERMS

Chemical restraint
Defensive tactics
Force continuum
Situated transaction
Objectively reasonable
Totality of circumstances

Discussion Questions

1. What role does the force continuum play in training officers?
2. What are some of the reasons that officer presence and verbalization can prevent some violence?
3. Discuss two of the types of force used by officers and contrast the training methods for those types.
4. What are the benefits of scenario-based training?

TRY THIS

Examine several law enforcement and correctional agency websites. Try to locate the training policy. List and discuss the factors that you found within the policy.

References

Andersen, J. P. and Gustafsberg, H. (2016). A training method to improve police use of force decision making. *SAGE Open*, 6(2).

Andersen, J. P., Papazoglou, K., Koskelainen, M., Nyman, M., Gustafsberg, H., and Arnetz, B. B. (2015). Applying resilience promotion training among special forces police officers. *Journal of Police Emergency Response*, 5, 1–8.

Andersen, J. P., Pitel, M., Weerasinghe, A., and Papazoglou, K. (2016). Highly realistic scenario based training simulates the psychophysiology of real world use of force encounters: implications for improved police officer performance. *Journal of Law Enforcement*, 5(4), 1–13.

Armstrong, J., Clare, J., and Plecas, D. (2014). Monitoring the impact of scenario-based use-of-force simulations on police heart rate: evaluating the Royal Canadian Mounted Police skills refresher program. *Western Criminology Review*, 15(1), 51–59.

Artwohl, A. and Christensen, L. (1997). *Deadly force encounters*. Boulder, CO: Paladin Press.

Birdwhistell, R. 1970. *Kinesics and context*. Philadelpha: University of Pennsylvania Press.

Birzer, M. L. (2003). The theory of andragogy applied to police training. *Policing*, 26(1), 29–42.

Blum, L. N. (2000). *Force under pressure: how cops live and why they die*. New York: Lantern Books.

Branco, M. C., Branco, G. C., and Vencesbrito, A. (2016). Introduction to data collection for performance analysis and their integration in martial arts training: a biomechanical and motor control perspective. *Revista de Artes Marciales Asiaticas*, 11(2), 19–21.

Bureau of Justice Statistics, State and Local Law Enforcement Training Academies. (2013). NCJ 249784. Retrieved from: www.bjs.gov/index.cfm?ty=pbdetail&iid=5684

Buttle, J. W. (2007). A constructive critique of the officer safety programme used in England and Wales. *Policing and Society*, 17(2), 164–181.

Glennon, J. (2010). *Arresting communication: essential skills for law enforcement*. Villa Park, IL: Lifeline Training.

Holoka, J. P. (1992). Nonverbal communications in the classics: research opportunities. In F. Poyatos (Ed.), *Advances in nonverbal communication*. Amsterdam/Philadelphia: John Benjamins.

Hough, R.M. and Tatum, K. M. (2012). An examination of Florida policies on use of force continuums. *Policing: An International Journal of Police Strategies and Management*, 35(1), 39–54.

IACP (International Association of Chiefs of Police). (2014). *Training key #685, Health and fitness: importance to law enforcement officers*. Alexandria, VA: IACP.

Lee, C. (2016). Race, policing, and lethal force: remedying shooter bias with martial arts training. *Law and Contemporary Problems*, 79(3), 145–172.

Lee, H., Jang, H., Yun, I., Lim, H., and Tushaus, D.W. (2010). An examination of police use of force utilizing police training and neighborhood contextual factors: a multilevel analysis. *Policing: An International Journal of Police Strategies and Management*, 33(4), 681–702.

Lim, H., Goodman, W., and Lee, H. (2015). The effects of supervisor education and training on police use of force. *Criminal Justice Studies: A Critical Journal of Crime, Law and Society*, 28(4), 444–463.

McAllister, B. (2015). FBI – Officer survival spotlight: foot pursuits: keeping officers safe. *FBI Law Enforcement Bulletin*, 14–17.

Makin, D. A. (2016). A descriptive analysis of a problem-based learning police academy. *Interdisciplinary Journal of Problem-Based Learning*, 10(1), 18–32.

Morrison, G. B. (2010). Deadly force in the United States. In J. B. Kuhns and J. Knutsson (Eds.), *Police use of force: a global perspective*. Santa Barbara, CA: Praeger, pp. 132–140.

PERF (Police Executive Research Forum). (2016). *Integrating communications, assessment, and tactics (ICAT)*. Washington, DC: Author.

Pinizzotto, A. J. and Davis, E. F. (1999). Offenders' perceptual shorthand. *FBI Law Enforcement Bulletin*, 68(6), 1–4.

Pinizzotto, A. J., Davis, E. F., and Miller, C. E. (2000). Officers' perceptual shorthand: what messages are offenders sending to law enforcement officers? *FBI Law Enforcement Bulletin*, 69(7), 1–6.

Quigley, A. (2008). Fit for duty? The need for physical fitness programs for law enforcement officers. *Police Chief Magazine*, June. Retrieved from: www.policechiefmagazine.org/magazine/index.cfm?fuseaction=display_arch&article_id=1516&issue_id=62008#11

Staller, M. S., Bertram, O., and Körner, S. (2017). Weapon system selection in police use-of-force training: value to skill transfer categorisation matrix. *Salus Journal*, 5(2), 1–15.

Young, M. (2016). What is a safe distance? *FBI Law Enforcement Bulletin*, 1–4.

8

USE OF FORCE IN LAW ENFORCEMENT

STUDENT LEARNING OUTCOMES

- Students will be able to analyze the frequency of use of force situations.
- Students will be able to describe some of the common factors of use of force encounters.
- Students will be able to critique the preparation for active shooter encounters.
- Students will be able to evaluate the types and frequency of violence against officers.
- Students will be able to explain the hypothesized dynamic of race and use of force.

Introduction

Each chapter has examined the use of force from a different angle, though each dimension touches others and has reciprocal and interacting effects. With this chapter's stated focus of use of force by law enforcement, and the next chapter as we look at correctional employees, we knit together a number of pieces of the overall fabric to comment on day-to-day force usage as a function, an outcome, and a tool. Authority to use force is an integral part of the officer's role in society. Along with his other parts, we perceive him as a whole, though we consciously and subconsciously regard the latent embodiment of force as more tangible than say, service functions. In truth, acquiescence to officer authority is ingrained in most people of the world as the officer's mere presence signals potential enforcement action. Whether in traffic, driving by a street-corner gathering, responding to a neighbor dispute, or quietly seated at a desk as an assigned School Resource Officer (SRO), the persistent aura of a uniformed officer is deference-inducing.

To be sure, we have established that few activities require an officer to actually employ physical force, yet he stands as someone capable through law, policy, training, and equipment, to use that force if he deems it necessary. So when do officers actually use force beyond mere influence? How much force is used and under what circumstances? We restate that force is not used frequently if we consider the tens of millions of interactions people have with police each year. Many researchers have studied the types of calls, locations and incidents where officers use force, the time of the day and days of the week, the attributes of the people who have force used on them and who use force, aspects of an agency and its policies, and many other potentially correlated variables. There is a lack of agreement that very many factors exist that provide an explanation for the use of force (Klahm and Tillyer, 2010). None of the following variables or categories is a singular pathway to force usage; some combination of things, or the occasional violent robber who does not want to be arrested, have to be considered.

Many Factors of Force Encounters

Which officers using which force options with which people at which times and in which places has been and remains of clear interest. What is less clear is a prescriptive that allows law enforcement to avoid or prevent all force usage, if that were even thought possible. Various studies in the last three decades and more have tried to understand the correlates of force usage. The Police Public Contact Survey (PPCS), a supplement to the National Crime Victimization Survey (NCVS), is administered by the BJS every three years (since 1999) and looks at a sample of contacts to examine the nature of the contacts and the outcome, including threatened or actual use of force. The Law Enforcement Management and Administrative Statistics (LEMAS) was another effort of the Bureau of Justice Statistics (BJS) to gather data on a variety of law enforcement issues gleaned from a sample of agencies with 100 or more officers. Both the PPCS and the LEMAS inquire of citizens and agencies, respectively, about complaints made against police including about the use of force. Hickman and Poore (2016) articulate the many challenges to accurate and valid measurement, including problems in the 2003 and 2007 LEMAS:

- Reporting total citizen complaints rather than the subset involving use of force;
- Combining citizen complaints with internal complaints;
- Combining or replacing citizen complaints with officer-reported uses of force;
- Reporting total force allegations within complaint cases, rather than cases involving any force allegation;

- Reporting total complaints investigated, rather than complaints received; and
- Undetected data entry error (either agency or data collection agent).

(p. 473)

Friedrich, writing nearly 40 years ago (1980), cited three categories of explanations for use of force: in terms of individual characteristics of officers; characteristics of the situation or encounter of citizen and officer; and organizational characteristics of the law enforcement agency. Bolger's (2015) meta-analysis of the major narrative evaluations of previous literature in force usage events, built on four categories of variables identified as included in prior research. These theoretical categories of correlates, as summarized by Bolger, are: "encounter, suspect, officer, and community character-istics" (p. 467). Bolger's meta-analysis provides a good gauge of the influence of various factors because it includes so many previous studies and the data on which they relied. The variables were clustered into the four categories or "predictor domains," yet one is reminded that since different variables are not measured uniformly across all studies that none forms an independent basis for a universal theory.

Where It Happens

Location, location, location. Whether it is your realtor or a use of force situation, it seems that *where* an incident occurs may be a key to *whether* something occurs (Terrill and Reisig, 2003; Lawton, 2007). The characteristics of an encounter have been identified as strongly correlated to force decisions (Bolger, 2015). Law enforcement officers respond to all manner of calls for service as well as initiating activity on their own based on observed behavior of individuals or in the course of patrolling assigned areas. While prediction of both crime and of danger remain elusive, we can examine the statistics regarding when force usage as well as officer assaults have occurred and talk about how officers prepare for these types of calls and circumstances. MacDonald, Manz, Alpert, and Dunham (2003) wrote an article that looked at the relationship between calls for service, subject resistance, and police use of force. While the data reflected the experience of just one Southeastern police department, it nonetheless illustrates a finding echoed by trainers in law enforcement: trying to arrest people often results in resistance and a concomitant need to use some level of force. In earlier work examining the same data, Alpert and Dunham (1999) found that suspects resisted arrest and thus initiated the use of force in 97 percent of force cases. Later research continued to highlight the all too obvious connection between subjects resisting and officers using force options (Terrill, 2003). The field continues to try to develop or utilize various devices such as OC and CEDs to lessen the risks and injuries to officer and citizens (Taylor and Woods, 2010).

It is not known with certainty if the outcomes of deadly force incidents are driven by the exact same set of variables as less lethal force usage. Research is mixed on lethal incidents, though there is a larger body of studies on the more serious fatal option. One study by Klinger, Rosenfeld, Isom, and Deckard (2015) indicated that the levels of violent crime in neighborhoods in St. Louis were more explanatory than either race or economic disadvantage. Others have discovered similar results when examining neighborhood level crime and the use of force by police (Terrill and Reisig, 2003; Lee, Vaughn, and Lim (2014) in combination with various other factors including subject resistance and age (Lee, Jang, Yun, Lim, and Tushaus, 2010). Crifasi, Pollack, and Webster, (2016) noted that fatalities of officers were higher when ambushed or when a person assaulted the officer unprovoked.

They also observed that officers who were disarmed by the subject were twice as likely to suffer fatal injuries. Again, much remains to be understood about circumstances where force is used but the implications of an environmental aspect beyond the direct control of police (and requiring the concerted efforts of many entities to improve) underscores the complexity of the force encounter as it moves across geographical, racial, and economic landscapes and while actors move into and out of the vignette.

When It Happens

Use of force may or may not occur during an arrest, but obviously during arrest is when most resistance will occur. The decision to arrest may be dictated by procedure or, procedure may allow for the discretion to not arrest. Where discretion does exist in the face of probable cause to arrest, the demeanor or actions of the subject may precipitate the confluence of factors that result in a force usage (Klinger, 1994; Terrill and Paoline, 2007). There have been some studies that examined the use of force across different types of calls in police work and the traffic stop, for example, is when many force events occur.

The side of the road is a less than ideal place to attempt to take someone into custody. Cars whizzing by, uneven ground, potential lighting and sound challenges – and just possibly an intoxicated, aggrieved, or secretly wanted individual resisting your attempt at handcuffing. Traffic stops and other initially brief encounters or detentions are often when force encounters occur. Traffic stops are also when most members of the public come into contact with police (Eith and Durose, 2011). The Supreme Court in *Terry v. Ohio* (1968) provided guidance for some aspects of those investigatory detentions and weapons pat-downs. The where of stopping people on the highway or in an alleyway blends with the when of the encounter to increase statistically the potential for resistance by someone or assault on an officer. Yet the volume of such interactions without a serious force usage is perhaps a more important "risk" in that officers may be lulled into complacency or the automaticity of missing an important threat signal when the last nine traffic stops had no significant element of confrontation. Why should the tenth one? In regards to the timing of force usage, it is also plausible that when officers arrive more quickly to a call of something in-progress, more participants are still present, emotions are still high, and the potential for conflict is thus greater (Cihan, 2015).

Who Is There

The human officer is incapable of knowing the mind of another person. Sometimes the struggle to restrain a person begins and stops, only to start again with more ferocity, followed by something else, each with a different force level within the same event (Mesloh, Henych, and Wolf, 2008). The officer is trained to an extent on physical and verbal signals that a person is agitated or under a psychological pressure. This is an imperfect process of assessment, but such assessments have saved many lives and allowed officers to short-circuit assaults and escapes. A seemingly obvious, but primary determinant of force usage is when a suspect resists (Alpert and Dunham, 1999; Leinfelt, 2005), which may result in part from the initial demeanor or actions of the officer (Terrill, 2003), but the resistance is also found to be at a higher level than the officer in many cases (Terrill, Leinfelt, and Kwak, 2008). Suspect behavior remains a focal point in explaining many uses of force (Hickman,

Piquero, and Garner, 2008) and it has been pointed out that the suspect's demeanor alone is not necessarily a predictor of officer force (Terrill and Mastrofski, 2002), but instead can be impacted by the criminal or other physical actions of the person (Klinger, 1994; Engel, Sobol, and Worden, 2000). Resistance to arrest or resisting charges are also higher in areas with higher calls for service rates (Belvedere, Worrall, and Tibbetts, 2005) which brings up the issue of various factors external to the officer.

In considering the characteristics of an individual whom an officer faces we must recognize that much is unknown to the officer. What has happened to bring the person and the officer together (e.g., robbery in progress, drunken fight, someone reported as acting crazy, any other 911 call)? Is the person under the influence of alcohol or some other substance? How much under the influence are they? Has the ingested substance or some other psychological or physiological condition rendered the person less sensitive to pain and therefore to many of the techniques an officer may employ?

Force was seen as more likely when police were dealing with people under the influence of drugs or alcohol and those who were dealing with mental illness (Kaminski, DiGiovanni, and Downs, 2004; NIJ, 1999). Law enforcement officers have been found to receive more severe injuries when dealing with individuals who are under the influence of alcohol or drugs (IACP/BJA, 2014). And while there seems to be a positive relationship between use of force and persons with mental illness (PMI), there is not necessarily greater injury incurred (Rossler and Terrill, 2017).

In the NIJ report it was noted that, "A small proportion of officers are disproportionately involved in use-of-force incidents" (p. viii). The authors cautioned that more research was needed and indeed assignment to specific tasks or units, time of day or day of week, and supervisory styles directing officers may all play into the volume of activity and attendant increase in force usage. Brandl and Stroshine (2012) also looked at the idea of some officers being associated with more force usage. They examined individual officer variables such as the officer's background, where the officer was assigned to patrol, and the officer's arrest activity. Their work reminds administrators to monitor selection practices, shift assignment methods, and to pay close attention to early warning methods that highlight correlates of relatively higher force usage. If there are multiple officers on-scene, force may be more likely (Lawton, 2007), but the presence of more than a single officer may also reflect the seriousness of the crime or the behavior of the individual involved. Agency policy does seem to impact use of force, with findings that stricter force policy is related to lower force usage (McEwen, 1997; Terrill and Paoline, 2017). Policies on force and training officers on methods as well as policy remain crucial elements in an agency's approach to force usage and legitimacy with citizens (Hough and Tatum, 2012).

A human officer following policy still makes mistakes. A use of deadly force may be a mistake of fact shooting; a perceived threat was something other than what the officer thought it was. Speed affects the ability to positively identify an object but someone reacts to the object based on context – gunshots, yelling, underlying situation that brought the officer to this location at this moment. There may be a report of someone who is likely armed, or someone does not comply with the officer's order, acts aggressively or in a manner not consistent with complying; there may be an offender in low light, or who says one thing and does another; there may be no time to clearly see an object; a person may be acting recklessly. All of these may confound the accuracy of the officer in arriving at a timely decision. The response decision may be likened to waiting to judge a pitch. You see some signals but you do not know which pitch you will get – even after the wind up and the pitcher's arm is in motion. The speed at which a weapon can be introduced is shockingly brief and the officer is acquiring information as the event unfolds.

Wherever or whenever it happens, an increase in the amount or level of force used may be necessitated as a situation gets worse. This does not define excessive force, but rather it may simply reflect the amount of resistance encountered or the failure of lesser controls to manage an individual's resistance. Cases where excessive force appears to have been used will likely attract public attention through various media, but brief passages of recorded footage will rarely provide adequate context to accurately assess what came before, what is occurring in the footage, and various other dynamics of a force event. The Supreme Court in its *Graham v. Connor* decision (1989) gave us a framework of four factors to use in analyzing the appropriate amount of force: the perceived threat, the severity of the offense, actual resistance offered, and whether the subject is attempting to escape.

Bonner (2015) identified themes related to officer decision-making that incorporated working rules impacted by the norms of the setting. Modes of policing and styles of officers, supervisors, and agencies have been offered as helpful categories to understand much decision-making. Force decision-making, similar to arrest decision-making, is bound by a number of factors and is not the unrestrained "do what you like" behavior depicted in television and movies. The essence of an American law enforcement officer is discretionary decision-making authority. Bittner's work (1970) is a touchstone for anyone writing on American police use of force as he states that such use is the defining characteristic of policing. In fact, force usage is but the most visible and consequential use of *discretion*, which can be identified (perhaps semantically) as the defining characteristic of a law enforcement officer. As noted elsewhere in the book, discretion flows from many sources: law, policy, training, education, experience, peer norms, maturity, and other factors.

As a practical matter, agencies would want to minimize the officer effect in the equation of force situations. In the meta-analytic study done by Bolger (2015), he commented that "if officers are systematically using force in an inappropriate manner, changes to training are more likely to be fruitful than changes to hiring practices" (p. 486). Bolger identified the "encounter characteristics" category as most correlated to force decisions. It seems that ongoing training efforts should incorporate self-awareness by the officer to avoid or enhance force encounter outcomes as well as enhance safety. Lawton (2007), in a single agency study, found that "the officer's prior use of force in the preceding year, the severity of the crime, the presence of multiple officers, and the citizens' behaviors and conditions seemed to drive the particular level of force reported" (p. 177).

The officer is obviously present, as well as one or more subjects. Some officer factors that have been examined include not having other officers present (Lawton, 2007). It is not entirely clear which incidents result in the suspect being encouraged to resist or attack because of only one officer, or because an officer uses more force because she feels the need to quickly control the risk of resistance. This is usually outside the control of an officer regarding timing, but it is worth noting when considering procedures for those calls that are amenable to advance planning, such as warrant arrests. However it is also a statistical certainty that among the nearly 800,000 law enforcement officers in the United States there are at least a few who default to the use of force, even when it is not warranted (Toch, 1996).

A common assumption by many is that college-educated police will use force less than their less formally educated peers. Rydberg and Terrill (2010) looked at this issue through analysis of observational data from two agencies and found a significantly lower use of force by college-educated officers while observing no effect on decision to arrest or to search. Rydberg and Terrill note that much of the previous literature on the impact of college on law enforcement has been inconsistent. It is also the case that while there have calls for greater college education for officers since Vollmer, the Wickersham Commission, and more, that few agencies require a recruit to have a degree. However it should also be pointed out that today far more officers do have some level of college education, and 15 percent of agencies have some college requirement (Reaves, 2015). While the link between less use of force and officer education is far from ironclad, the recruitment and utilization of college and university educated officers remains desirable for a host of reasons, and in fact possession of a degree or significant credit hours has increased among officers (Paoline, Terrill, and Rossler, 2015).

In another example of assumption, the role of women in policing continues to suffer from anecdotal accounts of what is gender-appropriate or expected of female officers. Paoline and Terrill (2004) examined the use of verbal and physical coercion by female officers in two police agencies and found few differences between male and female officers. Reexamining the same data, Rabe-Hemp (2008) noted that while women may not use as much "extreme controlling behavior, such as threats, physical restraint, search, and arrest" (p. 426), they also did not use stereotypically-assumed supporting behaviors. Rabe-Hemp and Schuck found evidence that female officers may be at an elevated risk of assault at calls of family conflict (2007). Each of these issues has implications for officer training and potentially for differential call response protocols.

Race and Force

The optics of media reports seem straightforward – white police use force, at least lethal force, against black males. And they do. But the relationship between race and the use of force is not simple. How a person historically arrived at a place and time to encounter a law enforcement officer is not dependent on that individual officer. How the officer acts or reacts in that encounter is also driven by any number of the factors discussed here – and possibly by a bias. The evidence of a bias *causing* a particular use of force is scant. Kahn, Steele, McMahon, and Stewart (2017), for example, looked at how bias may influence officer actions over the course of an interaction rather than just treating the entire encounter as one discrete unit. Their results demonstrated that black and Latino suspects receive more force in the beginning stages of the interaction, whereas encounters with white suspects escalated in level of force faster after initial levels (p. 1). However, research has generally found that with other incident factors controlled for, race/ethnicity and force are not significantly related (Jetelina, Jennings, Bishopp, Piquero, and Gonzalez, 2017; Lott and Moody, 2017; Klinger, Rosenfeld, Isom, and Deckard, 2015). A notable exception is the research by Paoline, Gau, and Terrill (2016) whose study found:

> Results revealed that black citizens were no more likely than white ones to display non-compliance, and the strength of their resistance did not vary across officer race. White officers used higher levels of force against black suspects (controlling for resistance), while black officers appeared unaffected by suspect race.
>
> *(p. 13)*

In their analysis the authors provide insight on a number of previous views and studies, but one important observation about the race of the officer–suspect dyad is that, "Resistive black suspects appear to respond to the uniform, not the race of the person inside it" (p. 12). And that, "White citizens were also no more likely to resist black officers than white ones" (p. 12). A large-scale study by Hickman and Piquero (2009) likewise did not find a relationship between minority representation and either complaints or sustained complaints. In other words, prior hypotheses about whether having more black and minority officers would significantly shift interaction between black citizens and police are called into question. People resist the uniform. To be sure, more black and minority officers and women are encouraged and important for reasons of representativeness, equal access, and inclusion – this should be achieved based on these reasons and not "based on erroneous assumptions or unrealistic expectations" (p. 14). This is underscored by the reality that many white people may view the appropriateness of police use of force (and other societal situations) through a lens of how they view racial minorities (Carter and Corra, 2016). It has been found that "racial attitudes predicted support for police use of excessive force invariably across political groups" (Silver and Pickett, 2015, p. 650). To highlight that the use of force can be complex when considering race, Fridell (2017) paraphrased a range of media headlines this way: "there is bias in the use of force," "there is no bias in the use of force," and "there is bias in some types of force, but not others" (p. 502).

Engel and Calnon (2004) called for police training to include exposure to empirical studies pointing out the general lack of effectiveness of minority-targeted searches and seizures. This anticipates improving police methods in locations where there has been disproportionate interaction with blacks or Hispanics that may signal bias-based policing. Jetelina et al. (2017) as noted above, found that when looking at less than lethal use of force in a sample of data from the Dallas Police Department in 2014 and 2015, that there were significant relationships between white officers and use of force with non-white subjects, but the statistical significance fell way when the researchers controlled for situational and individual factors.

Yet research over the last few decades illuminates various aspects of the police subculture (see e.g., Wilson, 1968; Bittner, 1970; Ingram, Paoline and Terrill, 2013), including what some call "exaggerating the dangers of the job" (Marenin, 2016). Police culture has been studied for a relatively long time, given the youth of the field of criminology and its somewhat older uncle sociology. With that attention, much has been written about perspectives on a "police subculture" or aspects of solidarity, similar to the military to some extent, and based purportedly on shared experiences that are unique and different from civilian experiences. Alignment with this culture has been viewed as a variable in the sometimes complex equation of force (Terrill, Paoline, and Manning, 2003). The crime-fighter image of police has been reinforced, and created to some extent, by entertainment media. Officers themselves often buy into the myth, partly because of unrealistic expectations when they enter the job and perhaps a measure of rationalizing the performance of a job that is not all non-stop excitement as they had initially believed. Schaefer and Tewksbury (2017) write that some contextual discussion of police use of force actions among police themselves can be "storytelling" when in a group setting, but more reflective or in the form of critique when done in the more intimate space of a squad car.

Excessive Force

When it comes to definitions, people often confuse excessive force with brutality. Timing and intention can be at play in evaluating the difference. The use of force by law enforcement is infrequent; the use of excessive force is even rarer (Ross, 2005). We know that when officers do use force in excess or egregiously, public confidence wanes and the legitimacy and moral authority of government can be called into question (Prenzler, Porter, and Alpert, 2013). Questions and observations regarding the unnecessary use of force by police, and other disrespectful or undesirable behavior, are not new in society (Wilson, 1968; Delattre, 1996; McCluskey, Terrill, and Paoline, 2005; Sparrow, 2016). So there must be something to this examination of when society's agents are tasked with enforcing the dictates of the other members of that society – and given the authority to force adherence in certain instances.

There are various behaviors by law enforcement officers that hold the potential for misuse (Klahm, Frank, and Liederbach, 2014), but the use of force is viewed as having the greatest likelihood of causing physical harm. How do officers view the use of force? Paoline and Terrill (2011) surveyed officers about how they used force on an everyday basis rather than strictly focusing on excessive force. They found what amounted to a "natural progression" similar to a use of force continuum, and that the officers expressed a "rather conservative" response to resistance schema. Phillips (2015) surveyed a single law enforcement academy class about the use of unnecessary force and, while only surveying a small sample, found that the type of unnecessary force impacted the recruits' views of acceptability. For some crimes the recruits' responses indicated that many would not report unnecessary force to supervisors; however, how the academy experience or patrol experience may change the views of that particular group is not known.

In many cases, an individual officer in a specific situation may not be fully versed in, or confident about the current state of the law. Judge Gould of the Ninth Circuit Court, in dissenting from the majority opinion in the *Brosseau v. Haugen* decision, wrote:

> [J]udges, unlike police officers, have the luxury of studying the constitutional issues in the calm of their chambers, with the benefit of lawyers' briefing, and after hearing oral arguments …. [J]udges should not expect police officers to read *United States Reports* in their spare time, to study arcane constitutional law treatises, or to analyze Fourth Amendment developments with a law professor's precision.

The Supreme Court reversed the denial of summary judgment of the lower court in this case.

As it turns out, the Supreme Court recognized this as well when it opined in *Graham v. Connor* (1989): "The reasonableness of a particular use of force must be judged from the perspective of a reasonable officer on the scene, rather than with the 20/20 vision of hindsight" (pp. 396–397). This caution against quick after-the-fact judgment of an officer's actions in using force is important in light of the potential to misinterpret what a body-worn camera (BWC) or witness takes in from a particular angle or perspective. Aside from the risk of an incorrectly arrived at gestalt of the force situation, camera recordings by citizens as well as BWCs can remind police to moderate their actions and introduce improvements that benefit all (Brown, 2016). In fact, there is evidence that what medium is used to take in information by the public (e.g., text, audio, video), and an officer's immediate reaction and how that is perceived by the member of the public influences that citizen's perception of force legitimacy (McCamman and Culhane, 2017). This may not be surprising but it seems to be something that everyone should think about in trying to sort subjective feelings from objective facts. The lived experiences of citizens and law enforcement officers are not wholly distinct. The public may well and rightfully look to criminal justice practices to be procedurally fair

(Meares, Tyler, and Gardener, 2016), but there is the question of whether or when members of the public grasp constitutional or policy appropriateness aside from the perception of fairness.

There are various behaviors of concern to citizens and police supervisors and administrators alike that are not strictly related to excessive use of physical force on citizens. Discourteous behavior and "coercion" are important in understanding the relation of complaints, officer activity, and the efficacy of early warning systems (McCluskey and Terrill, 2005). McCluskey and Terrill rely on previous research and theoretical foundations of sociology and psychology to explain how officers apply differential treatment of individuals. From a sociological perspective, an officer may be influenced by a person's status and action, say as a disrespectful, intoxicated, young person (to give only one example). The authors also note importantly that some researchers involve theoretical orientations such as Black (1976), while others "simply examine the influence of situational factors" (p. 515). The psychological approach McCluskey and Terrill comment on involves researchers looking at individual officer traits and how or whether they relate to different or similar responses in similar circumstances. Some of the situational factors they note as common measures "include: citizen race, gender, class, age, demeanor, and sobriety, as well as a number of legal variables (e.g. citizen resistance, presence of a weapon, degree of evidence)" (p. 515). With some mix of findings, McCluskey and Terrill do find support for the connection between a relatively high volume of officer complaints, including verbal discourtesy, and higher levels of force used. They note the limitations of their work and caution that not every agency (as noted above) will necessarily experience factors in the same way. Still, they advise administrators to contemplate the issues as they design policy and manage their agencies. A critical function of management is hiring, and there are findings that appropriate employment screening in combination with higher education requirements and appropriate levels of training are associated with lower levels of complaints (Stickle, 2016).

Law Enforcement Officers Killed and Assaulted

The fact and danger of attacks on officers or the likelihood of a violent arrestee may be in place as a more conscious concern on a daily basis for officers in some jurisdictions more than others. Busy jurisdictions with the interplay of the previously mentioned high-crime neighborhoods will see more activity and, by volume, more calls involving confrontations. Some of these confrontations turn deadly for either a citizen or an officer.

The FBI gathers data on officers assaulted through the Law Enforcement Officers Killed and Assaulted (LEOKA) program. When an officer is killed in the line of duty, the affected agency is asked to complete a comprehensive questionnaire about the circumstances of the death. The LEOKA also collects information about officers assaulted by examination of UCR data. Without question this method significantly underestimates the number of actual assaults on officers. Such incomplete data not only obscures the actual scope of a phenomenon, but impedes the understanding of the public or policy makers as to the actual risks and reality of law enforcement.

The National Law Enforcement Officer's Memorial Fund (NLEOMF) also gathers data on officer killed in the line of duty and reported that in the decade of 2006–2015, 521 officers were shot to death, twelve more were stabbed to death, three were strangled, and thirteen were killed by terrorist attack (NLEOMF, 2016).

TABLE 8.1 Deaths, Assaults and Injuries over the Decade 2004–2013

Year	Deaths*	Assaults**	Assaults with injuries**
2004	165	59,692	16,737
2005	163	57,820	16,072
2006	156	59,396	15,916
2007	192	61,257	15,736
2008	148	61,087	15,554
2009	125	57,268	14,948
2010	161	56,491	14,744
2011	171	55,631	14,798
2012	126	53,867	14,678
2013	107	49,851	14,565
Average per year	151	57,346	15,375

Sources: *National Law Enforcement Officers Memorial Fund. **Federal Bureau of Investigation.

Note: Updated September 15, 2015

WHAT-WHY

Department of Justice
Office of Public Affairs
FOR IMMEDIATE RELEASE
Friday, January 13, 2017

Justice Department Announces Findings of Investigation into Chicago Police Department
Justice Department Finds a Pattern of Civil Rights Violations by the Chicago Police Department

The Justice Department announced today that it has found reasonable cause to believe that the Chicago Police Department (CPD) engages in a pattern or practice of using force, including deadly force, in violation of the Fourth Amendment of the Constitution. The department found that CPD officers' practices unnecessarily endanger themselves and result in unnecessary and avoidable uses of force. The pattern or practice results from systemic deficiencies in training and accountability, including the failure to train officers in de-escalation and the failure to conduct meaningful investigations of uses of force.

(DOJ press release at: https://www.justice.gov/opa/pr/justice-department-a
nnounces-findings-investigation-chicago-police-department)

GOING GLOBAL

Officer safety in England and Wales was historically not seen as a focal concern. Recent trends in weapon acquisition by criminal gangs, and the tactics of terrorists, may have changed this view for those inside and outside of policing in the U.K. In a 2007 journal article, John Buttle examined the rationale and the limitations of officer safety training. Buttle argued that officer safety training emphasizes pre-emption in the use of force approach he observed. Safety for the public is desired as well as accountability of officers.

The myth of the good-natured Bobbie adopting a stern expression and telling ruffians to desist, has finally given way to a more realistic view that sometimes people are willing to harm officers to avoid arrest. Assaults increased against officers in the U.K. and so in the decade between 1990 and 2000, safety practices and training improved. Similar to many observers, the view was put forward that officers should be more "highly skilled" users of force, to reduce the number of mistakes made out of fear and to encourage lower levels of force used based on more confidence by the highly trained officer (Geller and Toch, 1996). The National Police Training added annual refresher training to what had been only self-defense instruction during initial recruit training.

ASSAULTS ON COLORADO LAW ENFORCEMENT OFFICERS SPIKE

The *Denver Post* (7/17) reports, "Police officers and sheriff's deputies in Colorado are increasingly under physical attack, according to new crime statistics, and they blame a number of factors." Factors cited by police include a "swelling population, an overall increase in crime, more interactions with the mentally ill, rising drug abuse and growing hostility toward police." Assaults on Colorado law enforcement officers have "increased nearly 42 percent between 2012 and 2016, according to the Colorado Bureau of Investigation's annual crime report, which was released Wednesday." Alamosa Police Chief Duane Oakes is quoted as saying, "I do feel like with what has been going on across the nation the last several years there are more people who are willing to be resistant to police." Oakes told the *Post* that more agencies are providing crisis intervention training and working to improve community relations in order to lessen attacks on officers.

(IACP's The Lead, July 19, 2017)

RESEARCH RESULTS

A review of the literature on police officers' use-of-force decision-making conducted by Bolger (2015), examined the strength and direction of the influence of correlates of use of force. The researcher conducted one of the most comprehensive efforts to date of locating studies that dealt with factors impacting the use of force decision by law enforcement officers. He observed that many studies have suffered from methodology problems through using too few sites to collect data. Based on further analysis Bolger conducted for a number of the previous studies cited, he determined that correlations asserted by the original researchers do not exist in some cases. The inclusion of quite a few variables in several studies was seen to perhaps confound a clear result. Bolger's work did not investigate interaction effects, and so he accepts that a fuller understanding of some variables cannot be determined from his study. An important strength of Bolger's work is his underscoring the need to constantly strive to improve research and methods.

Summary

Using physical force is an inescapable element of law enforcement. Force is used to control resistance and to defeat assault. We want officers and subjects to be safe. We train our officers in physical techniques, equip them with sundry devices, send additional officers when available or in anticipation of a problem, and then supervise and monitor their actions and incident outcomes. Still, the human officer at time errs or, in rare instances, acts maliciously. The human subject acts unpredictably, without restraint, and often in advance of the non-mind-reading officer.

Effective force principles and methods/techniques are not new. Interpersonal and tactical communications have received renewed interest, in part due to the efforts of PERF. Recognition of the need to consistently train officers in techniques to deal with persons in crisis has increased. Academy curricula, in-service training, and agency–community partnerships do much to assist officers in their duties and improve outcomes for citizens.

Methods of selecting officers are fairly well developed. The inappropriate or incompetent use of force is not seen as routinely coming from flawed selection. Training and sound supervision of officers should remain a priority for all agencies. It is important that officers and supervisors are furnished with clear policies and that these policies are reviewed on a scheduled basis, as well as when new legal developments occur or improved methods become available.

KEY TERMS

Body-Worn Camera (BWC)
Defensive tactics
Excessive force

Discussion Questions

1. Is it accurate to say that officer-involved shootings are frequent? Why or why not?
2. What are some of the common factors found about where and when officers use force?
3. Discuss the ways in which law enforcement prepares for and reacts to active shooter situations.
4. In considering violence against officers, why is it important that trainers and administrators present officers with comprehensive and balanced information?

TRY THIS

Examine several law enforcement agency websites. Try to locate an annual report summarizing the use of force. List and discuss the circumstances and the size of the jurisdiction.

References

Alpert, G. P. and Dunham, R. (1999). *The force factor: measuring and assessing police use of force and suspect resistance. Report to the National Institute of Justice: Use of force by police: overview of national and local data.* October-NCJ 176330. Washington, DC: U.S. Department of Justice, pp. 45–60.

Ariel (2016). Wearing body cameras increases assaults against officers and does not reduce police use of force: results from a global multi-site experiment. *European Journal of Criminology*, 13(6), 744–755.

Belvedere, K. , Worrall, J. L., and Tibbetts, S. G. (2005). Explaining suspect resistance in police–citizen encounters. *Criminal Justice Review*, 30(1), 30–44.

Bittner, E. (1970). *The functions of police in modern society*. Washington, DC: U.S. Government Printing Office.

Black, D. (1976). *The behavior of law*. New York: Academic Press.

Bolger, P. C. (2015). Just following orders: a meta-analysis of the correlates of American police officer use of force decisions. *American Journal of Criminal Justice*, 40, 466–492.

Bonner, H. (2015). Police officer decision-making in dispute encounters: digging deeper into the 'black box'. *American Journal of Criminal Justice*, 40(3), 493–522.

Brandl, S. G. and Stroshine, M. S. (2012). The role of officer attributes, job characteristics, and arrest activity in explaining police use of force. *Criminal Justice Policy Review*, 24(5), 551–572.

Brown, G. (2016). The blue line on thin ice: police use of force modifications in the era of cameraphones and youtube. *British Journal of Criminology*, 56(2), 293–312.

Buttle, J. W. (2007). A constructive critique of the officer safety programme used in England and Wales. *Policing and Society*, 17(2), 164–181.

Carter, J. S. and Corra, M. (2016). Racial resentment and attitudes toward the use of force by police: an over-time trend analysis. *Sociological Inquiry*, 86(4), 492–511.

Cihan, A. (2015). Examining the neighborhood effects on police performance to assault calls. *Police Practice and Research*, 16(5), 391–401.

Crifasi, K. C., Pollack, K. M., and Webster, D. W. (2016). Assaults against U.S. law enforcement officers in the line-of-duty: situational context and predictors of lethality. *Injury Epidemiology*, 3(29). doi:10.1186/s40621-016-0094-3

Delattre, E. J. (1996). *Character and cops*. 3rd ed. Washington, DC: American Enterprise Institute.

Eith, C. and Durose, M. (2011). *Contacts between police and the public, 2008*. Washington, DC: Bureau of Justice Statistics.

Engel, R. and Calnon, J. (2004). Examining the influence of drivers' characteristics during traffic stops with police: results from a national survey. *Justice Quarterly*, 21, 49–90.

Engel, R., Sobol, J., and Worden, R. (2000). Further exploration of the demeanor hypothesis: the interaction effects of suspects' characteristics and demeanor on police behavior. *Justice Quarterly*, 17(2), 235–258.

Fridell, L. A. (2017). Explaining the disparity in results across studies assessing racial disparity in police use of force: a research note. *American Journal of Criminal Justice*, 42(3), 502–513.

Friedrich, R. (1980). Police use of force: individuals, situations, and organizations. *Annals of the American Academy of Political and Social Science*, 452, 82–97.

Geller, W. A. and Toch, H. (1996), Understanding and controlling police abuse of force. In W. A. Geller and H. Toch (Eds.), *Police violence: understanding and controlling police abuse of force*. New Haven CT and London: Yale University Press.

Hickman, M. J. and Piquero, A. (2009). Organizational, administrative, and environmental correlates of complaints about police use of force. *Crime and Delinquency*, 55(1), 3–27.

Hickman, M. J., Piquero, A. R., and Garner, J. H. (2008). Toward a national estimate of police use of non-lethal force. *Criminology and Public Policy*, 7(4), 563–604.

Hickman, M. J. and Poore, J. E. (2016) National data on citizen complaints about police use of force. *Criminal Justice Policy Review*, 27(3), 455–479.

Hough, R. M. and Tatum, K. M.. (2012). An examination of Florida policies on force continuums. *Policing: An International Journal of Police Strategies and Management*, 35, 39–54.

Ingram, J. R., Paoline, E. I., and Terrill, W. (2013). A multilevel framework for understanding police culture: the role of the workgroup. *Criminology: An Interdisciplinary Journal*, 51(2), 365–397.

International Association of Chiefs of Police Center for Officer Safety and Wellness and Bureau of Justice Assistance. (2014). *Reducing officer injuries: final report*. Washington, DC: IACP.

Jetelina, K. K., Jennings, W. G., Bishopp, S. A., Piquero, A. R., and Gonzalez, J. R. (2017). Dissecting the complexities of the relationship between police officer–civilian race/ethnicity dyads and less-than-lethal use of force. *American Journal of Public Health*, 107(7), 1164–1170.

Kahn, K. B., Steele, J. S., McMahon, J. M., and Stewart, G. (2017). How suspect race affects police use of force in an interaction over time. *Law and Human Behavior (American Psychological Association)*, 41(2), 117–126.

Kaminski, R.G., DiGiovanni, C., and Downs, R. (2004). The use of force between police and persons with impaired judgment. *Police Quarterly*, 7(3), 311–338.

Klahm, C., Frank, J., and Liederbach, J. (2014). Understanding police use of force: rethinking the link between conceptualization and measurement. *Policing: An International Journal of Police Strategies and Management*, 37, 558–578.

Klahm, C. and Tillyer, R. (2010). Understanding police use of force: a review of the evidence. *Southwest Journal of Criminal Justice*, 7(2), 214–239.

Klinger, D. A. (1994). Demeanor or crime? Why 'hostile" citizens are more likely to be arrested. *Criminology*, 32, 475–493.

Klinger, D., Rosenfeld, R., Isom, D., and Deckard, M. (2015). Race, crime, and the micro-ecology of deadly force. *Criminology and Public Policy*, 15(1), 193–222.

Lawton, B. (2007). Levels of nonlethal force: an examination of individual, situational and contextual factors. *Journal of Research in Crime and Delinquency*, 44(2), 163–184.

Lee, H., Jang, H., Yun, I., Lim, H., and Tushaus, D. W. (2010). An examination of police use of force utilizing police training and neighborhood contextual factors: a multilevel analysis. *Policing: An International Journal of Police Strategies and Management*, 33(4), 681–702.

Lee, H., Vaughn, M. S., and Lim, H. (2014). The impact of neighborhood crime levels on police use of force: an examination at micro and meso levels. *Journal of Criminal Justice*, 42, 491–499.

Leinfelt, F. H. (2005). Predicting use of non-lethal force in a mid-size police department: a longitudinal analysis of the influence of subject and situational variables. *The Police Journal*, 78, 285–300.

Lott, J. R. and Moody, C. E. (2017). Do white police officers unfairly target black suspects?SSRN.com, July 21. Available at: https://ssrn.com/abstract=2870189. Accessed August 16, 2017.

McCamman, M. and Culhane, S. (2017). Police body cameras and us: public perceptions of the justification of the police use of force in the body camera era. *Translational Issues in Psychological Science*, 3(2), 167–175.

McCluskey, J. and Terrill, W. (2005). Departmental and citizen complaints as predictors of police coercion. *Policing: An International Journal of Police Strategies and Management*, 28, 513–529.

McCluskey, J., Terrill, W., and Paoline, E. (2005). Peer group aggressiveness and the use of coercion in police–suspect encounters. *Police Practice and Research*, 6, 19–37.

MacDonald, J. M., Manz, P. W., Alpert, G. P., and Dunham, R. G. (2003). Police use of force. examining the relationship between calls for service and the balance of police force and suspect resistance. *Journal of Criminal Justice*, 31, 119–127. doi:10.1016/S0047-2352(02)00219-2

McEwen, T. (1997). Policies on less-than-lethal force in law enforcement agencies. *Policing: An International Journal of Police Strategies and Management*, 20, 39–59.

Marenin, O. (2016) Cheapening death: danger, police street culture, and the use of deadly force. *Police Quarterly*, 19(4), 461–487.

Meares, T. L., Tyler, T. R., and Gardener, J. (2016). Lawful or fair? How cops and laypeople perceive good policing. *Journal of Criminal Law and Criminology*, 105(2), 297–343.

Mesloh, C., Henych, M., and Wolf, R. (2008). *Less lethal weapon effectiveness, use of force, and suspect and officer injuries: a five-year analysis.* Unpublished report to the National Institute of Justice, Washington, DC.

Morrow, W. J., White, M. D., and Fradella, H. F. (2017). After the stop: exploring the racial/ethnic disparities in police use of force during Terry stops. *Police Quarterly*, 20(3). doi:10.1177/1098611117708791

National Law Enforcement Officers Memorial Fund. (2017). *Preliminary mid-year law enforcement officer fatalities report.* Retrieved from: www.nleomf.org/facts/research-bulletins/

NIJ (National Institute of Justice). (1999). *Use of force by police: overview of national and local data (NCJ 176330).* Washington, DC: U.S. Department of Justice, Office of Justice Programs.

Paoline, E. A., Gau, J. M., and Terrill, W. (2016). Race and the police use of force encounter in the United States. *The British Journal of Criminology.* doi:10.1093/bjc/azw089

Paoline, E. A. and Terrill, W. (2004). Women police officers and the use of coercion. *Women and Criminal Justice,* 15, 97–119.

Paoline, E. A. and Terrill, W. (2011). Listen to me! police officers' views of appropriate use of force. *Journal of Crime and Justice,* 34(3), 178.

Paoline, E. A., Terrill, W., and Rossler, M. T. (2015). Higher education, college degree major, and police occupational attitudes. *Journal of Criminal Justice Education,* 26(1), 49–73.

Phillips, S. W. (2015). Police recruit attitudes toward the use of unnecessary force. *Police Practice and Research,* 16(1), 51–64. doi:10.1080/15614263.2013.845942

Prenzler, T., Porter, L., and Alpert, G. P. (2013). Reducing police use of force: case studies and prospects. *Aggression and Violent Behavior,* 18, 343–356.

Rabe-Hemp, C. E. (2008). Female officers and the ethic of care: does officer gender impact police behaviors? *Journal of Criminal Justice,* 36, 426–434.

Rabe-Hemp, C. E. and Schuck, A. M. (2007). Violence against police officers: are female officers at greater risk? *Police Quarterly,* 10(4), 411–428.

Reaves, B. A. (2015). *Local police departments, 2013: personnel, policies, and practices (NCJ 248677).* Washington, DC: U.S. Department of Justice, Office of Justice Programs, Bureau of Justice Statistics.

Ross, D. (2005). A content analysis of the emerging trends in the use of non-lethal force research in policing. *Law Enforcement Executive Forum,* 5, 121–149.

Rossler, M. T. and Terrill, W. (2017). Mental illness, police use of force, and citizen injury. *Police Quarterly,* 20(2),189–212.

Rydberg, J. and Terrill, W. (2010). The effect of higher education on police behavior. *Police Quarterly,* 13, 92–120.

Schaefer, B. P. and Tewksbury, R. (2017). The tellability of police use-of-force: how police tell stories of critical incidents in different contexts. *The British Journal of Criminology.* doi:10.1093/bjc/azx006

Silver, J. and Pickett, J. (2015). Toward a better understanding of politicized policing attitudes: conflicted conservatism and support for police use of force. *Criminology,* 53(4), 650–676.

Sparrow, M. (2016). *Handcuffed: what holds policing back, and the keys to reform.* Washington, DC: Brookings Institution Press.

Stickle, B. (2016). A national examination of the effect of education, training and pre-employment screening on law enforcement use of force. *Justice Policy Journal,* 13(1), 1–15.

Taylor, B. and Woods, T. (2010). Injuries to officers and suspects in police use-of-force cases: a quasi-experimental evaluation. *Police Quarterly,* 13, 260–289.

Terrill, W. (2003). Police use of force and suspect resistance: the micro-process of the police-suspect encounter. *Police Quarterly,* 6, 51–83.

Terrill, W., Leinfelt, F., and Kwak, D. (2008). Examining police use of force: a smaller agency perspective. *Policing: An International Journal of Police Strategies and Management,* 31, 57–76.

Terrill, W. and Mastrofski, S. (2002). Situational and officer based determinants of police coercion. *Justice Quarterly,* 19, 215–248.

Terrill, W. and Paoline, E. (2007). Non-arrest decision-making in police citizen encounters. *Police Quarterly,* 10(3).

Terrill, W. and Paoline, E. A. (2017). Police use of lethal force: does administrative policy matter? *Justice Quarterly,* 34(2), 193–216.

Terrill, W., Paoline, E., and Manning, P. (2003). Police culture and coercion. *Criminology,* 41, 1003–1034.

Terrill, W. and Reisig, M. (2003). Neighborhood context and police use of force. *Journal of Research in Crime and Delinquency,* 40(3), 291–321.

Toch, H. (1996). The violence prone police officer. In W. Geller and H. Toch (Eds.), *Police violence*. New Haven, CT: Yale University Press, pp. 94–112.

Wilson, J. Q. (1968). *Varieties of police behavior*. Cambridge, MA: Harvard University Press.

Cases Cited

Brosseau v. Haugen, 339 F.3d 857 (2003)

Graham v. Connor, 490 U.S. 386 (1989)

Terry v. Ohio, 392 U.S. 1 (1968)

9

USE OF FORCE IN CORRECTIONS

CHAPTER OUTLINE

Introduction
Prison and jail
Juvenile correctional facilities
Private facility employees
Probation and parole
Restraints
Excessive force
Summary
Features: What-Why, Going Global, Research Results
Key Terms
Discussion Questions
Try This
References

STUDENT LEARNING OUTCOMES

- Students will be able to discuss factors leading to the use of force in a correctional environment.
- Students will be able to describe the force options available to correctional officers.
- Students will be able to explain the role of policy in guiding force decisions in corrections.
- Students will be able to discuss the force training provided to correctional officers.
- Students will be able to explain the variation in force usage among facilities.

Introduction

There is a perception by many of the public that correctional facilities are rife with violence and that force usage by correctional staff is frequent, if not constant. While the environment of a locked facility can be dangerous at times, the reality of jail and prison life, while perhaps not pleasant, is rarely the ongoing violent place that movies and TV drama would portray. Nevertheless, the setting is by nature coercive and while each correctional officer is a de facto supervisor of others, one set of tools that may be called into play which differs from others used by those who supervise is that which involves force options. That correctional use of force incidents known to the public mainly in the form of television and movies is the result of a comparative lack of research, unlike force usage in policing.

The order maintenance goal of correctional staff observed by Sykes (1958) 60 years ago is accomplished through a consensus view of how to do one's time when incarcerated, namely following the established rules and generally acquiescing to the directions and orders of officers. Correctional officers have available, in addition to verbal direction, the coercive tools of restraint, placement in segregation cells, and the use of force that may accomplish such placement. A number of factors contribute to circumstances of force usage in corrections, including an inmate's behavior, the immediate environment within a locked facility or elsewhere, including the presence of other inmates or officers, options available to staff and articulated in policy, the limits of staff training, and perhaps the propensity to resolve situations through the use of force. An officer typically directs and controls the movements and actions of inmates throughout his shift without resorting to force (Griffin, 2002). Nonetheless, the implicit *ability* to threaten or use force is ever present. In 2009, the American Correctional Association (ACA) said this in its Public Correctional Policy on Use of Force:

> Correctional agencies are responsible for ensuring the safety in correctional programs. To achieve this goal, it may be necessary for correctional staff to use legally authorized force to respond to resistance and other situations.
>
> *(p. 90)*

Inmates arrive at a local jail via the mechanism of arrest. The arrest, as we have discussed elsewhere, is not likely to have involved the use of force, though it may have. The routinized process that occurs as someone is booked into a jail begins or continues an acculturation to rules and rule adherence that belies how a person arrived there in the first place – breaking the rules. Individuals who are arrested and incarcerated for violating society's expectations that carry sanctions, recognize that in the confines of a jail or prison disobeying rules or the instructions of staff carries more immediate consequences than is often realized in free society. Thus, order is generally maintained even though inmates are in a facility against their wishes.

Whenever staff members see inmates violate rules or physically refuse to follow instructions, a variety of factors may be at play. Some rule violations may occur without violence on the part of the inmate but rather stem from the belief that they can get away with it or that they are fulfilling an inmate role expectation. Other instances of rule breaking may include assaulting another inmate, engaging in a fight, or on occasion physically resisting an officer or assaulting one. Resistance to authority within a locked environment may seem and in fact generally be a futile gesture but we are still dealing with human beings – humans who are affected and driven by emotions and motivations just as they may be when outside of a locked environment. Rule violations by inmates may in some cases be affected by police use of force during their initial arrest. Klahm, Steiner, and Meade (2017) examined the correlation between police use of force and subsequent inmate rule violation. It is unsurprising that the researchers found that inmates have a greater likelihood of having force used against them than citizens who are free in society. It may also not come as a surprise that findings suggest that inmates who had force used against them during their arrest may have perceived the force as unnecessary (and it may have been more than what was required) and as a result of that act out through rule violations of various kinds. One implication of this effect can be that correctional staff members are only vaguely aware of the circumstances that resulted in the inmate's presence at the correctional facility. At the jail level, staff members working in the booking area may have witnessed some aspects of resistance by the arrestee but this knowledge may not be formally passed on to officers in a housing area. The perception of fairness or lack thereof by inmates of how they have been treated is seen as one potential source of rule violation. As always, we note that human behavior is complex and treatment at the time of arrest is but one variable that may impact someone's adherence to rules and their overall behavior once they are inside of a locked environment.

This perception of fairness is important. In part, officers are well advised to be cognizant of how inmates perceive their treatment and how they may act in response. A larger issue for the overall organization and how it deals with conditions of confinement and training, are the effects of procedural justice within the facility. Fairness in the processes of rule enforcement and punishment is important to those processes being accepted as legitimate, thus enhancing compliance. Results are mixed on how much impact such factors have on citizen behavior (Dai, Frank, and Sun, 2011), let alone what effect any derived approach may have on an inmate population. Regardless, staff should always be mindful that "95% of people incarcerated in prisons and jails will eventually return home to their communities" (Commission on Safety and Abuse in America's Prisons, 2006). People who are incarcerated can easily be said to live a frustrated existence; when to wake and sleep, when to eat, when and where to move, when to see loved ones – if there is an attempt by others to see the inmate – all are controlled by rules of the facility as enacted by individual corrections officers.

Juvenile offenders may be temporarily held in detention centers or for longer periods of time in residential treatment centers that approximate the adult prison setting. Holding cells in courthouses or police departments are also settings where people are detained by locked doors and the potential for force to be used against them if they try to leave. Deputy sheriffs, police officers, bailiffs, and corrections officers – all may interact with restrained individuals and potentially use force to gain compliance. For people under the supervision of correctional authorities the potential for use of force varies but is generally avoided through following the rules and instructions of staff.

The use of force within the corrections component of criminal justice takes a variety of forms. This is driven by the individuals that officers come into contact with, the officers themselves, the environment (jail, prison, probation office, etc.), and the circumstances of the transaction. The use of force in a locked facility is not entirely the same as during a street encounter by a law enforcement officer or a probation officer. Case law has drawn distinctions worth noting. But the danger faced by corrections staff is real (Konda, 2012) and many officers do have fear and perceive risk (Gordon, Proulx, and Grant, 2013) and adversity in various forms (Trounson, Pfeifer, and Critchley, 2016). The potential for violence or injury from inmates is perhaps the most obvious stressor in correctional work, but it is certainly not the only one (Higgins, Tewksbury, and Denney, 2012). Use of force incidents may come about through individual officers interacting with individual inmates, such as an officer who must force someone into or out of a cell. The use of force may be in breaking up two or more inmates fighting with one another. This in turn may necessitate or involve multiple officers and, potentially, non-lethal weapons such as OC (pepper spray), stun shield, or perhaps a tactical team in pads. Lethal weaponry is typically only carried or employed on the perimeter of a facility, during the transportation of inmates, or if an escape has occurred.

A component of the reality of the correctional environment is that officers are numerically out-numbered by the inmates in almost every setting. But each inmate individually may represent a threat based not only on his current and previous charges, but also based upon his state of mind on a given day. Officers direct inmates and obtain compliance mostly through the power of their legitimate position. Inmates recognize that the officer is "in charge" and it is appropriate to follow instructions. In addition to the position power as a staff member, competent officers also wield personal power, the ability to gain compliance through persuasion and being perceived as a fair officer who is performing within his or her role expectations. This point is important as administrators consider how to reduce attrition (Ferdik, Smith, and Applegate, 2014), and select training officers and supervisors.

Prison and Jail

Each type of locked facility serves its purpose in a somewhat different way. Prison security designations generally involve varying levels of access and some variation in the housing configuration and hardness of furnishings, fixtures, and equipment. The jail environment, while viewed by the general public as the less serious facility due to being geographically local and the shorter length of incarceration typical for its inmates, is well known to correctional professionals as fraught with security challenges based on the reality that each offender may move on to prison if convicted and sentenced in court. Everyone from the drug user to the murderer must first pass through the local jail. The classification concerns are often more complex in a jail compared to prison because of this catch-all nature of inmates housed in a jail (Hastings, Krishnan, Tangney, and Stuewig, 2011). Effectively, this makes every jail facility a maximum security environment. And of course within the walls of each facility are humans. Humans within a locked environment, even though they are aware of the rules, possess their individuality when it comes to deciding their behavior. Their actions and reactions can be shaped by their cir-cumstances as well. This may include intensified emotions and behaviors that would have been less extreme had they taken place outside of such a facility or set of circumstances.

For officers this means that an inmate's behavior may change on any given day based on that inmate's perception of her circumstances. Correctional professionals know, for example, that an inmate who has received bad news in court or from loved ones will often be depressed and this depression can be magnified due to the inability to have any influence over a court outcome or to be in contact with friends or loved ones outside of the facility. The psychological pressure that results from the stress of such goal blockage may lead an otherwise nonviolent inmate to act out against other inmates or staff, or even against herself. This dynamic of the locked environment is considered by competent staff members on a daily basis, and when classification and housing assignments are deter-mined. In a jail or juvenile detention center, an exception to generally knowing something about an inmate is in the booking area when an arrestee or detainee is first delivered (Shaffer and Ruback, 2002). The jail staff may have no previous information quickly available and will only be able to rely largely on whatever information an arresting officer provides. The likelihood of acting out, whether a minor rule violation or physical assault or resistance, may certainly be impacted by an inmate's history, status within the culture of a specific facility, or even perhaps partly by how the offender was treated, or perceived she was treated, during arrest (Klahm, Steiner, and Meade, 2017).

With jails housing inmates from the lowest security classification and threat potential up through the most violent criminals, it is expected that force will from time to time be used within the local correctional environment. Much of the public certainly thinks of violence in prisons as perhaps something that occurs more often. Television shows and movies have long dramatized inmates concealing shivs only to slip them into the back of another inmate or "guard" at an opportune moment. Unlike the largely unknown environment and subjects encountered by law enforcement officers, corrections officers are operating within a locked facility with settings that are known and inmates who are somewhat known to the staff members. This does not mean that inmates will not resist or assault officers (Lincoln et al., 2006), but it should encourage policies that require officers to clearly articulate in official reports what the circumstances were at the time of a force usage that mitigated the more controlled environment.

There are "group" concerns within corrections that are not entirely the same as those commonly experienced by officers on the street. Everyone in the facility has been arrested. In a jail they may be pre-trial and only stand accused, but they are among similarly situated accused. In the prison, everyone is a convicted offender. Prisons are more likely to have an active element of gangs, and this brings a particular set of challenges as individuals band together for protection or predation (Gaes, Wallace, Gilman, Klein-Saffran, and Suppa, 2002; Griffin and Hepburn, 2006). Juvenile inmates are generally more impulsive and within a facility are concentrated. Mental health inmates may be grouped for safety, therapeutic, or logistical reasons. All of these groups are therefore concentrated.

The dynamics of close confinement is a backdrop of unhappiness and frustration that informs much of the facility climate and which carries implications for violent encounters and force usage. Luckenbill (1977), in examining the causes of homicide, specifically referred to Goffman's (1967) male "character contest" in constructing six stages that two individuals go through in negotiating face-saving. Luckenbill said the character contest involved "a consensus among participants that violence was a suitable if not required means for settling the contest" (p. 177). An important component that Luckenbill comments on is the typically present "audience" in these types of confrontation. This is a frequent given within a jail, prison, or juvenile detention center, and experienced staff are readily familiar with the amplifying effect that the group of onlookers has in escalating some conflicts. These dynamics are not entirely gendered, and female inmates have proven their ability and inclination to be violent (Steiner and Woolridge, 2009). Programmed activity such as education, including frequent access to outdoor physical recreation yards, can have a mitigating effect on boredom-inspired behavior as well as actual opportunities for self-improvement (Lahm, 2009; Rocheleau, 2014).

There is no readily available source for records of force usage in the U.S.A.'s roughly 1,800 federal and state prisons, more than 3,000 local and county jails, or close to 1,800 juvenile facilities, many of which hold only a handful of youthful offenders. The federal and state systems have centralized policies on record-keeping, but the local and county agencies may follow a variety of practices for reporting the use of force. In addition, different organizations may use different definitions of force situations, which incidents require reporting, and in what format. As with law enforcement, there is no central reporting mechanism due to the state and local control of most agencies. National and state-level accrediting bodies require agencies to have use of force policies, including some method of record keeping for use of force, but they do not call for those records to be forwarded anywhere else. Some agencies pattern their policies and procedures after accreditation standards (see ACA, 2017) even if they are not pursuing full accreditation. Accreditation is largely a voluntary affair that can indicate that a facility or organization is following the generally accepted standards of the field.

Even without mandated central reporting to a state or national entity, documentation on the use of force in corrections has steadily increased over the years. This is the result of various factors including efforts at transparency and improved practices, lawsuits necessitating compilation of such records, and monitoring by external groups resulting from consent decrees or memoranda of understanding. The environment of the facility affects the behavior of inmates and officers alike. There have been efforts to gauge the views and perceptions of inmates as to how "fairly" a facility is run (Henderson, Wells, Maguire, and Gray, 2010), and the views of staff about the organization (Hemmens and Stohr, 2001) but (figuratively) penetrating the walls of a jail or prison to observe the dynamics has been a stubborn challenge. Research overall within corrections has been fairly robust, but the use of force by and against staff has received far less scholarly attention.

The National Institute of Corrections (NIC) is an agency within the U.S. Department of Justice, Federal Bureau of Prisons. The NIC's director is appointed by the U.S. Attorney General. Some of the work of the NIC has been to provide policy guidance as well as act as a repository for research and resources on a wide variety of corrections topics. Also, the National Center for Jail Operations, a component of the National Sheriff's Association, provides resources and training for jails from across the country. Corrections professional groups such as the American Correctional Association (ACA) and the American Jail Association (AJA) also provide resources, training, and policy guidance on use of force and virtually every other aspect of corrections. These groups are important to the continuing professionalization and progress of the field.

As an example, the ACA offers contract training that can come on-site to a facility and provide a range of courses. Here is the description of the week-long training course for Correctional Emergency Response Team instruction:

> Overview: These teams are highly trained jai/prison officers tasked with responding to incidents, riots, cell extractions, mass searches or disturbances in jails and prisons possibly involving uncooperative or violent inmates. Correctional Emergency Response Team (CERT) members are required to be contactable and available at all times. CET is founded upon a team concept and is made up of highly motivated and experienced prison/jail officers.

The course entitled "Use of Force and Due Process" is also a week long and is described thus:

> Given the nature of correctional environments, officers are allowed to use reasonable force in particular situations. Knowing when to use this force, as well as what type and how much to use is essential to defending yourself against allegations of improper use of force. Another area somewhat unique to corrections is the decision-making process for classification, transfers and discipline. These types of decisions affect the daily lives of offenders and may become the focus of claims of a "lack of due process." The guidelines provided will mark the boundaries of what force can be used, how much can be used, and when it can be used. The interactive exercises and practical case studies will help you apply the concepts to your job.

The ACA also offers courses in the force category with titles such as "Self-Defense and Personal Protection Techniques," Use of Force," "Introduction to Subject Control and Use of Force Training," "Firearms, Baton and Edged Weapons," "Chemical Weapons," and "Restraints."

WHAT-WHY: *BAILIFFS MURDERED AT COURTHOUSE*

In July 2016 two bailiffs were shot and killed and two other people were injured when an inmate tried to escape. The individual managed to disarm an officer and then use the firearm to kill the two bailiffs and wound a sheriff's deputy and a civilian.

The incident occurred inside the Berrien County Courthouse in St. Joseph, Michigan. The inmate was in jail for felony charges and when officers were in the process of moving him from a cell to the court room the individual was able to disarm one of them in a fight. Commentary in the news at the time was that the individual was not handcuffed, something that may have been an oversight, the result of local policy, or in some cases upon the instructions of the court who sometimes do not believe it appropriate to have someone in restraints in front of them.

(Associated Press)

Juvenile Correctional Facilities

Juveniles who are arrested by law enforcement officers are not routinely taken to the local jail or a juvenile detention center. Rather, such facility incarceration occurs only if the juvenile engaged in a violent offense or scored high on a risk assessment driven mainly by having multiple prior offenses and a lack of a capable guardian to take responsibility for them. And most juveniles charged also do not "score out" high enough based on crime seriousness, past record, or danger to the community, to warrant pre-trial detention in a juvenile facility. When a juvenile is detained the challenges for staff are somewhat different than those dealing primarily with adult inmates. The emotions and behavior of adolescents can differ from older and more experienced adults. This is also true in the correctional setting.

Juveniles of various ages can and do assault fellow inmates as well as juvenile custody staff members. While it may not be unusual for a juvenile to fight with others or commit minor offenses, violent resistance or assault on officers by juveniles in facilities is not uncommon (Trulson, DeLisi, and Marquart, 2011). It is important to ensure that a discussion of youthful offenders and their behaviors, especially violent ones, does not hang on a questionable adherence to what chronological age classifies a person as a minor, as opposed to what the behavior of that particular person actually is. In considering the objective reasonableness standard for the use of force against anyone, the Supreme Court did not make a distinction based on the number of years a person has lived. Rather, it considered such factors as size of a subject and the officer, the ability of the subject to cause harm, the availability of weapons, etc.

The use of force in a juvenile correctional facility is inevitable. However it is incumbent on administrators to ensure officers are well trained in de-escalation techniques and the dynamics of impulsive behavior. Clear policies on force usage and reporting are important, as is the training of officers and the work of supervisors to properly guide and monitor staff actions. As in any correctional facility, proper inmate classification is a factor that impacts inmates, staff, and overall facility safety and climate (Berk, Kriegler, and Baek, 2006). Information about potential rule violating or danger may become somewhat known through *assessments* (Reidy, Sorensen, and Davidson, 2016; Walters and Crawford, 2014), but these will not happen immediately. To the extent possible based on facility architecture, inmates should be grouped according to objective criteria. The use of appropriate seclusion rooms when needed is a safety matter. Such seclusion is not intended for long-term solitary confinement, and practices should address mental health and self-harm issues when individual confinement away from the normal sleeping cells is used.

Of ongoing concern is the psychological impact of the use of force as well as the use of restraints, and of lengthy solitary confinement for younger inmates. Within the context of both adult and juvenile confinement settings, solitary confinement can be considered under the rubric of control, if not force. There is no shortage of commentary from groups and individuals about the need to eliminate or severely curtail the use of solitary confinement within juvenile corrections (see for example the ACLU (2014) and Feierman, Lindell, and Eaddy, 2017). In a 2014 video on the website of the Department of Justice, then U.S. Attorney General Eric Holder spoke out against the excessive use of such confinement specifically used for those youth with disabilities. Holder noted, as many do, that juvenile inmates may need to be removed for a limited period of time to protect staff, other inmates, and the juvenile himself, but pointed to the need to closely monitor and not overuse the practice.

Private Facility Employees

The use of private providers in the field of corrections is neither new nor unusual. For-profit companies offer incarceration services for juvenile offenders, adult jail inmates, and prisons. Private security employees also perform functions such as transporting inmates to and from court as well as transfer between facilities. It has generally been observed that employees of most private correctional facilities are paid less on average than their public sector counterparts. Private companies may also provide fewer benefits, which lowers overheads and is part of the formula that allows shareholders to make a profit. Of concern is that employees of private facilities can have a higher turnover rate, be subject to less stringent hiring criteria, and receive less than ideal training. The assertion by companies of saving money for citizens and government is debated, though not a specific part of our discussion here.

An additional concern raised by the practice of private firms running correctional facilities is managing the incarceration of fellow citizens for profit (Lindsey, Mears, and Cochran, 2016). For many people inside and outside of government this concept raises an ethical and philosophical objection. The private company does not take on the entirety of civil liability for mistreatment or harm that may come to the people held in their facilities. Many citizens incorrectly believe that with the transfer of supervisory function from government to private sector, that legal responsibility is transferred as well. The relative invisibility (to the public consciousness) of corrections is all the more reason why accountability measures should be robust (Volokh, 2013). Far too little research or data exist regarding the frequency or level of use of force by private sector employees compared to the direct governmental employees in the majority of jails and prisons.

RESEARCH RESULTS: *CORRECTIONAL OFFICER FEAR*

Gordon and Baker (2015), using the concepts of fear facilitators and inhibitors, examined a sample of 901 male and female officers from 40 different institutions in an effort to better understand fear experienced by those officers. Members of the general public are often found to have a fear of victimization. In a similar way, officers fear becoming victims of a violent assault (crime) at the hands of inmates. The researchers looked into the various organizational and individual factors that contribute to fear, through various facilitators of emotional fear of inmates, along with the cognitively understood actual risk of being victimized by inmates. Importantly, the research underscored the potential for fear, an important job stressor, to contribute to job dissatisfaction, reduced productivity, and possible inappropriate behavior by officers. The authors noted that "social support and a sense of belonging to the institution may serve as fear inhibitors" (p. 7). Female officers were found to experience greater levels of fear, especially if those officers perceived the organizational structure as inadequate.

Probation and Parole

Community corrections officers, usually probation or parole, interact with offenders who are under the control of the court but not confined to a locked facility. Officers are challenged by the fact that many community control offenders do not view themselves as "inmates" and see themselves as ordinary citizens burdened with the inconvenience of reporting in to a probation or parole officer. This sometimes attitudinal and psychological mindset of offenders is to view themselves as possessing all the rights of a citizen not under court supervision because they live among those people. Such a view held by some probationers and parolees contributes to the potential for resistance to lawful actions by community corrections officers. Efforts at developing staff safety training have been ongoing at the federal and state levels (see e.g., Thornton, 2003) and officers routinely train with other criminal justice agencies in various safety skills and procedures.

In addition to the mindset dynamics that officers face with those under community corrections control, the settings where encounters occur can vary. While it is normal for probationers and parolees to meet with officers at the official premises of an agency, probation and parole officers will at times also visit offenders in their home, workplace, or other setting. The home visits are perhaps those with the most potential for danger or a use of force, if the officer makes a decision to take the offender into custody. The officer is not uniformed and does not typically have any devices other than perhaps handcuffs. Some states allow for probation or parole officers to carry firearms. While the carrying of firearms is debated, probation and parole officers have been killed on duty by those they are tasked with supervising (Schweer, 2016). Some officers may arrange to have a law enforcement officer accompany them if they know they are going to try and take someone into custody.

GOING GLOBAL

The use of restraints for youth in custody stirs the emotions of many people around the world. In England many of the same concerns raised in the U.S. have been debated for more than a decade. Tragic instances of juveniles dying in custody have occurred in both countries. In 2004, two teenage boys died after restraint; one committed suicide following the restraint. Investigation following the incidents pointed to various systemic problems in the running of juvenile custody facilities. Gooch (2015) reports that ten years on from these incidents, restraint of youth in custody remains a serious concern of governmental agencies and advocacy groups alike.

Restraints

Persons arrested are typically restrained through the use of handcuffs, placed into the back of a locked squad car with security partitions, and delivered to the booking suite of a jail or juvenile detention center. Each step of the way involves the use of restraint devices. A resistant subject may also be sprayed with OC or have a conducted energy device used to restrain him or gain compliance. Once an individual has been delivered to a facility, his behavior may invoke the use of further restraints. While it is understood that the individual is now inside of a locked facility without freedom of movement, additional restraints that may be employed include solitary confinement, restraint chairs, four-point restraints, shackles, chemical spray or conducted energy device again, or restraint belts. Officers and facilities must be cautious not to use such restraints as punishment (Cohen, 2015; Collins, 2012).

The use of temporary placement in a single cell may arise from the behavior of an inmate violating rules, such as fighting or destroying property within the facility. Such cells are likely even more spartan than a standard cell and may have only a stainless steel toilet/sink combination unit and a steel or concrete bunk, or no bunk and the inmate may simply be supplied a mattress. The average citizen outside of a correctional facility is rarely aware of the physical environment inside a jail, prison, or detention center and is likely unconcerned unless there is a media report of something gone wrong, or they have a friend or loved one who has been incarcerated. Leaving aside separation in a special cell, most discussion of restraints centers on devices or methods intended to immobilize the individual. Tools such as a restraint chair or four point medical restraints are intended to be used as a way of keeping the individual inmate from harming himself or others while acting in an uncontrolled manner. Even though the intent of such methods and devices is to keep individuals from harm, restraint, as with any use of force, carries the potential for injury or complication. The design of devices and the intent of methods can be used inappropriately, in excess, or with intent to punish rather than restrain. All of these may result in harm as well as civil liability, or even incur criminal charges against a staff member who intentionally misuses force or equipment to harm an inmate.

The use of solitary confinement or equipment such as a restraint chair should be guided by written policy and procedures of the facility. An important component of such a policy is due process. Protections afforded through the due process of a corrections procedure may be in the form of an after the fact review by higher authority of the necessity to use restraints on an individual. While we often think of due process as occurring prior to an action, the immediacy of a dangerous situation may call for the retroactive examination of correctional staff decisions as well as any subsequent disciplinary sanction imposed on an inmate. Agencies should always be mindful of the proper monitoring and documentation of the use of such devices or practices, as the use may give rise to a legal action or outside inquiry.

Use of restraints in a correctional facility may be the result of rule violations followed by forcible removal from a cell or other location when an inmate resists voluntary movement, to a disciplinary cell. Such circumstances may involve a so-called cell extraction, where correctional officers using prearranged and practiced tactics enter the location of the inmate, pin the individual and isolate his limbs, and then restrain him and move him to the desired location. This may be accomplished by a correctional emergency response team (CERT) or by multiple members of the shift working in a facility. Schwartz (2009) comments on how some correctional agencies utilized canines to force an inmate from a cell. He also notes at least one agency that he was familiar with that utilized noise flash diversionary devices followed by the entry of a cell extraction team to secure and move a disruptive inmate. He rightfully points out that cell extraction is usually an example of a planned force usage that has likely received a supervisor's approval before it occurs and therefore presents the opportunity to have sufficient staff including a supervisor and medical personnel standing by when the extraction takes place.

Restraint can occur with the assistance of various tools and devices, including chemical or pepper spray and electronic devices such as stun shields and handheld conducted energy devices. Batons, both short and the longer riot baton variety, are still available in most facilities for use in limited circumstances, including the chaos that gave rise to the lengthy baton's name. In older facilities there may still be fire hoses that could also be utilized in the event of a large-scale disturbance. Modern construction and fire regulations have seen most facilities switch to using overhead sprinkler systems, even though their function in a largely concrete and steel building can be questioned when many schools have waivers to avoid having to install such fire suppression apparatus.

Nonlethal Weapons

Corrections officers are aware of the inherent risks of the environment and of some inmates. Officers are also aware of the fact they are at almost all times outnumbered if multiple inmates should choose to attack them. While this is a thankfully infrequent occurrence in corrections, the introduction of non-lethal devices over the years was logical and, for the most part, helpful. Hepburn, Griffin, and Petrocelli (1997) examined one setting to evaluate the introduction of pepper spray, CEDs, and the training that accompanied the two options. The researchers noted that in the county jail setting they were evaluating, initial resistance did give way to overall acceptance as fears of effectiveness of the devices and the risk of inmates taking the OC and CEDs and using them against staff dissipated. The usage at this evaluation site gradually increased and reflected a reduction in the use of hands-on control methods.

The use of pepper spray in many corrections facilities has been common for 25 years. While the use of OC in law enforcement or corrections can prevent physical injury to officers and subjects, it can also be misused if applied wantonly within corrections to an already restrained inmate or perhaps one suffering from mental illness where a different approach may be more effective (Martin, 2006; Felson, Silver, and Remster, 2012). Most policies will call for the decontamination of affected inmates (and staff) subsequent to use of OC or chemical restraint. This may also involve video recording the process or examination by facility medical personnel.

Trying to maintain or restore order is daunting work at times and necessitates the use of force. Corrections Emergency Response Teams (CERTs) are generally not available to smaller facilities the same way that SWAT teams are not on duty in most police jurisdictions, based on size and staffing. Cell extractions will likely be accomplished by multiple officers, but they may not have the same training, equipment, or numbers to perform as a tactical team would. Personnel may have some specialized equipment or clothing available to facilitate some force actions, even if there are no tactical team members to handle a particular task or incident.

Excessive Force

While the use of force is occasionally necessary in corrections, there may be instances of excessive force just as there are in law enforcement. When considering whether force was excessive, the courts look at the need for the use of force, including the officer's perception, the amount of force an officer used, and perhaps what other efforts were made by staff. If there was no apparent force needed in a situation, or if force did not stop or deescalate proportional to the actions of the offender, this may indicate a knowing misuse of force and a source of liability for the agency and the officer (Rembert and Henderson, 2014). Within corrections, as in law enforcement, some shift and officer assignments are more active than others and may statistically see more force usage. Still, officers who are involved in force usage events more frequently than similarly situated colleagues may be overusing force due to poor training, overreaction, or bad intent.

Similar to in-car video in the policing environment, correctional facilities frequently have camera coverage. A perennial goal of corrections architecture is to improve the sight lines that allow staff to effectively monitor inmate activity and ensure the safety of everyone in the facility (Morris and Worrall, 2010). Important, however, is that just as with a car camera, video coverage inside or outside of a facility rarely if ever can view or record all activities. And also as with car cameras, the video recording will not be able to convey all aspects of an incident and what led to it.

Summary

If there is a paucity of information and available data on the use of force in law enforcement and corrections, the view within the walls is even more obscure. If an inmate is victimized during incarceration, the impact this might have on her future interactions with citizens and criminal justice employees upon release can be profound (Boxer, Middlemass, and Delorenzo, 2009). There is an influence of procedural justice perceptions on inmate behavior and subsequent need for the use of force (Henderson, Wells, Maguire, and Gray, 2010). This raises the issue of what such considerations hold for policy and training in correctional academies and in facilities. If officers are well trained in both techniques and human factors and dynamics, the use of force in correctional facilities may be minimized even though it will likely never be eliminated entirely.

There is both a different and higher use of force standard in a correctional facility because it is a locked building that offers little chance of an inmate escaping. Tight spaces are not unique to jails and prisons, but the frequency with which they are the setting for fights or resisting inmates makes them an important consideration in selecting tactics. In addition to the close quarters of cells, the gathering places of inmates (e.g., dining halls, chapel, recreation yards) present the potential for planned or spontaneous disruptions between or among inmates or against correctional staff (DeLand and Billings, 2010). At times an officer can wait until he has conferred with a supervisor who is likely on-site (Schellenger, 2013), formulate a plan, and then enter an area where an inmate must be controlled or moved. This is not always the case and a well-trained officer will still have to rely on his training and experience in the heat of the moment.

While we have pointed out that the correctional facility is a coercive environment by nature, efforts can be made to minimize inmate violence as well as the need for staff use of force. No facility administrator or correctional organization wants the publicity or liability for circumstances in which inmates and correctional staff may be injured. Behavior expectations for inmates during their intake, comprehensive training of correctional staff members, well written policies and procedures, and active and informed supervisors can all reduce or mitigate instances and after-effects of force usage in corrections. Even more so than within the law enforcement community, there is a lack of central or perhaps even systematic collection of use of force information. Part of this is the result of agencies being relatively independent, as they are in law enforcement.

This reality of legal, public, or even criminal liability or publicity has led to a more risk-management approach to many policies inside of correctional agencies, including those that address the use of force. Elected officials and appointed administrators want staff and inmates to be safe while the inmates' term of incarceration runs its course. Proper staff selection and training, clear and complete policies, competent supervision, and strong and informed administration can provide the environment to allow for a well-run facility or program in corrections.

KEY TERMS

Chemical restraint
Physical restraint
Defensive tactics
Honor contests

Discussion Questions

1. Why should we consider the context of the secure facility as we examine jail and prison violence and the use of force by staff?
2. Who are the employees of private for-profit facilities and how are they trained?
3. Discuss the factors affecting juvenile inmates that can lead to increased use of force incidents.
4. What policy options are recommended in regards to use of force for probation and parole officers?

TRY THIS

Examine several correctional agency websites. Try to locate the use of force policy. List and discuss the factors that you found within the policy.

References

ACA (American Correctional Association). (2017). *Manual of accreditation policy and procedure.* March 15, Washington, DC.

ACLU (2014) *ACLU National Prison Project and ACLU Center for Justice, Advocacy Toolkit: Ending the solitary confinement of youth in juvenile detention and correctional facilities.* June. http://njdc.info/wp-content/uploads/2014/10/ACLU-Advocacy-Toolkit-Ending-the-Solitary-Confinement-of-Youth-in-Juvenile-Detention-and-Correctional-Facilities.pdf

Berk, R. A., Kriegler, B., and Baek, J. H. (2006). Forecasting dangerous inmate misconduct: an application of ensemble statistical procedures. *Journal of Quantitative Criminology,* 22, 131–145.

Boxer, P., Middlemass, K., and Delorenzo, T. (2009). Exposure to violent crime during incarceration: effects on psychological adjustment following release. *Criminal Justice and Behavior,* 36(8), 793–807.

Cohen, F. (2015). Constitutional test for excessive force on detainees: the U.S. Supreme Court speaks. *Correctional Law Reporter*, 27(3), 33–40.

Collins, W. C. (2012). Use of restraints: current law and best practices. *Corrections Managers' Report*, 18(2), 19.

Commission on Safety and Abuse in America's Prisons. (2006). *Confronting confinement*. Washington, DC: Vera Institute of Justice.

Dai, M., Frank, J., and Sun, I. (2011). Procedural justice during police-citizen encounters: the effects of process-based policing on citizen compliance and demeanor. *Journal of Criminal Justice*, 39, 159–168.

Felson, R., Silver, E., and Remster, B. (2012). Mental disorder and offending in prison. *Criminal Justice and Behavior*, 39, 125–143.

DeLand, G. W. and Billings, R. (2010). Use of force in corrections facilities. *Corrections Managers' Report*, 16(3), 33.

Feierman, J., Lindell, K. U., and Eaddy, N. (2017). Unlocking youth: legal strategies to end solitary confinement in juvenile facilities.. Philadelphia: Juvenile Law Center.

Felson, R., Silver, E., and Remster, B. (2012). Mental disorder and offending in prison. *Criminal Justice and Behavior*, 39, 125–143.

Ferdik, F.V., Smith, H.P., and Applegate, B. (2014). The role of emotional dissonance and job desirability in predicting correctional officer turnover intentions. *Criminal Justice Studies*, 18, 4–20.

Gaes, G. G., Wallace, S., Gilman, E., Klein-Saffran, J., and Suppa, S. (2002). The influence of prison gang affiliation on violence and other prison misconduct. *The Prison Journal*, 82, 359–385.

Goffman, E. (1967). *Interaction ritual: essays on face-to-face behavior*. Garden City, NY: Doubleday.

Gooch, K. (2015). Who needs restraining? Re-examining the use of physical restraint in an English young offender institution. *Journal of Social Welfare and Family Law*, 37(1), 3.

Gordon, J. and Baker, T. (2015). Examining correctional officers fear of victimization by inmates: the influence of fear facilitators and fear inhibitors. *Criminal Justice Policy Review*, 1–26.

Gordon, J., Proulx, B., and Grant, P. (2013). Trepidation among the "keepers": gendered perceptions of fear and risk of victimization among corrections officers. *American Journal of Criminal Justice*, 38(2), 245–265.

Griffin, M. L. (2002). The influence of professional orientation on detention officers' attitudes toward the use of force. *Criminal Justice and Behavior*, 29, 250–277.

Griffin, M. L. and Hepburn, J. R. (2006). The effect of gang affiliation on violent misconduct among inmates during the early years of confinement. *Criminal Justice and Behavior*, 33, 419–448.

Hastings, M. E., Krishnan, S., Tangney, J. P., and Stuewig, J. (2011). Predictive and incremental validity of the Violence Risk Appraisal Guide scores with male and female jail inmates. *Psychological Assessment, 23*(1), 174–183.

Hemmens, C. and Stohr, M. K. (2001). Correctional staff attitudes regarding the use of force in corrections. *Corrections Management Quarterly*, 5(2), 27–40.

Henderson, H., Wells, W., Maguire, E. R., and Gray, J. (2010). Evaluating the measurement properties of procedural justice in a correctional setting. *Criminal Justice and Behavior*, 37, 384–399.

Hepburn, J. R., Griffin, M. L., and Petrocelli, M. (1997). *Safety and control in a county jail: nonlethal weapons and the use of force*. National Institute of Justice Grant 94-IJ-CX-K006. Washington, DC: U.S. Department of Justice.

Higgins, G. E., Tewksbury, R., and Denney, A.S. (2012). Measuring work stress among correctional staff: a Rasch measurement approach. *Journal of Applied Measurement*, 13(4), 394–402.

Klahm, C. F., Steiner, B., and Meade, B. (2017). Assessing the relationship between police use of force and inmate offending (rule violations). *Crime and Delinquency*, 63(3), 267–295.

Konda, S., Reichard, A., and Tiesman, H. (2012). Occupational injuries among U.S. correctional officers, 1999–2008. *Journal of Safety Research*, 43, 181–186.

Lahm, K. (2009). Educational participation and inmate misconduct. *Journal of Offender Rehabilitation*, 48, 37–52.

Lincoln, J.M., Chen, L-H, Mair, J.S., Biermann, P.J., and Baker, S.P. (2006). Inmate-made weapons in prison facilities: assessing the injury risk. *Injury Prevention*, 12, 195–198.

Lindsey, A. M., Mears, D. P., and Cochran, J. C. (2016). The privatization debate. *Journal of Contemporary Criminal Justice*, 32(4), 308.

Luckenbill, D. F. (1977). Criminal homicide as situated transaction. *Social Problems*, 25(2), 176–186.

Martin, S. J. (2006). Staff use of force in U.S. confinement settings: lawful control tactics versus corporal punishment. *Social Justice*, 33(4), 182–190.

Morris, R. and Worrall, J. (2010). Prison architecture and inmate misconduct: a multilevel assessment. *Crime and Delinquency*, 60, 1083–1109.

Policies and resolutions. (2009). *Corrections Today*, 71(2), 87–92.

Reidy, T. J., Sorensen, J. R., and Davidson, M. (2016). Testing the predictive validity of the Personality Assessment Inventory (PAI) in relation to inmate misconduct and violence. *Psychological Assessment*, 28(8), 871–884.

Rembert, D. A. and Henderson, H. (2014). Correctional officer excessive use of force: civil liability under section 1983. *The Prison Journal*, 94(2), 198–219.

Rocheleau, A.M. (2014). Prisoner coping skills and involvement in serious prison misconduct. *Victims and Offenders: An International Journal of Evidence-Based Research, Policy and Practice*, 9(2), 149–177.

Schellenger, D. (2013). Situational awareness: an officer's perspective revisited. *Corrections Today*, 75(3), 18–20.

Schwartz, J. A. (2009). Come and get me. *American Jails* (July/August), 17–26.

Schweer, R. G. and Thornton, R. (2016). Officer deaths in probation, parole, and community corrections: a summary of what we know. *Perspectives* (0821–1507), 40(3), 20.

Shaffer, J. and Ruback, B. (2002). *Violent victimization as a risk factor for violent offending among juveniles*. Juvenile Justice Bulletin. Washington, DC: U.S. Department of Justice, Office of Justice Programs, Office of Juvenile Justice and Delinquency Prevention.

Steiner, B. and Wooldridge, J. (2009). Individual and environmental effects on assaults and nonviolent rule breaking by women in prison. *Journal of Research in Crime and Delinquency*, 46, 437–467.

Sykes, G. M. (1958). *The society of captives: a study of a maximum security prison*. Princeton, NJ: Princeton University Press.

Thornton, Robert L. (2003). *New approaches to staff safety*. 2nd ed. Washington, DC: U.S. Department of Justice, National Institute of Corrections.

Trulson, C., DeLisi, M., and Marquart, J. (2011). Institutional misconduct, delinquent background, and rearrest frequency among serious and violent delinquent offenders. *Crime and Delinquency*, 57, 709–731.

Trounson, J. S., Pfeifer, J. E., and Critchley, C. (2016). Correctional officers and work-related environmental adversity: a cross-occupational comparison. *Applied Psychology in Criminal Justice*, 12(1), 18–35.

United States Department of Justice. (2014). Combatting excessive use of juvenile solitary confinement. Remarks by Attorney General Eric Holder, May 13. https://www.justice.gov/opa/video/combating-exces sive-use-juvenile-solitary-confinement

Volokh, A. (2013). Prison accountability and performance measures. *Emory Law Journal*, 63(339).

Walters, G. D. and Crawford, G. (2014). Major mental illness and violence history as predictors of institutional misconduct and recidivism: main and interaction effects. *Law and Human Behavior*, 38(3), 238–247.

10

FORCE BY TACTICAL TEAMS

CHAPTER OUTLINE

Introduction
SWAT
CERT
HNT
RIOT
Active shooter and tactical patrol response
Tactical emergency medical services
Militarization: tactics, equipment, mindset
Summary
Features: What-Why, Going Global, Research Results
Discussion Questions
Try This
References

STUDENT LEARNING OUTCOMES

- Students will be able to discuss factors that call for the use of a tactical team.
- Students will be able to describe what capabilities that SWAT provides to an event.
- Students will be able to explain the role of specialized equipment.
- Students will be able to discuss the use of hostage negotiators.
- Students will be able to explain the militarization debate.

Introduction

Variously called SWAT, SRT, HNT, CERT, ESU, SORT, and others, tactical teams are necessary resources in any country's criminal justice system. There are times when line officers in both law enforcement and corrections are confronted with challenges not easily overcome by one or even several officers equipped with standard training and tools. This may be a barricaded hostage situation in a bank or an apartment, a developing or occurring large-scale disturbance in a jail or prison, or perhaps a street demonstration that was co-opted by violent individuals with their own agenda to disrupt the peace. High-risk arrest and search warrant actions are also examples of tasks where tactical teams have been employed to manage or mitigate resistance or violence.

When these types of incidents occur, greater numbers of officers with specific training and enhanced devices are typically called upon if available. However, most agencies are not large enough to maintain, even on a part-time basis, such tactical response teams. By default, line officers are often called upon to try and control crowd movement and behavior or confront the immediacy of an armed or barricaded person, including active shooters in a school or other setting. Officers assigned to specialized functions such as SWAT or CERT, require extensive training in tactics, tools, and thought processes.

School shooting situations shown on television have provided the public with an image of the type of armed response of the tactical team in the law enforcement setting. The scenes show officers wearing black or camouflage uniforms and bulky gear moving in military fashion towards an objective. While officers have been trained to await a tactical team if one is available for relatively static situations where an armed individual is held up, it is not always within the control or choice of the officer to stand by waiting for specially equipped support or any backup at all. In addition to this, active shooter training has swung toward immediately entering the area where a shooter is believed to be located in order to try and stop the threat before he can cause more harm.

The intentional and calculated assaults on officers in Dallas, Texas and Baton Rouge, Louisiana, in the summer of 2016 graphically illustrate the dangers presented by killers trained in or familiar with tactics and well-equipped with substantial weaponry. The mirror image of this is the need for officers to have available adequate defensive and offensive tools when confronting such threats. After the infamous 1986 Miami FBI shoot-out with two rifle- and pistol-wielding and tactically savvy bank robbers, agencies across the country reviewed their selection of issued firearms. The two bank robbers used an assault rifle, a shotgun, and .357 handguns to at times pin down FBI agents and eventually kill two, Agents Ben Grogan and Jerry Dove, and wound five more agents. Both killers were military veterans with relevant training and experience. Five of the eight FBI agents involved in the gunfight were armed with revolvers, while only three had semi-automatic pistols.

Police tactics have not been well studied by the academic community, and this extends to team tactics. This is to say that while specific tactics have been used effectively in many locations over long periods of time, they have drawn the attention of relatively few researchers (see e.g., Kraska and Paulsen, 1997; Kappeler and Kraska, 2015) or the application of appropriate sample research, perhaps drawing on the literature in motor learning and performance. A number of non-academic books have been written by (largely) practitioners who have been involved in tactical teams and their training for a considerable length of time (see for example Blair, Nichols, Burns, and Curnutt, 2013; Mijares and McCarthy, 2008). The information presented in many of these books may be useful to officers, trainers, and agencies, even without empirical evidence of efficacy. The authority of some authors relies on their experience and anecdotal success with techniques and strategies they teach. Some attempts at evaluation or measurement have been conducted (Blair and Martindale, 2014; O'Neill, O'Neill, and Lewinski, 2017), though few replication studies exist to provide solid support. Crisis management and decision-making during large scale events or with multiple agency response is tangibly different from the decision-making that individual officers exercise during most calls for service (Crichton, Flin, and Rattray, 2000). The decision-making of agencies and government to address crowd events is drawing greater scrutiny and commentary (Gorringe, Stott, and Rosie, 2012).

WHAT-WHY

A gunman in Baton Rouge, Louisiana, deliberately targeted police officers, ambushing them with an assault rifle as they responded to reports of the suspicious individual on a public roadway. That the killer knew his firearm would defeat the ballistic vests worn by the officers is clear, based on his U.S. Marine Corps training and familiarity with his weapon.

In response to the increased attacks on law enforcement, Miami-Dade police in Florida acquired upgraded steel-plated vests and 500 high-powered rifles.

GOING GLOBAL

On Bastille Day, 2016, an individual driving a truck intentionally plowed through a crowded area of Nice, France, killing at least 84 civilians, including women and children, and injuring hundreds more.

In response, officials in Europe commented on a potential new norm of lone individuals using unconventional weapons such as the large truck to carry out such attacks. This type of attack illustrates the challenges of prevention as well as response during an assault. Security specialists and police officials know that planned attacks with limited advance communications among multiple conspirators challenge the possibility of intervening.

Trucks and cars have increasingly been used as makeshift explosive devices. While many government buildings around the world have added physical barriers and devices to thwart or at least limit such attacks, the practicality of retrofitting every possible target is questionable.

SWAT

The most well-known and universally visible tactical group is the Special Weapons and Tactics (SWAT). Originally attributed to the Los Angeles Police Department, most such units are trained in a curriculum consistent with the Tactical Response and Operations Standard for Law Enforcement Agencies (2015) outlined by the National Tactical Officers Association (NTOA). The NTOA SWAT standard document delineates recommended training topics based on what capabilities and functions a team is designed to undertake, including high-risk warrant service and apprehension, dignitary protection, sniper operations, hostage rescue, and barricaded subjects. Each of these potential operational capabilities is matched to recommended training courses available through the NTOA and others. When a tactical team integrates with a bomb squad, the organization recommends additional considerations to ensure proper coordination.

Many organizations are not large enough to staff a tactical team such as SWAT on a full-time basis. This challenge can be met through inter-local agreement with a larger agency that has a SWAT team, or by a multi-agency team. The departments organize the local or regional team while paying close attention to mutual aid agreements and applicable laws. The NTOA notes that teams should incorporate, when appropriate, the following elements: tactical command; containment team; entry team; sniper team; and, tactical emergency medical support, or TEMS. Extra considerations exist for tactical canine support, manned and unmanned aviation support, and hazardous material (HAZ-MAT) support.

Tactical team elements for SWAT typically include entry, containment, sniper, and medical support components. Most people are aware through media and movies of the visible role of the entry team as they are shown going into a building in a well-practiced series of maneuvers to quickly identify and suppress threats. But in the layers of space surrounding a SWAT action, patrol officers and others fulfill the important role of containment around the central point or points of an operation. Ubiquitous in SWAT over the years has been the sniper component. Highly trained officers may provide precision shooting to effectively suppress a threat to hostages, citizens, and officers. The challenges of officers being ambushed can be within the incidents where counter-sniper fire is required (De Groot and Fachner, 2014). A medical component rounds out the contemporary tactical team. While EMS is often staged nearby if a planned SWAT operation is about to commence, most teams incorporate medics or even SWAT-trained medical doctors as part of their response.

"The first step in good management [of tactical teams] is supplying adequate training" (George, 2012, p. 20). All of the training and team readiness should be grounded in agency policy (or multiple agencies' policies) and reflect hours devoted monthly to developing and maintaining capabilities consistent with the agency's stated tactical team mission. Basic new member training should be at least 40 hours and be followed by a field training program modelling the same mentorship afforded new patrol officers. Monthly training of 16–40 hours may be appropriate, based again on the tasks identified by the agency as ones the team may undertake, as well as by the volume or frequency of performing those tasks. Specialized assignments, such as sniper, will require additional skills training. An operational assessment should be a component of all training (NTOA, 2015). Consideration of tactical team training has been ongoing for decades and focuses on the processes of tactics (Gray, 1983). Training may be sought from private providers composed of retired or former military and law enforcement tactical specialists. Agencies must ensure that any such training and subsequent use of tactics taught by these entities conforms to law and agency policy (Mijares and McCarthy, 2008).

The selection of personnel is of obvious importance due to the discipline necessary to properly fulfill the roles of tactical team members. The esprit de corps and work ethic of team members, "operators" in the parlance of tactical units, has been important since their inception. The thought processes of team members and those who direct the actions of teams are important to consider as training, operations, and debriefings are carried out (Girodo, 2007). How this evolves with the introduction of millennials and the eventual passing of the baton completely to those born since the early 1980s remains to be seen, as generalized observations of attitudes to work assignments and militarization of civilian police functions meet the hard reality of the specialized unit's needs (Lang, 2017; Kappeler and Kraska, 2015). Women in policing and corrections, while not employed at a rate representative of their numbers in the general population, have been involved for quite some time. Resistance to their inclusion in tactical teams was predictable, yet they have made progress over the last several decades (Strandberg, 2016).

CERT

Generally equivalent to a SWAT team is the Correctional Emergency Response Team (CERT), or Special Operations Response Team (SORT). Used in jails, detention centers, and prisons, the CERT is generally trained and equipped to deal with riots, forced cell moves and extractions, high-risk prisoner transport, escapes and attempted escapes, and other duties involving a coordinated team response in situations with more potential danger (and liability) than other situations routinely encountered in a locked environment (Ross, 2017). CERT training has also been used in some mental health institutions to provide employees working with sometimes volatile patients the techniques to work together in a practiced manner to control and safeguard patients and staff.

Similar to SWAT teams, a CERT is composed of volunteer staff members trained in specified tactical procedures and specific team responsibilities. Selection criteria are generally stringent and include physical and psychological screenings and standards. Team management and organization may be centralized as in the Federal Bureau of Prisons (BOP) or any of the state departments of corrections, or the team may be a local one such as within a county jail system. The latter are typically members of a sheriff's office or county department of corrections. Some special response teams may respond from a number of locations to quell a disturbance at a specific location. The training for team members would allow them to "have enough common knowledge to work together for the successful resolution of an emergency" (Federal Bureau of Prisons, 1999, p. 1).

As with all other teams, clear policies and procedures, consistent training, and proper supervision are all components of successfully completing assigned tasks and operations. Managers and administrators within correctional organizations are responsible for acquiring adequate budget resources and the training and oversight of teams and their operations. Given the characteristics of a locked facility, team members often include a specialist in locking systems and security equipment as well as someone with extensive knowledge of facility layouts and infrastructure. The CERT will integrate with hostage negotiation team (HNT) members who specialize in responding to incidents where staff or other inmates are being held to try and safely free hostages. Joint training between CERT and HNT reinforces the need to work together during hostage situations.

CERT utilizes specialized equipment and, like SWAT, team members may keep some of the personal protective equipment with them when they are not working their normal duty shift. This allows members to respond to a facility incident with their gear. Other equipment will typically be maintained at individual facilities in an armory or other assigned storage area. This equipment may include shields, pepper spray or other chemical sprays and deployment devices, electronic control devices (ECD), breaching tools and cutting torches, and in some cases, firearms.

In the 1960s and 1970s, riots drew the attention, and resources, of state corrections departments. Injuries and the loss of life, facility disruption, and the damage to property were significant, and tactical teams helped quell disturbances. Ironically, the success of CERT/SORT and riot squads, while important and needed, may have reduced the visibility of some legitimate complaints and concerns raised by inmates (Bernstein, 2013).

HNT

The Hostage Negotiation Team (HNT) or Crisis Negotiation Unit (CNU) may be a stand-alone unit or a component within a larger tactical team such as SWAT or CERT. Whether joint or separate, the crisis negotiators should receive adequate initial training and maintain that level (Mijares, 2006; Mijares and Liedtke, 2007).

Officers already on scene at a hostage incident should make efforts to try and maintain calm at the location, with an emphasis on listening skills and possibly some basic negotiation tactics (Magaletta, Vanyur, and Digre, 2005; Norton, 2006). Once HNT members arrive they will try to establish contact with the hostage-taker(s) or take over from the initial personnel. There are different models of communications that the hostage negotiator will follow as they interact with the subject who is barricaded or has taken a hostage (Madrigal, Bowman, and McClain, 2009; Marques-Quinteiro, Curral, Passos, and Lewis, 2013). As with so much in law enforcement and corrections, academic research on hostage negotiations methods has been limited and has largely focused on the psychology of the hostage taker (Norton and Petz, 2012) and some consideration of the stress and mental health effects on negotiators (Fullard, 2007). What is known in many organizations is that when two or more units have overlapping responsibilities, tension or coordination issues may arise (Vecchi, 2002). Agencies must have policy, training, and internal leadership to ensure that none of these predictable organizational behaviors compromises the work done by the groups.

The taking of a hostage in the community may be the result of a crime that went wrong or when law enforcement arrives before the criminal can leave the scene of a crime. Within the correctional environment, an inmate or a group may have had a good bit of time to work out the planned hostage taking. Corrections officials know the inmates and may be aware of the past violence of individuals involved (Peak, Radli, Pearson, and Balaam, 2008). In either setting the suspect and the negotiator attempt to exert control and influence, and this is an important focus of learning and practice for negotiators in their training curriculum (Borowsky, 2011). Few correctional facilities have a hostage negotiator on each shift, if at all. This in itself may not be problematic as there is not always a mandate to employ one. This holds true in patrol or corrections if the area is not one that has needed hostage negotiators, or has one available from a neighboring agency (Perkins and Mijares, 2003).

Riot, Disturbance, Event, and Crowd Management

A riot squad or disturbance control team (DCT) is sometimes found in either the law enforcement or correctional environments. This may also be accomplished through the additional training of many or most officers in the operations components of agencies in crowd dynamics and coordinated group movements to control crowds. Rallies, demonstrations, the aftermath of sporting events, and civil unrest may all necessitate the use of officers in a coordinated fashion or *en masse*. Mass arrest protocols have been developed by many agencies and detail how to efficiently detain and transport arrestees and to document the event and actions taken by officers.

Law enforcement is called upon to safeguard protestors at 1st Amendment protected events, which gives officers the important role of protecting those expressing their views and working to maintain the peace. The Department of Justice published guidelines in 2011 for such events and recommends that agencies approach them in stages: pre-event; operational; and post-event. This is a familiar and generally effective formula to conceptualize natural and man-made disasters as well. The Incident Command System (ICS) known to almost all public safety personnel in the U.S. is often utilized to organize and manage resources when responding to incidents of varying scale.

While protective gear for officers is important, there are some items and modes of response that can be questioned for practical, visual, and liability reasons. In the type of congested setting that is a crowd, the use of ECWs or chemical agents/pepper spray may affect the wrong individual or many people who are not being disruptive. Fire hoses or water cannon may cause injuries. The sheer size of their horses may make it difficult for mounted officers to maneuver around people on foot. Motorcycles may also present a simliar challenge. Long-Range Acoustic Device (LRAD) technology is being used by some agencies to discourage hostile individuals from a distance. Innovation is always on the minds of team commanders and technology continues to provide new tools that extend from intelligence and information such as "geospatial holograms" (Fuhrmann, Smith, Holzbach, and Nichols, 2009), to more commonly thought of devices such as battering rams and breaching tools. Skirmish lines, arrest teams, and documentarians all come into play when training to meet large-scale event challenges.

Crowd management has been a function of law enforcement almost since the beginning of organized police forces. Preparing for known events as well as responding to spontaneous crowds (or mobs) is an important responsibility of agencies. During an August, 2017 rally and counter-protest by white supremacists, violence broke out and one man was arrested and charged with murder and other crimes for ramming his car into counter-protestors. Both the "white nationalists" and the protestors criticized the Charlottesville, Virginia Police and Virginia State Police, saying they stood by and allowed the encounter to get out of control until the man drove into the crowds and the Virginia governor declared a state of emergency. A number of observers stated that law enforcement officers were not close enough to the groups and did nothing to keep them separated.

Many areas have faced the social media-facilitated phenomena of flash mobs/crowds. The obvious challenge here is the spontaneous nature of crowds assembled in this way. The ever-increasing impact of social media technology can inform policy and practice in addressing groups, crowds, and mobs. This includes considerations of law enforcement monitoring social media, or posting messages to social media or, conversely, dampening the cellular signals in an area to block postings. A joint survey conducted by the International Association of Chiefs of Police and the Urban Institute (Kim, Oglesby-Neal, and Mohr, 2017) found that 89 percent of agencies use social media to make the public aware of safety concerns. The study cites the recommendation of the President's Task Force on 21st Century Policing as one factor encouraging the use of social media to boost community engagement through technology.

Active Shooter and Tactical Patrol Response

Examples exist where the response of patrol officers to immediately seek control of a deteriorating situation with an armed individual has prevented the loss of life. Other examples can be pointed to where it seems that the more sound decision would have been to contain a person or area and await the arrival of the tactical team (Blair, Nichols, Burns, and Curnutt, 2013). The Columbine High School shooting in the spring of 1999 changed the view of most law enforcement in the U.S. regarding how to deal with an "active shooter." The two teenagers, who had extensively planned the carnage they initiated at their school, were certainly not the first to carry out violence against classmates and staff, and the weapons they were able to access and use marks their act as massive, quick, and gruesome.

What changed following Columbine was the realization that patrol officers typically lacked sufficient tactical training to engage these types of shooters but also that officers were typically expected to contain the perimeter of such situations as best they could and await the arrival of a SWAT team.

Regardless of the hypothetical outcome of any given situation, had different tactics been used, the tragedy served to present a different model: enter a location if it is feasible and attempt to stop the threat before it can do more harm (PERF, 2014). The Columbine massacre, and other incidents, made it clear that officers in a position to act cannot always wait for the arrival of a tactical team.

Recognizing the need to equip line officers with the tactics to face these types of challenging situations brings with it the need to determine appropriate methods, design the training for those methods, and then select and utilize appropriate personnel to teach those tactics. And while businesses and organizations may have missed early signs of a pre-attack assessment (Doherty, 2016), law enforcement must still deal with the situation as it occurs. This model will logically not be the extensive and complex movements and interactions backed by countless hours of drilling as an integrated unit. Rather, fluid techniques based on situational cues and solid decision-making are the order of the day for the patrol officer thrust into certain tactical scenarios. To add to this challenge is the fact that the basic and specialized tools of tactical teams will not be readily available to the line-level officer. It is not uncommon to have an uninformed person opine that all law enforcement agencies should utilize helicopters during car pursuits. Such an individual can usually be educated quickly to appreciate the size of most agencies, the expense of helicopters and pilots, and the brief duration of most pursuits which renders any type of aircraft involvement irrelevant. Similarly, the idea of securing the perimeter of an active shooting, waiting on the arrival or instructions of command staff, and the assembly of the specialized tactical team, may be unrealistic. In an examination of all active shooter events between the years 2000 and 2010, Blair et al. (2013) found that nearly three quarters of all shooters in the 84 incidents were stopped within 9 minutes of the incident first being reported. The median response time for law enforcement was about 3 minutes. The first responding patrol officers are likely to face the prospect of trying to quickly stop a person or persons who is/are actively killing or seriously injuring others.

The FBI has studied reports of active shooter incidents in the United States between 2000 and 2015 and published reports late in 2014 and in 2016 (Blair and Schweit, 2014; Schweit, 2016). The FBI utilized a widely agreed upon definition of an active shooter as "an individual actively engaged in killing or attempting to kill people in a confined and populated area" (Blair and Schweit, 2014, p. 5). The 2013 study examined 160 unique active shootings with a total of 1,043 killed and wounded victims, and noted the following characteristics

Incidents

- An average of 11.4 incidents occurred annually.
- An average of 6.4 incidents occurred in the first 7 years studied, and an average of 16.4 occurred in each of the last 7 years.
- 70.0% of the incidents occurred in either a commerce/business or educational environment.
- Shootings occurred in 40 of 50 states and the District of Columbia.
- 60.0% of the incidents ended before police arrived.

Shooters

- All but 2 incidents involved a single shooter.
- In at least 9 incidents, the shooter first shot and killed a family member(s) in a residence before moving to a more public location to continue shooting.

- In at least 6 incidents, the shooters were female.
- In 64 incidents (40.0%), the shooters committed suicide; 54 shooters did so at the scene of the crime.
- At least 5 shooters from 4 incidents remain at large [at the time of the study].

(Blair and Schweit, 2014, pp. 6–7)

Sadly, there are many active shooter examples in the United States as well as around the world that illustrate how suddenly a single individual or sometimes more can disrupt and destroy the peace of the schoolyard, shopping mall, nightclub or open air venue. In the evening hours of October 1, 2017, a gunman opened fire on a crowd of concert goers at the outdoor event in Las Vegas, Nevada. A lone gunman firing from the 32nd floor of the Mandalay Bay Casino used an automatic weapon to fire down on the lighted area several hundred yards from his location. At least 59 people were killed and more than 500 were reported injured in what is considered the most deadly mass shooting in modern U.S. history. Law enforcement officers were able to locate the room where the man was conducting his deadly assault. The man fired through his hotel room door at officers but when SWAT officers breached the door, they found the 64-year-old white male dead inside, along with multiple firearms and ammunition (IACP, 2017; CNN, 2017). When shooters are armed with long guns capable of killing over significant distances, law enforcement agencies must have the equipment and weapons to confront the conditions they face. The shooter who spends more time preparing for an attack likely poses greater challenges to responding officers (Capellan, 2015), though each incident is filled with the potential for significant loss of life and injuries. Orlando Police and other local law enforcement faced a similar horrific mass shooting, now considered the second most deadly in modern U.S. history, in June 2016 as a 29-year-old man killed 49 people and wounded scores more in what was labelled a terrorist attack and hate crime. Armed with a semi-automatic rifle and pistol, the killer entered the Pulse Nightclub around 2:00 a.m. and indiscriminately shot patrons. After the gunman entered the women's restroom where he shot more people, he remained in that area until SWAT members breached the wall from the outside. Officers engaged in a gun battle with the man until he was killed. Looking at the experiences of the U.S. and other countries, police, citizens, and government officials in the United Kingdom are struggling with the policy question of how many officers should be firearms trained and equipped, and where to post those officers.

GOING GLOBAL: *2011 BRITISH RIOTS*

Police in England and Wales faced the rioting of several thousand people during an approximately one-week period in August 2011. Widespread rioting occurred following the shooting death of a 29-year-old British man who was under investigation by London's Metropolitan Police for firearm possession and suspicion of planning an attack. The man who supplied the firearm to the deceased was later convicted for that crime.

The riots resulted in five deaths, a number of other people injured, and an estimated £200 million worth of damage to both property and the local economies of several areas. Notably and sometimes overlooked, the cost to the Metropolitan Police of their response and subsequent large-scale investigation was estimated at £34 million. In addition to the police response to the rioting, larger issues were highlighted such as economic woes, race and class tensions, an increase in the gang culture in the U.K. and what seems to be the inevitable "excuse" for some people to loot.

In contrast to the rioting that sprang to life following the above incident, in March 2011 in Sheffield, a large group gathered at the Liberal Democratic Party Conference to protest recommended budget cuts and student tuition increases. During the two days of protest South Yorkshire Police used traditional patrol officers for security but supplemented the force with 15 members of a Police Liaison Team (PLT) of officers in a lighter shade of blue uniform. In addition, police used Twitter, Facebook, and other social media to tamp down rhetoric that was intended to incite protestors. The actions of the PLT were generally seen as legitimizing the police role (Waddington, 2013) in the event because they "mingled" with protestors and "quickly cultivated a relationship of mutual trust and rapport" (p. 63).

The officers on the scene of an active shooter have the priority tasks of neutralizing the threat and at the same time caring for the injured. It has long been taught to police academy recruits that arriving on the scene of any crime in progress or reported as over with, requires care as the incident may not have ended and a threat may still be present. Officers in the field, just as combat-deployed soldiers, require some level of medical knowledge, often referred to as first responder training. Applying basic skills in wound management has saved many lives over the years whether carried out by civilians at the scene of a traffic accident, an officer at the location of an active shooter, or on a faraway battlefield when administered by a fellow soldier.

Tactical Emergency Medical Service/Support (TEMS)

Civilian law enforcement tactical teams have increasingly shown a desire to move to a model of SWAT paramedics with the recognition that members with such experience may be needed on any callout (Weiss and Davis, 2007). These medically trained team members accompany the tactical team into many circumstances where the potential for injuries is notable. Some of the interest in TEMS comes from the continued debate over the timing of EMS entry to a scene that may still have an active threat (Foreman, 2010; Erich, 2017). Entering a known area where danger is likely to be present, but without medical support right there to assist with injuries, has influenced many law enforcement agencies to add medically-trained members to their tactical teams (Zink and Geary, 2007).

There is no set formula for how many personnel are trained and to what level of emergency medical care (Schreiber, 2009). TEMS may play a role in injury prevention as well as caring for injuries at a tactical event, with some teams able to include physicians in their team configuration (Young, Sena, and Galante, 2014). EMS, whether entering a warm scene or waiting, trains for active shooter and other dangerous events as well (Gates, 2017; Molloy, Newlin Jr., and Racht, 2017).

Militarization: Tactics, Equipment, Mindset

There is a refrain from some that policing in the democratic society of modern America is increasingly militarized. This assertion is pejorative and there is a further implication that style of uniform and manner of equipment signal a mindset by peace keepers that they may be viewed as occupiers, at times of, communities rather than community servants and partners. Where is the balance between rhetoric and reality? There is room for misperception by both citizens and agencies about which police duties may call for specialized equipment and extra protective measures when confronted with or predicting an "extra-dangerous" situation.

Law enforcement organizations have a long history (back to Robert Peel himself) of hiring former military members to don the uniform of civilian police. There are good reasons for this, having to do with a presumably stable work history, the understanding of "mission," the ability to comprehend and follow technical manuals, familiarity with the chain of command, etc. On the downside, some have observed that many former military members have been indoctrinated into a black-and-white worldview that impedes the effective transition to the gray haze of policing fellow citizens. Leaders and supervisors have to be mindful of mindset.

Some time back, many agency heads began to allow specialized unit members to wear battle-dress uniforms (BDUs) during specific operations such as a SWAT response. The wearing of various non-traditional uniforms has undergone sartorial creep over time under the guise of nighttime-casual, long-shift-comfortable, and bad-ass impressionable. The role of leadership, managers, supervisors, and field training officers, should not be ignored in properly reminding officers that they are not an occupying army, nor a military contingent of any sort and that carries an awareness of appearance that goes beyond how fit one looks. A headline from the *Star Tribune* in Minneapolis reflected one agency's attempt at change: "Minneapolis SWAT teams get less militarized look: it's hoped that changing color of uniforms and gear will soften units' intimidating appearance" (Libor, 2016).

Weapons carried by hand or in the vehicles of many contemporary agencies mirror those which are seen in movies or on television shows. This is neither surprising nor indicative of anything in and of itself. If, however, officers are not provided guidance by policy and competent supervision on when to access which weapons and tools, a risk may exist for misuse of a weapon and the related liability, and the strain of or further deterioration of already strained citizen confidence. Technology facilitates, but does not replace, the work of human officers. Knowing when to use which tools is still essential (Garrett, 2010). The misuse of a tool may come from having the item in your hands at the time of need to use force. When case law does not require the least force, but that only "reasonable" force be used, this may not present a particular problem. However, when there is adequate time, in other words when it is *feasible* that an officer or officers acquire specific tools for a known challenge, then it would behoove them to do so. In management science, somewhat famously attributed to the psychologist Abraham Maslow (1966) is the statement: "I suppose it is tempting, if the only tool you have is a hammer, to treat everything as if it were a nail" (p. 254). The implication of the quote used here would be to use a weapon, say an automatic weapon, when a sidearm would do. There are commentators who have described what seems to them a disturbing rise of the military mindset (Balko, 2014; Kraska and Kappeler, 1997; Kraska and Paulsen, 1997). If the officer has lawful grounds to employ lethal force she may very well have used a spear, but we would not want her to spray everyone with OC because it is in her hands when people could be verbally directed first without significant risk to the officer. Kraska and Cubellis, writing in 1997, asserted:

> To many people, even among academics, the military model represents constraint, discipline, honor, control, competence, and even a type of patriotism. To others it stands for tyranny, state violence, human rights abuses, war, and an ideology which stresses that problems are best handled by technologized state force. Some will see the rise and normalization of PPUs as a

necessary and rational approach to today's crime, gang, and drug problems; others will view it as bureaucracy building and as evidence of a government in crisis moving towards a police state.

(p. 627)

The tactics used by law enforcement are, well, tactical. Each vehicle that an officer approaches potentially holds a threat. Certainly not most of the cars and trucks, but which one? Interesting that when various lay-people are afforded the opportunity to participate in law enforcement scenario training and they are faced with the shoot–don't shoot dichotomy, many role-players go down in a blaze of incorrect threat assessment. This is not a fair apples-to-apples comparison perhaps since the journalist, academician, or lawyer does not think every "shift" about the risks of the job, nor do they contemplate and know that their uniform, badge, and even weapons, will not always keep them safe.

An armored rescue vehicle pulling onto a residential street with a team of tactically garbed and equipped officers on the running rails can be an upsetting sight to residents. Yet the arrival of specially trained and specifically equipped officers may spell the difference between a violent outcome and one where safety is maximized and even the suspect is taken into custody without harm (O'Brien, Weiss, and Davis, 2013). Criticism remains, and the provision of equipment to civilian public safety personnel by the military is seen by some as something that "uses a military approach that threatens to transform the traditional police mandate of protecting and serving into one of engaging and defeating" (Rahall, 2015, p. 1785). Yet a balance is needed. Even before the post-9/11 era there existed a need for specialists within agencies to deal with special situations. Contemporary terrorism underscores a necessity for domestic law enforcement to have resources beyond intelligence gathering to counter physical attacks (Brooks, 2010; O'Brien, Weiss, and Davis, 2016). Teams should be activated for the appropriate event, and should be properly selected, trained, and managed. It may still be seen as ironic that having more or sufficient teams may result in more peaceful outcomes.

The appeal in belonging to an elite tactical unit is fairly straightforward. The assignment comes with the best and latest equipment, more extensive and specialized training, the cachet of inclusion in a group whose standards are likely the highest in an agency, the respect of most members of the public, and perhaps even a pay supplement. The equipment includes specialized weapons and protective gear, body armor and tactical shields, sophisticated communications technology, and night vision equipment to name a few. How about the ReconRobotics Throwbot XT Reconnaissance Robot? Introduced in 2012, the Throwbot at that time could survive a throw of 120 feet, weighed in at only 1.2 pounds, and was built for the use of SWAT teams or military units (ReconRobotics, 2012).The mindset of officers in most tactical units is one of pride, teamwork, and camaraderie. This esprit de corps is to be expected and is desirable in so far as it aids the mission and lends to the competence of team members. A potential morale issue within an agency is that the proliferation of specialized units, including some investigative ones, may undermine the view that patrol officers have of their role in the organization.

RESEARCH RESULTS

Researchers examined three methods of interfacing a robotic device with SWAT operations at a department in Mississippi (Lalejini, Duckworth, Sween, Bethel, and Carruth, 2014). The team, based at Mississippi State University, conducted a test of supervisory control methods of an "autonomously operated mobile robot system" using: (1) hand gestures via Microsoft Kinect,

(2) an interactive android application on a hand-held mobile device, and (3) verbal commands issued through a headset. These methods of supervisory control were compared to a tele-operated robot using a gamepad controller (p. 1). The article describing the study talked about the efforts over the last two decades to utilize the capabilities of robot helpers while reducing the downside of taking a SWAT team member offline to remotely control the device. This may be especially important for smaller teams with no extra human resources to spare during an operation. The touchscreen device was found to have the easiest interface and provide "the most enjoyable, satisfying, and engaging interface of the four user interfaces evaluated" (p. 1). The use of robots is not new in law enforcement, where they have facilitated surveillance, delivering smoke or gas, providing a video feed to officers, and distracting a suspect. Drone technology also represents another initially military tool that made its way to the civilian public safety environment. With the use of a remotely operated robot delivering C4 plastic explosives, Dallas police killed a sniper with military training as he gunned down twelve police officers, killing five, in July 2016.

Summary

Any agency that utilizes either tactical teams or a coordinated response protocol is well-advised to develop sound policy and engage in appropriate training of its affected members. Tactical team capabilities continue to advance due to both improved and increased training as well as technological developments. Failure to train tactical officers in relevant procedures can lead to liability actions under Section 1983, Title 42 US Code. Training is recommended to be held monthly with coverage of policy and procedures as well as simulations to approximate realistic scenarios that teams may face.

Each specialized team, unit, or group of trained officers, requires procedures for documenting its response after being activated. Agency report forms along with video and photographic recordings are typical. These considerations fulfill legal and public trust concerns and allow for trainers and commanders to review and debrief personnel for improved responses and accountability of actions. The perceived legitimacy of criminal justice agencies is closely tied to the question of citizens viewing their law enforcement agencies as inappropriately or over-militarized.

Discussion Questions

1. What are the common features of most tactical teams?
2. Who are the members of tactical teams? Why do they join tactical teams?
3. Discuss the reasons for using tactical teams.
4. What makes the availability of a crisis intervention team a potential benefit?
5. Analyze the arguments in favor of and against the use of fortified tactical teams.

TRY THIS

Visit the web page of the Justice Technology Information Center at: https://justnet.org/resources/Excess-Federal-Property.html. After reading the brief description, look at the inventory listings of the Defense Reutilization and Marketing Service (DRMS). Find your state and look at some examples of equipment acquired under this program. What are your thoughts about local and state agencies having the ability to acquire these items after they have been purchased and used by the federal level of government?

References

Balko, R. (2014). *Rise of the warrior cop.* New York: Public Affairs.

Bechky, B. A. and Okhuysen, G. A. (2011). Expecting the unexpected? How swat officers and film crews handle surprises. *Academy of Management Journal*, 54(2), 239–261.

Bernstein, J. (2013). Why are prison riots declining while prison populations explode? *Atlantic*, 312(5), 1.

Blair, J. P. and Martindale, M. H. (2014). *Evaluating police tactics: an empirical assessment of room entry techniques.* Abingdon and New York: Routledge.

Blair, J. P., Nichols, T., Burns, D., and Curnutt, J. R. (2013). *Active shooter events and response.* Boca Raton, FL: CRC Press.

Blair, J. P. and Schweit, K. W. (2014). *A study of active shooter incidents, 2000–2013.* Washington, DC: Texas State University and Federal Bureau of Investigation, US Department of Justice.

Borowsky, J. P. (2011). Responding to threats: a case study of power and influence in a hostage negotiation event. *Journal of Police Crisis Negotiations*, 11(1), 1–19.

Brooks, B. E. (2010). Law enforcement's role in US counterterrorism strategy. *Police Journal*, 83(2), 113–125.

CNN (Cable News Network). (2017). October 3.

Capellan, J. A. (2015). Lone wolf terrorist or deranged shooter? A study of ideological active shooter events in the United States, 1970–2014. *Studies in Conflict and Terrorism*, 38(6), 395–413.

Crichton, M. T., Flin, R., and Rattray, W. R. (2000). Training decision makers: tactical decision games. *Journal of Contingencies and Crisis Management*, 8(4), 208.

De Groot, A. and Fachner, G. (2014). Protecting officers from ambush attacks: key insights from law enforcement executives. *The Police Chief*, 81, 10–11.

Doherty, M. (2016). From protective intelligence to threat assessment: strategies critical to preventing targeted violence and the active shooter. *Journal of Business Continuity and Emergency Planning*, 10(1), 9–17.

Erich, J. (2017). EMS World Roundtable: Optimizing active-shooter response. *EMS World*, 46(3), 26–34.

Federal Bureau of Prisons. (1999). *Special Operations Response Team guidebook: revised by the Office of Emergency Preparedness.* Washington, DC: U.S. Department of Justice.

Foreman, K. (2010). Basic elements of a tactical team. *Kentucky Law Enforcement Magazine*, 9(3), 48–49.

Fuhrmann, S., Smith, N. J., Holzbach, M., and Nichols, T. (2009). Investigating geospatial holograms for special weapons and tactics teams. *Cartographic Perspectives*, 63, 5–19.

Fullard, D. A. (2007). A protocol for comprehensive hostage negotiation training within correctional institutions. *Federal Probation*, 71(3), 10–17.

Garrett, R. (2010). Part man part machine all cop. *Law Enforcement Technology*, 37(5), 8–14.

Gates, H. (2017). Gathering of eagles, part II: Responding to active-shooter events, part II. *EMS World*, 46(7), 44–47.

George, C. (2012). Managing the tactical unit. *Sheriff*, 64(1), 20.

Girodo, M. (2007). Personality and cognitive processes in life and death decision making: an exploration into the source of judgment errors by police special squads. *International Journal of Psychology*, 42(6), 418–426.

Gorringe, H., Stott, C., and Rosie, M. (2012). Dialogue police, decision making, and the management of public order during protest crowd events. *Journal of Investigative Psychology and Offender Profiling*, 9(2), 111–125.

Gray, W. D. (1983). Engagement simulation: a method of tactical team training. *Training and Development Journal*, 37(7), 28.

IACP (International Association of Chiefs of Police). (2017). *The Lead*, October 2.

Kappeler, V. and Kraska, P. (2015). Normalising police militarisation, living in denial. *Policing and Society*, 25(3), 268–275.

Kim, K., Oglesby-Neal, A., and Mohr, E. (2017). *Law enforcement use of social media survey*. Alexandria, VA: International Association of Chiefs of Police and the Urban Institute.

Kraska, P. B. and Cubellis, L. J (1997). Militarizing Mayberry and beyond: making sense of American paramilitary policing. *Justice Quarterly*, 14(4), 627.

Kraska, P. B. and Kappeler, V. E. (1997). Militarizing American police: the rise and normalization of paramilitary units. *Social Problems*, 1, 1.

Kraska, P. B. and Paulsen, D. J. (1997). Grounded research into U.S. paramilitary policing: forging the iron fist inside the velvet glove. *Policing and Society*, 7(4), 253.

Lalejini, A., Duckworth, D., Sween, R., Bethel, C. L., and Carruth, D. (2014). Evaluation of supervisory control interfaces for mobile robot integration with tactical teams. 2014 IEEE International Workshop on Advanced Robotics and its Social Impacts, Evanston, IL, 2014, pp. 1–6.

Lang, M. (2017). Millennials on the SWAT team. Cover story. *Law Enforcement Technology*, 44(4), 18.

Lawhead, R. (2016). Augmented reality: organized deterrence and adaptive policing. *Journal of California Law Enforcement*, 50(3), 6.

Libor, J. (2016). Minneapolis SWAT teams get less militarized look: it's hoped that changing color of uniforms and gear will soften units' intimidating appearance. *Star Tribune* (Minneapolis, MN), February 3.

Madrigal, D. O., Bowman, D. R., and McClain, B. U. (2009). Introducing the four-phase model of hostage negotiation. *Journal of Police Crisis Negotiations*, 9(2), 119.

Magaletta, P. R., Vanyur, J. M., and Digre, K. (2005). On the consequences of listening: hostage incidents in the Federal Bureau of Prisons. *Corrections Today*, 67(5), 90–92.

Marques-Quinteiro, P., Curral, L., Passos, A. M., and Lewis, K. (2013). And now what do we do? The role of transactive memory systems and task coordination in action teams. *Group Dynamics: Theory, Research, and Practice*, 17(3), 194–206.

Maslow, A. (1966). *The psychology of science: a reconnaissance*. New York: Harper and Row.

Mijares, T. C. (2006). Beyond Canton versus Harris: further mandates for continued crisis negotiation training. *Journal of Police Crisis Negotiations*, 6(2), 105.

Mijares, T. C. and Liedtke, R. (2007). Standards of the industry continued: Langford v. Gates and the role of documentation during police crisis negotiation training. *Journal of Police Crisis Negotiations*, 7(2), 117–122.

Mijares, T. C. and McCarthy, R. M. (2008). *The management of police specialized tactical units*. 2nd ed. Springfield, IL: Charles C. Thomas.

Molloy, D., NewlinJr.S., and Racht, E. (2017). Preparing for active shooters and hostile events. *EMS World*, 46(3), 35–42.

Norton, S. C. (2006). Hostage negotiation in jail facilities: first responder. *American Jails*, 20(3), 65.

Norton, S. C. and Petz, M. (2012). Hostage negotiators: managing psychological stress. *Journal of Police Crisis Negotiations*, 12(1), 28–38.

NTOA. (2015). *Tactical response and operations standard for law enforcement agencies*. Washington, DC: National Tactical Officers Association.

O'Brien, B., Weiss, J., and Davis, M. (2013). Police armored rescue vehicles in a time of global security concerns. *Journal of Counterterrorism and Homeland Security International*, 19(1), 44–47.

O'Brien, B., Weiss, J., and Davis, M. (2016). The role of local law enforcement in counterterrorism: the Cleveland, Ohio, police experience. Cover story. *Journal of Counterterrorism and Homeland Security International*, 22(1), 30–35.

O'Neill, J., O'Neill, D. A., and Lewinski, W. J. (2017). Toward a taxonomy of the unintentional discharge of firearms in law enforcement. *Applied Ergonomics*, 59, 283–292.

Peak, K. J., Radli, E., Pearson, C., and Balaam, D. (2008). Hostage situations in detention settings: planning and tactical considerations. *FBI Law Enforcement Bulletin*, 77(10), 1–14.

PERF (Police Executive Research Forum). (2014). *The police response to active shooter incidents*. Critical Issues in Policing series. Washington, DC: Police Executive Research Forum.

Perkins, D. B. and Mijares, T. C. (2003). Organization and structure of the crisis negotiation unit and related legal aspects. *Journal of Police Crisis Negotiations*, 3(2), 73–77.

Rahall, K. (2015). The green to blue pipeline: defense contractors and the police industrial complex. *Cardozo Law Review*, 36(5), 1785–1835.

ReconRobotics. (2012). Recon robots assist SWAT teams in Washington DC area. *Robotics Business Review*, May 3.

Ross, D. L. (2017). Examining the administrative liability issues of correctional tactical teams. *American Jails*, 31(2), 34.

Schreiber, S. (2009). Medics with guns. *Law Enforcement Technology*, 36(10), 28–33.

Schweit, K. W. (2016). *Active shooter incidents in the United States in 2014 and 2015*. Washington, DC: Federal Bureau of Investigation, U.S. Department of Justice.

Strandberg, K. W. (2016). The new changing norm – women in tactical units. Cover story. *Law Enforcement Technology*, 43(1), 14.

Vecchi, G. M. (2002). Hostage/barricade management: a hidden conflict within law enforcement. *FBI Law Enforcement Bulletin*, 71(5), 1.

Waddington, D. P. (2013). A "kinder blue": analysing the police management of the Sheffield anti-"Lib Dem" protest of March 2011. *Policing and Society*, 23(1), 46–64.

Weiss, J. and Davis, M. (2007). Training tactical medics: special-ops teams need specialized medical support. *EMS Magazine*, 36(10), 86–90.

Young, J. B., Sena, M. J., and Galante, J. M. (2014). Physician roles in tactical emergency medical support: the first 20 years. *Journal of Emergency Medicine* (0736–4679), 46(1), 38–45.

Zink, L. and Geary, P. (2007). Tactical medical team within the sheriff's office? *Sheriff*, 59(1), 20–21.

11

FORCE AND SPECIAL POPULATIONS

CHAPTER OUTLINE

Introduction
Mental illness
Developmental disability
Jails and prisons
Suicidal individuals
Stress/emotion/agitation
Alcohol, drugs, and physical distress
Age or physical condition
Summary
Features: Going Global
Key Terms
Discussion Questions
Try This
References

STUDENT LEARNING OUTCOMES

- Students will be able to discuss factors observed in force situations with special populations.
- Students will be able to describe the types of special populations with potential physical or psychological considerations during force usage.
- Students will be able to explain the role of alcohol and drugs in use of force encounters.
- Students will be able to discuss the influence of mental illness in force incidents.
- Students will be able to explain the impact age may have force considerations.

Introduction

The terminology of "special population" connotes a variety of features within society in referring generally to disadvantaged or vulnerable groups. Within criminal justice specifically, the reference is often to individuals possessing one or more physical or psychological characteristics that can present situational challenges for law enforcement, correctional, or other public safety interactions. Much, if not most, of the attention for such interactions involves those with a mental illness, diagnosed or undiagnosed, yet there are a number of others that bring a need for awareness of potential behaviors. Officers deal frequently with people who are behaviorally affected by such mental illness or other circumstances. This is not always, or even mainly, of a violent nature, but can often lead others to contact law enforcement to respond. Officers also routinely deal with individuals impaired by alcohol or other ingested substances. Additionally, the very young and the older members of society may have physical or mental considerations that bear upon interactions with, and the use of force by, officers.

As officers are trained in academy and in-service settings, including field training and evaluation programs, and as officers gain experience, they gain insight into behavior causation and they learn effective techniques to deal with many scenarios. Officers are frequently the first responders for cases involving someone with a mental illness, developmental disability, impairment, or in a highly agitated state. Calls for service or incidents that bring officers together with people who must be viewed, in the "tactical mind" of the officer, as possessing an added layer of complexity are to be approached with caution. The potential for force usage, should that become necessary, carries certain considerations.

Training to equip officers with knowledge to aid in such interactions has improved over time. Laws protect individuals and classes of people from discrimination. In the 1990s the Americans with Disabilities Act (ADA) began re-shaping much of the law in the U.S. regarding people with a physical or mental impairment that limits major life activities. From the standpoint of public safety personnel, the implication is that the same level of services be provided to those with limitations. In addition to safeguarding the rights of an individual with a disability during an arrest, officers may need to take into consideration physical limitations of mobility, vision, hearing or other, as well as mental or emotional processes that affect comprehension and interaction.

Certain individuals affected by mental illness, intoxication, or emotion may present with reduced sensitivity to pain during a force usage, with the result of injury from increased force used by officers to overcome resistance. In an arrest situation this may be relevant and impact force decisions, including when to switch from one approach or technique to another. There may also be a limitation of communication that obscures the intention of an individual or impacts the ability to understand or respond to questions or instructions. An officer may be trying to assess many such factors with an unknown individual while simultaneously assessing threat in a dynamic environment.

Mental Ilness

Mental illness is presented in various ways and manifests in behaviors that may bring a person in contact with law enforcement officers during calls for service or on the street, with correctional officers in a booking suite or in facility population, or medical or security personnel prehospital or in an emergency room setting. The National Institute of Mental Health reports that in 2015 nearly 10 million non-institutionalized adults, or 4 percent of adults in the U.S., had a Serious Mental Illness (SMI) (NIMH, 2015). It is not uncommon for officers to interact with those challenged by some mental illness (Cordner, 2006; Watson, Swartz, Bohrman, Kriegel, and Draine, 2014), though the danger believed by some to exist at high levels is likely exaggerated (Morabito and Socia, 2015). The use of force with this population does occur in some instances, especially when confounded by co-occurring conditions or circumstances (NIMH, 2015). Those with mental illness are more often victims than offenders, and those who come into contact with the criminal justice system often do not fare well (Myers, 2017; Schulenberg, 2016).

That law enforcement and corrections officers are called upon as first responders and care-givers to those with a mental illness is in itself not at all new (see for example, Goffman, 1961; Bittner, 1967).With the movement of the 1960s and 1970s to deinstitutionalize the mentally ill, more people freed from civil commitments that had lacked meaningful due process ended up on the streets of America. While the release of so many people wrongfully held was hailed as a major accomplishment in mental health rights, the liberated were often still in need of resources and treatment which were largely absent on the "outside." With the reduced population of mental health institutions, government funding dropped appreciably but was not transferred to community-based programs to treat the newly released or those individuals already in society who were in need of mental health services. During this same period more scrutiny was given to the civil commitment mechanisms that allowed for people to be taken into custody in the first place for forced assessment and treatment.

When called to a location where a fellow citizen is exhibiting abnormal behavior, law enforcement officers must determine whether anyone (including the individual who was subject of another citizen's call) is potentially at risk or in need of help. This may involve the use of force in controlling the immediate situation, making an arrest if called for, or taking someone into custody for further mental health evaluation (Jennings and Hudak, 2015). Criminal justice system administrators and trainers are by now familiar, if uncomfortable, with the phrase "lawful but awful." This generally refers to the optics of a force interaction between officers and a subject that involves actions that are within policy and law, but simply look dreadful because of injuries to the subject or the apparently excessive force used to control that person. Lawsuits settled between plaintiffs and agencies often fall within this category, with the notion by risk managers or agency defendant attorneys fearing the look of the available information on a case will simply be too challenging to explain or too risky to take before a state or federal court jury or judge.

There can be an intersection of persons with an impaired state, behaviors they exhibit that draw attention, and other citizens expressing some version of Bittner's admonition that the situation is "something-that-ought-not-to-be-happening-and-about-which-someone-had-better-do-something-now" (1974, p. 30) And thus, the arrival of the peace officer. A broader dimension of such encounters is the interaction of police officers with those suffering from mental illness, beyond just the use of force (Morabito, Socia, Wik, and Fisher, 2017). One approach commented on by these authors and others, is that of the Crisis Intervention Team (CIT). In their work, Morabito et al. examined more than 4,000 incidents from the Portland Police Bureau over a 4-year span, examining the use of force not only with those identified as having a mental illness but those with additional behavioral health disorders and issues of substance abuse. In this study, the individuals who presented with co-occurring disorders were also seen as more frequently violently resisting, with resulting police use of force. A similar finding by Johnson (2011) was that individuals with a mental illness resist more often as well as being under the influence of alcohol or illegal drugs. Suspected drug intoxication was seen as more of an influence in combination with other factors than was mental illness or alcohol (Kaminski, Digiovanni, and Downs, 2004).

The study by Morabito et al. (2017) compared the use of force by police department members who had completed CIT training with those who had not. The study categorized incidents with individuals having "co-occurring disorders, those who have only mental health or only substance use disorders, and those perceived as having no disorders" (p. 32). We are reminded by the authors that the use of force is rare in any event, and that has complicated the research into the use of force involving people identified as having a mental illness. In addition, use of force in such situations is typically something at the lower end of the spectrum and this of course may not be reported or aggregated as to types of force incidents.

Crisis Intervention Team (CIT) utilization and effectiveness is still not widespread, though officers exposed to the training have reacted positively (Bonfine, Ritter, and Munetz, 2014). A recurring difficulty with any effort to produce a comprehensive response to many issues of an emergency nature is the relatively small size of law enforcement agencies who are asked to deal with the sometimes volatile and often sensitive nature of mental health-related calls for service. The practicality of having each officer of the 18,000 some law enforcement agencies in the U.S. receive 40 or more hours of advanced crisis intervention team training is questionable. Still, most state criminal justice academies have added or increased basic training in symptomology of behavioral disorders. It is also important to train officers in general approaches to those suspected of mental illness such as the orientation of procedural justice so that the subject perceives the police as legitimate (Ferdik, 2014; Kara, 2014), and to conduct research into how officers view those with mental or emotional disturbances so as to incorporate their views or biases into training (Watson et al., 2014). It is challenging to identify someone with a mental illness through brief contact (Alpert, 2015), but an officer need not be capable of *diagnosing* a mental illness to be able to recognize that certain behaviors may emanate from the broad category of mental illness or impairment and act accordingly. Recognizing that individuals with co-morbid disorders have encountered more physical force than any other category individually suggests not only that the ongoing training and law enforcement is important, but that government and society as a whole must devote adequate attention and resources to assist those suffering from such conditions while reducing stigma and the misperception that those with a mental illness engage in routinely violent behavior (Kesic and Thomas, 2014).

To examine this connection to the use of force, researchers in Australia obtained a random sample of more than 4,000 cases over a period of more than a decade from a police use of force register and matched it against a public mental health database (Kesic, Thomas, and Ogloff, 2013). This study found that some 38 percent of the people on whom force was used had a recorded history of a mental disorder, and that there was an overrepresentation among subjects as suffering from psychosis and schizophrenia. The over-represented individuals were seen as potentially representing "a sub-group of people with mental disorders presenting with aggressive and otherwise problematic behaviours coupled with histories of criminal offending" (p. 225). The authors rightfully point out that this represents an ongoing challenge for law enforcement. In a separate commentary, the same authors identified an over-representation of those fatally shot as having disorders with acute symptoms of "severe mental disorders of psychosis and schizophrenia" (Kesic, Thomas, and Ogloff, 2010, p. 463). This study from Australia is echoed in the U.S. by news reporting in the *Washington Post* (2016) that nearly 25 percent of those shot and killed by law enforcement in 2015 suffered from mental illness (Kelly, Lowery, Rich, Tate, and Jenkins, 2016).

With a somewhat different focus and finding, Johnson (2011) used officer self-report data from two agencies and found that for individuals perceived to have mental instability, there was no greater likelihood of receiving some force, but when there was force used, they were more likely to receive serious force than the individuals seen as being mentally stable. Again, there were potential multiplier effects from some individuals also being correlated with "using alcohol or drugs, displaying an abusive demeanor, possessing a weapon, and serious resistance by striking officers" (p. 137). Notable is the point that in an era of mental health deinstitutionalization, it is not uncommon that law enforcement and correctional officers and staff frequently come into contact with people with some type of mental illness.

Upper- and middle-class neighborhoods are often mistakenly thought not to harbor the myriad challenges of those in lower socio-economic areas. Drug use, intimate partner violence, alcohol and mental illness – all may be less frequently reported to law enforcement officers because of the structural characteristics of the neighborhood. In lower-income neighborhoods or housing, people often live in closer proximity which allows neighbors or passersby to be aware of activities or problems that are audible or visible. These dynamics result in more frequent calls to police that do not emanate from the affected residence, but from neighbors (Krishan et al., 2014).

Regardless of the neighborhood or setting, police may be called upon to take individuals into custody using state authority to protect the person or others, whether through court order or a criminal violation being charged. Non-criminal proceedings are likely those of civil commitment which come into play with juveniles or those who appear incapable of taking care of themselves or who may harm themselves or others. Many states allow law enforcement officers to take someone described this way into custody and deliver them to a mental health receiving facility, so that psychiatric personnel can perform an assessment to further determine what action or treatment may be in the best interests of the person. Generally, a standard of "danger to self or others" has been used for civil commitments, though the interpretation of what exactly this means has varied somewhat across states. Regardless of the definitional debate, due process has been held to apply when a person has been involuntarily hospitalized (*Jones v. United States*, 1983). The danger posed by the individual is assessed in different states along dimensions of type, immediacy, and likelihood (Schug and Fradella, 2015).

The accuracy of such initial assessments by law enforcement officers may logically be insufficient for a long-term commitment, which is why the second level of assessment by certified mental health professionals is required, with potential court review, to ensure due process is observed. The initial law enforcement tool is time-limited to perhaps no more than 72 hours before the person must be further evaluated. The issue of potential threat to self or others encapsulates the problems of risk assessment and the inherent lack of perfect prediction based on human behavior. Nonetheless, a democratic society concerned with the safety of all and respect for individual rights is left to address the treatment of those presenting with indications of possible danger, in ways arrived at through the best work of professionals from several disciplines.

Developmental Disability

A developmental disability is typically a permanent impairment of intellect or behavior which may or may not be included in a given state's mental illness definition of civil commitment (Schug and

Fradella, 2015). These types of disabilities, like almost any other, are not direct causal links to dangerous behavior. But public safety personnel may encounter behavior or communications challenges requiring a flexible approach. Individuals with an intellectual disability vary in the severity of the disability and in their coping mechanisms. The different social skills and methods of communication shown by those with an autism spectrum disorder (ASD), for example, can be misinterpreted by others, including public safety personnel. Some of the self-stimulating behaviors of ASD individuals can help calm them when stressed, and include:

- Visual: staring at lights, repetitive blinking, moving fingers in front of the eyes, hand-flapping
- Auditory: tapping ears, snapping fingers, making vocal sounds
- Tactile: rubbing the skin with one's hands or with another object, scratching
- Vestibular: rocking front to back, rocking side-to-side
- Taste: placing body parts or objects in one's mouth, licking objects
- Smell: smelling objects, sniffing people.

(Edelson, 2017, retrieved from https://www.autism.com/symptoms_self-stim)

The Autism Research Institute website also notes that:

Communication with individuals on the autism spectrum is complicated – law enforcement officials will benefit from training focusing on recognition and response to affected individuals.

- Do not rely on facial expression or body language
- Do not expect normal eye contact
- Be aware of potential for self-stimulating behaviors which may help calm the individual
- Self-stimulating behaviors may include hand flapping, finger flicking, eye blinking, rocking, pacing, repetitive noises, or echolalia
- Be aware of special communication devices the individual may use.

(https://www.autism.com/law_enforcement)

Jails and Prisons

It is well-known in the corrections component of the criminal justice system that a significant percentage of inmates suffer from some form of mental illness (Al-Rousan, Rubenstein, Sieleni, Deol, and Wallace, 2017; Sloan and Efeti, 2017; James and Glaze, 2006). Nearly two million individuals suffering from a mental illness are arrested and jailed annually (NAMI, n.d.). Such illnesses range from anxiety disorders and depression to serious psychotic disorders. The person with function-impairing mental illness is often faced with one or more concurrent challenges. These may include a criminal record, substance dependence or abuse, health, housing, and employment problems. Correctional facilities house large numbers of people who would benefit from and should have access to mental health services, yet such places are not funded, staffed, or programmatically designed in most cases to administer such services.

Unsurprisingly, inmates with serious mental illness have spent more time in restrictive housing within facilities, reported higher rates of being sexually victimized by other inmates, (BJS, 2007), initiated a suicide attempt (Gates, Turney, Ferguson, Walker, and Staples-Horne, 2017), and have engaged in rule violations or fighting (Srivastava et al., 2014; Walters, and Crawford, 2014). This reality brings greater need for officers to be well-trained and to use appropriate inmate management techniques when dealing with mentally ill offenders (Sloan and Efeti, 2017). Agencies should consistently provide training about mental health signs, symptoms, and strategies.

Suicidal Individuals

A phrase common to public safety personnel and the general public is "suicide by cop." This connotes a person who has decided to end his own life but the method he has chosen is to compel a law enforcement officer to carry out the act. Within contemporary law enforcement training, officers are familiarized with behavior that indicates mental illness and someone who is possibly suicidal, though no one should expect officers to predict such outcomes or actions. In few criminal justice functions is it more apparent that officers are tacitly expected to have capabilities in so many things. Staff are not expected to have the knowledge (let alone credentials) to diagnose, but the intention of training is to equip officers with adequate information to recognize the signs and symptoms of potential mental illness or suicidal intent.

Anyone may act in an unpredictable way, but a suicidal or mentally ill person may do so as part of a longer sequence of precipitating incidents or thought process. The Police Executive Research Forum (PERF) in their recently launched model of Integrating Communications Assessment and Tactics (ICAT) emphasizes this need to recognize behavior and adjust communications and tactics accordingly.

Stress/Emotion/Agitation

The consideration of those in an emotional or agitated state as a category of special population is more for reiteration of the dynamics rather than a classification of people with unique behaviors. The very fact of strong emotion is often a factor in many police–citizen encounters. With that said, consider the effects of stress, emotion, or significant levels of agitation or anger on the individual and his or her judgment and behavior. If someone is angry she may act out verbally or physically. Decision-making is likely not the same as when she is calm. Some stress responses are also muted by their long-term nature.

The phrase most people may quickly connect to stress is Post-Traumatic Stress Disorder or PTSD. And while many individuals suffer the effects of PTSD, there is a common public perception of military combat veterans as suffering a disproportionate occurrence of symptoms. This has implications for the training of officers and the continuing need to employ de-escalation techniques where practical (Weaver, Joseph, Dongon, Fairweather, and Ruzek, 2013). To be sure, those ex-military individuals who have served in combat may have a challenge or disability that is noticeable and diagnosed, or more subtle and possibly undiagnosed or untreated. PTSD is, however, far from unique to combat veterans. Millions of children are exposed each year to traumatic experiences that may affect them over the long term (Harris, Lieberman, and Marans, 2007; Miller-Graff, Scrafford, and Rice, 2016), and when considering violence and problem behaviors of at-risk youth (Logan-Greene, Nurius, and Thompson, 2012). The effects of PTSD on victims of intimate partner violence are quite well established (Schmidt, 2014; Glass, Perrin, Campbell, and Soekin, 2007; Perez, and Johnson, 2008). There is a nexus of PTSD-suffering veterans and intimate partner violence (IPV) that is important for care providers to understand as they help families deal with emotional and psychological stressors (Finley, Baker, Pugh, and Peterson, 2010). Police officers too are exposed to psychologically stressful and traumatic experiences over their career and there may be interplay between these stressors and IPV as well (Zavala, Melander, and Kurtz, 2015). This reality and the need for officers to be constantly vigilant and hypersensitive to their environment leave them vulnerable to PTSD (Covey, Shucard, Violanti, Lee, and Shucard, 2013).

It would be a shocking thing indeed if people began to call their local law enforcement agency and ask to have an officer drop by because everyone was happy and getting along with one another. Instead, in addition to myriad calls about various needs the public feels law enforcers should be able to address, bad behavior is high on the list. Circumstances in which emotions are running high and people are agitated take up their share of calls for service and incidents within the confines of a correctional institution. Often the person calling for a law enforcement response wants the situation to stop with no further action. The elegance of simply making things "stop" is not always an option afforded the officer when he or she arrives on scene. Someone in the grip of anger and the potentially compromised job being done by the prefrontal cortex of the brain, may react to an insult or perceived aggressive act of another by lashing out physically. Other emotional upsets can bring anger that subsequently brings police. The agitation, one feels, may bring on aggression. Yet aggression does not necessarily lead to violence. In any event, it is not an excuse to commit a criminal act and it is frequently why law enforcement is summoned to maintain the peace.

Alcohol, Drugs, and Physical Distress

While some people are described as "happy drunks," there is a body of research that describes the frequent connection between alcohol use and aggressive behavior. As with any single variable, we would not assert that alcohol *causes* violence or aggressive behavior. Effects that have been linked to various levels of consumption and the physical state of the person imbibing include reduced inhibitions, reduced sensitivity to pain, and the already mentioned aggression. As in the discussion of high emotion, the presence of alcohol seems commonplace in the interactions of police and booking room personnel with subjects brought to their attention. Alcohol and other substances may alter behavior and complicate any interaction between officers and individuals. This long established link between alcohol and aggression can manifest in how some people respond to officers on the street or as they arrive to a booking location after arrest (Goldstick et al., 2015). The National Crime Victimization Survey (NCVS) reported for 2007 that "about 26% of victims of violence reported that the offender was using drugs or alcohol" (BJS, 2007). The Bureau of Justice Statistics (BJS) has studied the association of drugs and alcohol for offenders and reported that high percentages of offenders were under the influence at the time of their offenses (BJS, 2007).

Various ingested substances can trigger violent or uncontrolled behavior (Vilke et al., 2012). Medical examiners, emergency room medical personnel, EMS and other first responders have dealt with the many facets of such substance-induced behavioral crises for a long time. Medical first responders and law enforcement also confront cases of excited delirium syndrome (ExDS), which is "characterized by extreme agitation and aggression in a patient with altered mental status. Patients with ExDS display violent behavior, increased pain tolerance and superhuman strength. These patients are difficult to physically restrain and continue to struggle even once restrained" (Ordoobadi and Kivlehan, 2017). Because these ExDS events and their risk of sudden death are rare, the presenting condition for first responders is challenging to diagnose and therefore address (Strote, Walsh, Auerbach, Burns, and Maher, (2014).

Physical distress or an acute medical condition or crisis may cause any of us to act in a bizarre fashion that appears to others to be out of control or dangerous. As an example, someone suffering from a panic attack may act frantically, quite unable to control the overwhelming feelings generated from the body's systems. The perceived suffocation symptom the person might feel may be induced by a variety of real or unknown triggers, but manifest as panic. The afflicted individual may appear unable to control his movement as he tries to "escape" the sensations he is experiencing. A person who is resisting, struggling, or acting in a bizarre fashion may be experiencing a medical emergency.

City of Canton v. Harris (1989), discussed in a previous chapter, bears a few reminders here. The issue the Supreme Court addressed in this case was the failure to train law enforcement officers. *Canton* involved police who had been assigned temporarily to jail duties without adequate training. The incident involved a woman who was incoherent and repeatedly fell down while in custody. The officers did not summon medical aid and the woman filed suit against the city. Arrived at via the underpinning of Title 42 U.S. Code, Section 1983, *Canton* established that a municipality or county could be held liable if it was shown that the entity's policies, practices, or customs caused an officer's unconstitutional behavior. The Court held that the basis of such a finding of liability would be that a failure to train would have to rise to the level of a "deliberate indifference to the rights of persons with whom the police come into contact." This does not leave lower courts with crystal clear guidance or a formulaic template, but it does leave continued attention to the training of officers and the rights of citizens.

Age or Physical Condition

Very young persons or older individuals may not be as robust physically as those in the range of young adult to middle age. Consideration, where feasible, should be given to apparent frailty or potential structural weaknesses when attempting to control a person through physical means or devices. Someone of small stature can and has killed another person much larger than himself and so there is no set calculus for when to use which type of force in controlling a person whom officers have authority to control. There are examples that seem to defy common sense: the elderly person felled by a conducted energy device (CED), the eight-year-old sprayed with OC, etc. Conflicting results from examinations of use of force methods and citizen and officer injuries do not provide a clear formula for what to use when. This may never come. However, if a person presents as exceedingly frail, has no apparent weapon, but manages to wheeze, "I'm not coming with you," it is probably best not to risk a collapse injury by deploying a CED. Circumstances are always going to vary, and this is why agency policy, officer training, official reporting, levels of review, and transparency of documentation for the benefit of the public and the courts, are important.

Young people, juveniles, children – individuals under the age of eighteen, are generally considered as a status-defined population. There is mixed motivation between those who focus on the legal standing established in Western law, and the psychological-maturational assumptions about younger people in society. The life course trajectory of most teens brings them into decision scenarios they are ill-equipped by experience to effectively handle. Unfortunately, with little life know-how, many do make poor decisions. We all hope to learn from these judgment errors. Along the way, however, teens' seeming lack of concern about consequences involve the making of decisions with a shallow reservoir of experience to draw upon. But simple choice mistakes are not the greatest concern of the many people tasked with addressing the consequences of juvenile actions. Juveniles commit delinquent acts that bring them into contact with both the criminal and juvenile justice systems, often with police first.

The use of force is based in large part on objective reasonableness, not age per se (Thornton and Schweer, 2016). One category of juvenile response is resistant behavior that may induce a force usage by a law enforcement officer, generally during an arrest. Another circumstance is resistant or violent behavior during a period of incarceration.

GOING GLOBAL

An examination of fatal force usage in Victoria, Australia between 1982 and 2007 showed that while policy and practice changes in Australia have reduced shooting fatalities by police overall, the overrepresentation of people with severe mental disorders is concerning (Kesic, Thomas, and Ogloff, 2010). A significant number of those killed had previous contact with the public mental health system, but more than 80 percent had previous contact with criminal justice.

In this study of the 48 people killed by law enforcement in Victoria over a 25-year period, researchers point to an overall lowering of such fatalities following a policy intervention by Victoria Police. Yet the rate of those with serious mental illness being killed did not drop. Resultant recommendations included an emphasis on the need for partnering between police and mental health providers to continue, and that police receive ongoing training to assist them in dealing with persons with mental illness.

Summary

Given the research pointing to a connection between mental health and inmate behavior (James and Glaze, 2006), the training of officers, as well as policy construction, should reflect what is known and how this knowledge might influence the escalation or reduction of resistance or violence in any given situation. Immensely important work in neurobiology and neurocriminology by writers such as Robert Sapolsky and Adrian Raine has re-expanded the previously shrunken horizons of earlier forays into biological explanations of behavior à la physiognomy, phrenology and atavistic man. Altered mental status due to intoxication or medical emergency can come with bizarre or aggressive behavior. Regardless of the early or late origin of behavior, quite often it is the officer on the beat or in the booking suite who is called upon to deal with the behavior itself. Sometimes this contact further involves a use of force.

Training for criminal justice employees continues to improve, not least in the area of mental illness and considerations related to special populations. When making force decisions, an officer must gauge to the extent possible the subject's ability to understand and comply with the officer's commands. Officers may know little or nothing about a person's mental condition, leaving them with witness or family member statements and the observable behavior of the subject. The witnesses and family members may be mistaken, incorrect, or lying when they tell call-takers or officers about someone's past or instant behavior – whether aggravating or mitigating. Even if a corrections officer (for example) was familiar with the previous behavior of an inmate, circumstances may have changed and led to unpredictable or violent behavior by that inmate. Similarly, a person on the street previously encountered by a law enforcement officer may not act as they did on a previous encounter, whether cooperative or resistant/hostile.

Agencies must have policies that address interacting with special populations. Agency training must be integrated with the policies, and it would be beneficial as officers work to become more knowledgeable about such individuals that supervisors be available to support them in their interactions.

KEY TERMS

Crisis Intervention Team (CIT)
Impairment
Mental illness
Liability
City of Canton v. Harris

Discussion Questions

1. Select one form of mental illness and explain how it may influence behaviors that cause people to contact public safety employees.
2. How does the type of substance a person is consuming potentially affect how they may behave?
3. Discuss the challenges in arriving at the scene of an unknown trouble call with only a report of someone "acting crazy."
4. What makes the use of force with someone very young or very old particularly challenging?

TRY THIS

Go to the website of the National Institute of Mental Illness (NAMI) at https://www.nami.org/Learn-More/Public-Policy/Jailing-People-with-Mental-Illness. Find "The Stepping Up Initiative," go to the page for the program, and listen to the one-minute animation that describes the program.

References

Alpert, G. (2015). Police use of force and the suspect with mental illness: a methodological conundrum. *Criminology and Public Policy*, 14(2), 277–283.

Al-Rousan, T., Rubenstein, L., Sieleni, B., Deol, H., and Wallace, R. B. (2017). Inside the nation's largest mental health institution: a prevalence study in a state prison system. *BMC Public Health*, 17(1), 342.

Bittner, E. (1967). Police discretion in emergency apprehension of mentally ill persons. *Social Problems*, 14, 278–292.

Bittner, E. (1974). Florence Nightingale in pursuit of Willie Sutton: a theory of the police. In H. Jacob (Ed.), *Potential for reform of criminal justice*. Beverly Hills, CA: Sage, pp. 17–44.

BJS (Bureau of Justice Statistics). (2007).*Drug and crime facts, criminal victimization in the United States, 2007*. Statistical tables, table 32. Washington, DC.

Bonfine, N., Ritter, C., and Munetz, M. R. (2014). Police officer perceptions of the impact of Crisis Intervention Team (CIT) programs. *International Journal of Law and Psychiatry*, 37 (Police responses to persons with a mental illness: international perspectives), 341–350.

Cordner, G. (2006). *People with mental illness*. Problem-Oriented Guides for Police: Problem-Specific Guides series, no. 40. Washington, DC: COPS Office.

Covey, T. J., Shucard, J. L., Violanti, J. M., Lee, J., and Shucard, D. W. (2013). The effects of exposure to traumatic stressors on inhibitory control in police officers: a dense electrode array study using a Go/NoGo continuous performance task. *International Journal of Psychophysiology*, 87 (Electrophysiological and neuroimaging studies of cognitive control: evidence from go/nogo and other executive function tasks), 363–375.

Edelson, S. M. (2017). *Self-stimulatory behavior*. Autism Research Institute. https://www.autism.com/symptoms_self-stim

Ferdik, F. V. (2014). The influence of strain on law enforcement legitimacy evaluations. *Journal of Criminal Justice*, 42, 443–451.

Finley, E., Baker, M., Pugh, M., and Peterson, A. (2010). Patterns and perceptions of intimate partner violence committed by returning veterans with post-traumatic stress disorder. *Journal of Family Violence*, 25(8), 737–743.

Gates, M. L., Turney, A., Ferguson, E., Walker, V., and Staples-Horne, M. (2017). Associations among substance use, mental health disorders, and self-harm in a prison population: examining group risk for suicide attempt. *International Journal of Environmental Research and Public Health*, 14(3).

Glass, N., Perrin, N., Campbell, J. C., and Soeken, K. (2007). The protective role of tangible support on post-traumatic stress disorder symptoms in urban women survivors of violence. *Research in Nursing and Health*, 30, 558–568.

Goffman, E. (1961). *Asylums: essays on the social situation of mental patients and other inmates*. Garden City, NY: Anchor Books.

Goldstick, J. E., Lipton, R. I., Carter, P., Stoddard, S. A., Newton, M. F., Reischl, T., and Cunningham, R. M. (2015). The effect of neighborhood context on the relationship between substance misuse and weapons aggression in urban adolescents seeking ED care. *Substance Use and Misuse*, 50(5), 674–684.

Harris, W. W., Lieberman, A. F., and Marans, S. (2007). In the best interests of society. *Journal of Child Psychology and Psychiatry*, 48(3–4), 392–411.

James, D. J. and Glaze, L. E. (2006). *Mental health problems of prison and jail inmates*. No. NCJ 213600. Washington, DC: U.S. Department of Justice, Office of Justice Programs, Bureau of Justice Statistics.

Jennings, W. G. and Hudak, E. J. (2015). Police response to persons with mental illness. In R. G. Dunham and G. P. Alpert (Eds.), *Critical issues in policing: contemporary readings*. 5th ed. Long Grove, IL: Waveland.

Johnson, R. (2011). Suspect mental disorder and police use of force. *Criminal Justice and Behavior*, 38(2), 127–145.

Kaminski, R., Digiovanni, C., and Downs, R. (2004). The use of force between the police and persons with impaired judgment. *Police Quarterly*, 7(3) 311–338.

Kara, F. B. (2014). Police interactions with the mentally ill: the role of procedural justice. *Canadian Graduate Journal of Sociology and Criminology*, 3(1), 79–94.

Kelly, K., Lowery, W., Rich, S., Tate, J., and Jenkins, J. (2016). Fatal shootings by police remain relatively unchanged after two years. *Washington Post*, December 30. Retrieved from: https://www.washingtonpost.com/investigations/fatal-shootings-by-police-remain-relatively-unchanged-after-two-years/2016/12/30/fc807596-c3ca-11e6-9578-0054287507db_story.html?utm_term=.faa91ff55f18

Kesic, D. and Thomas, S. D. (2014). Do prior histories of violence and mental disorders impact on violent behaviour during encounters with police? *International Journal of Law and Psychiatry*, 37 (Police responses to persons with a mental illness: international perspectives), 409–414.

Kesic, D., Thomas, S., and Ogloff, J. (2010). Mental illness among police fatalities in Victoria 1982–2007: case linkage study. *Australian and New Zealand Journal of Psychiatry*, 44(5), 463–468.

Kesic, D., Thomas, S., and Ogloff, J. (2013). Estimated rates of mental disorders in, and situational characteristics of, incidents of nonfatal use of force by police. *Social Psychiatry and Psychiatric Epidemiology*, 48(2), 225–232.

Krishan, S., Bakeman, R., Broussard, B., Cristofaro, S. L., Hankerson-Dyson, D., Husbands, L., and Compton, M. T. (2014). The influence of neighborhood characteristics on police officers' encounters with persons suspected to have a serious mental illness. *International Journal of Law and Psychiatry*, 37 (Police responses to persons with a mental illness: international perspectives), 359–369.

Logan-Greene, P., Nurius, P. S., and Thompson, E. A. (2012). Distinct stress and resource profiles among at-risk adolescents: implications for violence and other problem behaviors. *Child and Adolescent Social Work Journal*, 29(5), 373–390.

Miller-Graff, L. E., Scrafford, K., and Rice, C. (2016). Conditional and indirect effects of age of first exposure on PTSD symptoms. *Child Abuse and Neglect*, 51, 303–312.

Morabito, M. and Socia, K. (2015). Is dangerousness a myth? Injuries and police encounters with people with mental illnesses. *Criminology and Public Policy*, 14(2), 253–276.

Morabito, M. S., Socia, K., Wik, A., and Fisher, W. H. (2017). The nature and extent of police use of force in encounters with people with behavioral health disorders. *International Journal of Law and Psychiatry*, 50, 31–37.

Myers, C. A. (2017). Police violence against people with mental disabilities: the immutable duty under the ADA to reasonably accommodate during arrest. *Vanderbilt Law Review*, 70(4), 1393–1426.

NAMI. (n.d.) *Jailing people with mental illness*. National Alliance on Mental Illness. Retrieved from: https://www.nami.org/Learn-More/Public-Policy/Jailing-People-with-Mental-Illness

NIMH. (2015). *Serious mental illness (SMI) among U.S. adults*. National Institute of Mental Health.

Ordoobadi, A. and Kivlehan, S. M. (2017). Excited delerium: ExDS is characterized by extreme agitation and aggression in a patient with altered mental status. *EMS World*, 46(5), 26–32.

Perez, S. and Johnson, D. M. (2008). PTSD compromises battered women's future safety. *Journal of Interpersonal Violence*, 23, 635–651.

Schmidt, I. D. (2014). Addressing PTSD in low-income victims of intimate partner violence: moving toward a comprehensive intervention. *Social Work*, 59(3), 253–260.

Schug, R. A. and Fradella, H. F. (2015). *Mental illness and crime*. Thousand Oaks, CA: Sage.

Schulenberg, J. L. (2016). The dynamics of police–citizen encounters with mentally ill persons. *Criminal Justice and Behavior*, 43(4), 459–482.

Sloan, B. L. and Efeti, D. E. (2017). Taking care of the mentally ill. *Corrections Today*, 79(3), 42–44.

Srivastava, P., Eqbal, S., Kiran, M., Kumar, P., Kumar, P., Mishra, S. K., and Singh, A. R. (2014). Personality traits and problem solving ability among mentally ill offenders. *Dysphrenia*, 5(2), 98–105.

Strote, J., Walsh, M., Auerbach, D., Burns, T., and Maher, P. (2014). Medical conditions and restraint in patients experiencing excited delirium. *American Journal of Emergency Medicine*, 32(9), 1093–1096.

Thornton, R. and Schweer, R. (2016). It's not the age – it's the action: juveniles and the use of force. *Perspectives* (0821–1507), 40(1), 26–32.

Vilke, G. M., DeBard, M. L., Chan, T. C., Ho, J. D., Dawes, D. M., Hall, C., and Bozeman, W. P. (2012). Excited Delirium Syndrome (ExDS): defining based on a review of the literature. *The Journal of Emergency Medicine*, 43(5), 897–905.

Walters, G. D. and Crawford, G. (2014). Major mental illness and violence history as predictors of institutional misconduct and recidivism: main and interaction effects. *Law and Human Behavior*, 38(3), 238–247.

Watson, A. C., Swartz, J., Bohrman, C., Kriegel, L. S., and Draine, J. (2014). Understanding how police officers think about mental/emotional disturbance calls. *International Journal of Law and Psychiatry*, 37, 351–358.

Weaver, C. M., Joseph, D., Dongon, S. N., Fairweather, A., and Ruzek, J. I. (2013). Enhancing services response to crisis incidents involving veterans: a role for law enforcement and mental health collaboration. *Psychological Services*, 10(1), 66–72.

Zavala, E., Melander, L. A., and Kurtz, D. L. (2015). The importance of social learning and critical incident stressors on police officers' perpetration of intimate partner violence. *Victims and Offenders*, 10(1), 51–73.

Cases Cited

City of Canton v. Harris (1989)

Jones v. United States, 463 U.S. 354 (1983)

12

THE FUTURE IS NOW

CHAPTER OUTLINE

Introduction
The media and society
Increased training
Use your words
Technology
Use of force by people not employed in criminal justice
Procedural and organizational justice
Summary
Features: What-Why, Going Global
Key Terms
Discussion Questions
Try This
References

STUDENT LEARNING OUTCOMES

- Students will be able to evaluate factors observed in media coverage of use of force situations.
- Students will be able to apply the concept of procedural justice to use of force policy.
- Students will be able to explain the role of technology in force encounters.
- Students will be able to contrast the influence of law and policy with training and individual behavior on force outcomes.
- Students will be able to explain the hypothesized dynamic of militarization of police.

Introduction

The future is a precarious place to go, but what choice do we have? The need to use force is present in the work done by public safety professionals. This reality will not change within the foreseeable future, if ever. There is no lack of pithy sayings regarding the future and how it is unknown or will be different than today. What we do know with some level of certainty are a number of realities that impact the use of force in society. Throughout history in organized society there have been individuals designated to keep peace and enforce the laws or rules of that society.

As we reflect on the use of force, it is important to remember that there are more than 20,000 separate police and corrections agencies that make up the American criminal justice "system." We know that some of these agencies have been changing their approaches to the use of force. In the last two decades many law enforcement agencies have sharply curtailed vehicle pursuits as they examined the reasons why many pursuits are ill-advised. Some police organizations such as Camden County, NJ have adopted a statement of "sanctity of life" to their use of force policies that might be seen as trying to extend the timeline of action indefinitely to avoid the use of lethal force. This may appear appropriate as a statement of philosophy. It will be left to the varied agencies and communities to reflect on whether the phrase represents an actual paradigm shift in approaching the use of force, or at least lethal force in certain situations. Similarly, some agencies incorporate into policy the language of "use the minimum amount of force necessary." This verbiage can have ramifications for litigation and the potential to be misconstrued in the post hoc evaluation of force usage. The U.S. Supreme court in *Graham v. Connor* (1989) required law enforcement officers to use "reasonable" force based on the totality of the circumstances known to the officer. The issue moving forward will be how this new approach to the use of force by some agencies might impact the perception of reasonableness as required by the courts

We have come back time and again throughout the text to comment on the decentralized nature of the criminal justice system and what impact that has on policy, training, and the gathering of meaningful data to improve both. The FBI's UCR program gathers a certain amount of gross crime data. The decades-long interrupted effort at passing the torch to the National Incident-Based Reporting System (NIBRS) remains incomplete. The occasional and emotional calls for central recording of lethal police force events are notable but not new (see Shane, 2016). Ultimately, such calls for better data tracking may not spur the vast and decentralized criminal justice agencies and the governmental entities that fund them to create or complete the infrastructure and hire the people needed to gather the information to create a clearer picture of the use of force. We therefore do not know the full picture of the use of force.

Small agencies with inexperienced chiefs and sheriffs as administrators impact the development and implementation of appropriate and forward-looking policies. Large agencies with a great distance between administrators and officers may not achieve sufficient alignment between espoused principles and street or cellblock practices. Efforts such as the President's Task Force on 21st Century Policing (2015) initiated by President Barack Obama detail recommendations and potential best practices to continue the work on community-police engagement. The first line in the introduction to that report is this: "Trust between law enforcement agencies and the people they protect and serve is essential in a democracy" (p. 1). Many administrators believe (correctly or incorrectly) that *their* public in their local community has faith in what the agency is doing. This mindset of "not us" enables a common organizational phenomenon of inertia as you perceive *others* as the ones who need to change, to improve.

The apprehension of lawbreakers may involve the use of varying levels of force, dictated generally by lack of cooperation by the offender. Breaches of the peace, which may also result in a criminal charge, may require more than the arrival and visible presence of law enforcement to prevent them. Restraining inmates who are fighting or resisting is not uncommon in a corrections facility. This state of affairs has existed throughout recorded history and will likely extend to the far distant future. What then can provide more clarity to agencies and officers and knowledge to the public and lawmakers about the state-sanctioned use of force by authorized actors? In this final chapter, let's consider a few ideas and directions for those involved in the production of force usage events.

In March, 2012, the International Association of Chiefs of Police (IACP) and the Community Oriented Policing Services office of the U.S. Department of Justice published a summary report of a use of force symposium they had convened in May 2011. In their conclusion, the group suggested the following topic areas be addressed to help inform the public perception of excessive force and guide agencies in their approach to force issues:

- *Officer mindset*: Hold regular briefings at both the command and officer level to fully understand how officers think about force issues, including policy adherence, liability, internal force reviews, public perceptions, and suspects' use of force against officers. Their perceptions will have a direct impact on how they use or do not use force.
- *Force policy and training*: Conduct a review of force policies, looking at both state and local policy models, to ensure currency and comprehensiveness. Revise and enhance all policies as needed. Make sure all use of force training is entirely consistent with policy and it both reinforces and further articulates policy intent.
- *Force reporting*: Review current use of force reporting policies in the context of both state and national models, and update or revise those policies as appropriate or needed. Proactively use that data to conduct annual use of force reviews that can influence policy and training enhancement.
- *Communications strategy*: Review local communications strategies to ensure preparedness and transparency in the event of a use of force incident that necessitates public commentary. On a regular basis, seek opportunities to gauge public perception on general use of force issues, absent of any recent incident.
- *Media*: Work with local media to educate them on use of force policy, training, and practices so they view and report on future incidents in an informed, contextual manner. Share that education with governing body leaders so they have the same contextual information as they review use of force incidents.

(p. 29)

As we look ahead at use of force issues, we discuss these and other topics in this final chapter.

The Media and Society

In an age of widespread electronic devices, connection to various sources of information is ubiquitous but not without peril. The proliferation of so-called news blogs and the myriad websites filled with outright false information can be challenging for the average citizen to navigate and for the many well-established professional news organizations to contend with. And yet the public relies on its chosen outlet of information or the media for most of its information about criminal justice matters (Dowler and Zawilski, 2007). We know that a majority of young people get their news only from social media and that this presents problems. Problems that are not merely that a large number of people may be mis- or under-informed, but that a fundamental imperative to seek a thorough recounting of an incident or statements that have undergone editorial review and verification are unknown or unimportant to much of a generation of citizens. This reality presents a challenge for government agencies and leaders who have a sincere and honest interest in providing factual information and context on a wide range of issues that are of interest to the public. Not the least of these would be furnishing accurate information in the wake of a serious use of force incident.

The sometimes tense relation between media and law enforcement can be a complicating factor to timely and accurate provision of information to the public. The two have different goals and timetables. It is typically appropriate that criminal justice agencies take time to gather facts and assemble a narrative of what occurred in a particular situation. Media organizations generally are driven to get *some* information out quickly and ahead of competitors for viewership or readership. In addition, a criminal justice agency is providing stark prose while the news wants an eye-grabbing headline and a story of an occurrence to interest readers. Thus, a fundamental difference in approach.

> Agency representatives may spend a great deal of time and effort explaining why certain details cannot be released in a case for fear of damaging the investigation only to have media say or print a terse, "Police refused to release information." The media may use this phrase to create an appearance of secretiveness or lack of cooperation by an agency.
>
> *(Hough and Tatum, 2014, p. 72)*

News stories have various impacts, including on how officers view themselves and their perceptions of how the public views them. Negative publicity has been linked to lower feelings of self-legitimacy in police (Nix and Wolfe, 2017), and this may relate to lowered motivation for the work. Those first 7–10 minutes of the nightly newscast (for those who watch) stoke the mean-world view of much of the public and provide little in the way of nuanced insights as to the circumstances involved in the majority of force usage events. News organizations have a tremendous opportunity, and responsibility, to show an issue as important as the use of force in a balanced way. It may be less dramatic but media members should be cautious to not take actions, isolated incidents, or incomplete facts out of context. News media organizations and representatives should not be apologists for criminal justice agencies, yet they should offer accurate statistics about the rarity of force usage.

Agencies for their part should try to provide information as expediently as possible. This has successfully taken the form of meeting with community or religious leaders in sessions closed to the media to show available evidence early in an investigation to help the community understand what may have occurred without simply providing a two-minute story on the news. The very real liability considerations for agencies temper the inclination to overshare information before a clear picture is available. Counsels general and government risk managers warn against the "liability of apology."

Increased Training

In this consequential, if infrequent, area of public safety responsibility referred to as the use of force, agencies must review and update policies as needed and provide the training, supervision, and leadership to equip and support officers so they in turn can appropriately serve the public. In the chapter on training we discussed not only the use of force but also a bit about the complexity of the role of a law enforcement or corrections officers in contemporary Western democracies. Training should be on a scheduled basis and when qualifications of various types are needed to document ongoing proficiency, this should not supplant actual training. In other words, firing a qualifications round that reflects marksmanship is not the same as scenario training or review of agency policy and legal updates. Similarly, sign-off sheets for corrections or law enforcement officers that document receipt of new or updated policies or procedures is not the same as conducting physical training or participating in interactive scenarios.

The force response training provided for recruit officers in a basic academy is not sufficient if officers do not receive refresher training. Such basic training and in-service training for officers should include verbal interaction skills, dynamics of dealing with the mentally ill or those impaired by substance use, potential for racial bias in force decision-making, threat assessment, and the use of physical control techniques and devices, to name a few important topics. The Police Executive Research Forum (PERF), in its training guide for Integrating Communications, Assessment, and Tactics (ICAT) (2016), observes: "Throughout our research on use of force, one critical issue surfaced repeatedly – the need for better and more consistent training of police officers" (p. 5). Part of threat assessment involves the idea of predicting danger. This does not automatically lead to the ability either to predict force or to select a non-forceful alternative to suit every circumstance. Criminal justice officers do face violent and potentially violent people and encounters. "Nature of the work" is a simplistic and familiar phrase. What do we mean at a deeper more consequential level? The "work" is about being called to places and circumstances imbued with tension, conflict, uncertainty, potential danger, and the opportunity for things to shift dramatically in mere moments. The U.S. Supreme Court explained in *Graham v. Connor* that

> The calculus of reasonableness must embody allowance for the fact that police officers are often forced to make split-second judgments – in circumstances that are tense, uncertain, and rapidly evolving – about the amount of force that is necessary in a particular situation.
>
> *(1989)*

Violence and aggression must at times be met by force usage when officers seek to control or take into custody various individuals or intercede in a group conflict. The prediction of violence is an inexact science. Public safety personnel assess and act based on the people and circumstances they encounter. The human officer can and does err at times, sometimes with tragic consequences. Researchers have found that individuals faced with a potential threat are more often to perceive such a threat if its focus is a black person (Lee, 2016; Nix, Campbell, Byers, and Alpert, 2017). This implicit bias, as well as instances of intentionally inappropriate profiling, has been chronicled in all manner of criminal justice system actions from stop-and-frisk, to prosecutorial decisions, to sentencing. Training, policies aimed at reduction of inadvertent or intentional practices, and vocal leadership on racial bias are crucial and can have positive results (Lee, 2016). Agencies in the 21st century must commit fully to addressing unconscious bias, implicit bias, and racism in order to best prepare officers to perform their duties. Training and open dialogue are key, and so are educational efforts for the media and through the media to inform the public.

WHAT-WHY

On July 28, 2017, President Donald Trump delivered a law-and-order speech ostensibly aimed at efforts to combat the gang MS-13. While attempting to convey a message of support to law enforcement, the president praised "rough" tactics in arresting people and said that police should not protect people's heads as they put them into squad cars, saying "You can take the hand away." President Trump added, "Please don't be too nice." Law enforcement agencies across the U.S. pushed back against the president's remarks and reinforced the need and commitment to treating people, including people arrested, properly. The International Association of Chiefs of Police, in a statement posted the same day, said in part: "Managing use of force is one of the most difficult challenges faced by law enforcement agencies .... Law enforcement officers are trained to treat all individuals, whether they are a complainant, suspect, or defendant, with dignity and respect. This is the bedrock principle behind the concepts of procedural justice and police legitimacy."

(Statement from the International Association of Chiefs of Police on Police Use of Force, July 28, 2017)

GOING GLOBAL

In the U.K. practitioners, politicians, academics, and the public all are in a period of reflection and searching as they consider the traditional mode of the police officer as not being armed with a gun. Certainly the increased threat of domestic and international terrorist actors creates in the minds of many people an exception to the historic model. The interaction of the average citizen with the average non-Authorized Firearm Officer (AFO) is neatly separated in the minds of many. But is this something of an artificial dichotomy? A truism of policing is the unpredictability of what you will face next. Squires and Kennison (2010), writing about this most crucial aspect of policing, observed: "The difficulties associated with spontaneous and unpredictable events increases the likelihood that mistakes and errors will be made. Yet we know that violence in shooting, even when practiced by seasoned professionals, is hazardous and surrounded by tensions, pressures and various perceptual distortions" (p. 2).

   With more time spent using any tool or performing any function, there is a statistical increase in undesirable outcomes. So too an increase in recent years of gang-related crime and violence must be considered. The law enforcement challenges of the Schengen Area are not inconsequential. With little to no passport or physical controls at the mutual borders of the participating European states, the comfort that many British citizens find in living in a non-gun culture may be largely illusory.

   The people in the process of confrontation and control are individuals and officers. The circumstances may start out calm enough or without foreknowledge of an arrest. Things can change in an instant as an officer realizes that someone must be arrested or someone realizes he is to be arrested. The intense emotion and physical exertion that may erupt during the transaction are integral components of detaining a person against their will. The stress on officers of anticipating such dynamics, as well as in the moments of engagement, can have immediate and long-lasting effects. Stress is particularly common among officers and it is connected to health and cognitive concerns. With the stress–induced production of cortisol, the obesity and general decline in fitness from shift work and sedentary periods of time between tasks, officers are at risk of diabetes, cardiac diseases, and unhealthy compensatory habits such as substance abuse (Christopher et al., 2016). These physical manifestations may intertwine symbiotically with psychological challenges. Depression is not uncommon for many who work in professional roles that bring them constantly into contact with people in tragic circumstances or in the grip of strong emotions. Suicide and short lifespan are both elevated among officers as compared to the general population.

That officers' decision-making may be negatively affected by various physical and psychological realities is unsurprising. Many of the sympathetic nervous system (SNS) responses that any human experiences are known to modify bodily functions and mental processes. Efforts to introduce physical fitness programs are always promising, and initiatives such as mindfulness training, breathing exercises, or even yoga and tai chi, are not New Age nonsense nor snake-oil. Focused techniques to assist the parasympathetic nervous system (PNS) in returning the body and mind to normal functioning can benefit most people, let alone the peace officer. In future, agencies must emphasize health and wellness programs for their officers as a way to influence force usage.

Use Your Words

The old wine of "interpersonal communication" in the new bottle of "de-escalation" remains an important focus for officers trying to convince people to do this or that. Under a rubric of tactical communications, officers learn and practice principles of how to most effectively use phrases, body language, and various verbal strategies to defuse potentially violent situations. It is certainly important to remember that it is not the efforts of an officer alone that determines whether a citizen or citizen inmate acts out physically or creates a hazardous situation for the officer or others. The "use of force-fulness" discussed earlier in the book, is an important skill that develops and is refined over time as an officer gains experience in either law enforcement or corrections. The command presence of an officer is effectively coupled with dialogue to interact and direct individuals with the intention of guiding them away from confrontation or arrest.

Such "use of force-fulness" has been known throughout history as a way to gain control of many situations and give direction to and gain compliance from people who are upset, scared, or confused. A dimension of forcefulness or command presence can be the appearance or actual employment of focused anger or intensity. Isn't anger a bad thing? It certainly is when the emotion disengages inhibitory mechanisms in the mind of someone who may flow from angry words to anger-fueled action. Yet some degree of focused anger has long been known to augment a persons fighting ability or provide a survival edge, whether confronting a saber-tooth tiger in a forest or an armed felon in an alley or on a roadside at 3 a.m. As an encounter transitions from the period of survival or threat-management to a control mode, the human officer must overcome and channel chemicals in his system to scan the environment for additional danger, regrouping attentional resources and working to regain fine motor skills.

That physiological and psychological reactions and responses combine and sometimes collide as they encounter and are engulfed in resistance is an evolutionarily-informed dynamic. The event termination response (ETR) (Hough, 2017) of both a person pursued and his pursuer is often fraught with danger, and there is certainly the potential for inexact decision-making and the less-than-perfect physical performance that every physical skills trainer warns trainees about, as they transfer from the controlled environment of a training venue to the roadway or back alley of the real pursuit. Continued rigorous research is needed that can provide guidance in training efforts and human performance and self-regulation.

Threat assessment is, ideally, ongoing. While taking a tactical pause before fully engaging in the dynamics of a call, the officer is working to assess the scene and the people present. The efforts of the Police Executive Research Forum (PERF) in developing the approach and training of Integrating Communications, Assessment, and Tactics (ICAT) is an important example of a professional organization of leaders focusing their efforts on a critical aspect of the police function – the use of force. It is notable that the organization stresses that this is not a panacea nor a method that should put officers in harm's way through hesitation or scrambling for the "right" technique at the wrong moment. PERF is clear that this is not about confronting a person who is wielding a firearm and trying to strike up a casual conversation.

But many opportunities for a studied approach to certain call types or individuals involve the nexus of force usage and encounters with those exhibiting signs and symptoms of a serious mental illness (SMI), frequent in both law enforcement and corrections settings. Those with diagnosed or undiagnosed serious mental illness (SMI) are typically unknown to public safety personnel unless through their behavior or a family member's call (McTackett and Thomas, 2017). There continues to be great promise in continuing training related to physiological and psychological responses related to the use of force, and agencies can access a wide variety of sources to provide education and training.

Technology

The Technology Policy Framework put forward by the International Association of Chiefs of Police (2014) provides an important reminder regarding the use of technology:

> Realizing the value that technology promises law enforcement can only be achieved through proper planning, implementation, training, deployment, use, and management of the technology and the information it provides. Like all resources and tools available to law enforcement, the use of new technologies must be carefully considered and managed. Agencies must clearly articulate their strategic goals for the technology, and this should be aligned with the broader strategic plans of the agency and safety needs of the public. Thorough and ongoing training is required to ensure that the technology performs effectively, and that users are well versed in the operational policies and procedures defined and enforced by the agency.
>
> *(p. 7)*

One group of researchers has referred to body-worn camera video as a "world-wide uncontrolled social experiment taking place" (Ariel et al., 2015). Their multi-site study showed a 14 percent higher rate per 1,000 of assaults *against* officers equipped with cameras. The same study found no change in use of force rates *by* officers. This may represent the type of unrelated factor that differs from a hypothesized or hoped for outcome such as reduced force usage *because* of wearing cameras. We must also caution against the "CSI Effect of BWC." There is a grossly exaggerated expectation that having a single (or even multiple) point recording of some of the activity in an encounter is tantamount to *understanding* the entire encounter. That commentators or critics across the spectrum may naively exhort people to "believe your own eyes" profoundly leads astray those who sincerely want or need to understand what happened. Support for the benefits BWC may provide to citizens, officers, and agencies should not be equated with the ability to make an accurate assessment of an event (Culhane, Boman, and Schweitzer, 2016).

Researchers in Washington, DC conducted a seven-month study of the effects of body-worn cameras (BWC) on documented use of force, complaints filed by citizens, and the use of discretion by officers as indicated by certain types of arrests (Yokum, Ravishankar, and Coppock, 2017). The researchers randomly assigned just over 1,000 Metropolitan DC officers with BWC and compared them to a second group of 1,000 officers who did not have the cameras. The study found no statistical difference between the two groups, and provides added information to consider in deciding whether to go to the expense of this particular technology and the complications of public records availability, storage costs, and additional personnel to manage the data. Absent evidence of effectiveness, many jurisdictions have to carefully weigh the pros and cons of such a policy decision.

Drones and many robotic devices are essentially remote-controlled tools. While very few agencies can either afford or need a helicopter and all of its attendant expenses, we can see that drones equipped with camera, thermal, GPS, and perhaps weapons are already within reach of many if not most agencies (Straub, 2014; Gettinger, 2017). Miniaturization, expanded capabilities, and cost reduction is an axiom for technology; there still remain opportunities for criminal justice agencies to acquire and utilize civilian-appropriate military surplus to facilitate many tasks. The beginnings of autonomous technology introduction into the public safety field are underway with various surveillance devices (e.g., facial recognition software to complement CCTV) and investigative tools (e.g., AI to augment case-management software for detectives). Crowd monitoring to predict movement and deploy resources is in use, and such efforts may help prevent losing control of large groups and thereby reduce the likelihood of some force usage.

WHAT-WHY

Since first authorized in 1990, the federal government's "1033 program" has funneled surplus equipment valued at $5.4 billion to local public safety agencies. Originally intended under the National Defense Authorization Act to bolster local agency capabilities in the "Drug War," items sometimes too expensive for the budgets of America's predominantly small agencies have come to be used for responding to different circumstances such as the 2015 San Bernardino shooting incident where two individuals, a man and a woman, shot and killed 14 people and wounded 21 more. Such shooting incidents that last long enough to activate teams with specialized equipment are rare, but law enforcement agencies believe it is better to be prepared.

There were cutbacks under the administration of President Obama after concerns voiced by some citizens that police departments appeared too militarized. However, in August 2017 President Trump signed an executive order to rescind the previous directive.

So again we look at views of those who feel the deployment of SWAT teams is either too frequent or perhaps disproportional to the potential danger. We examine the safeguards in place in the form of agency policy and oversight to ensure that when force is used it follows policy and law. Law enforcement and correctional agencies are already considered paramilitary by the use of rank structure, uniforms, and the authority to use arms. Of course law enforcement differs from the military because we grant our police the authority to use force against *us*, the citizenry. At the moment of employing force, the question turns on objective reasonableness, not choice of weapon. Technology continues to hold promise but its future impact on the use of force is not yet clear. Body-worn cameras will increase transparency, though not automatically understanding context. Whether BWCs will influence use of force by reducing or minimizing it, or improving or speeding up the review response or complaint and litigation landscape, is unknown. There is a need to continue monitoring and researching BWC issues. Various other technologies will help the overall efforts of criminal justice agencies and, by extension, the public.

Use of Force by People Not Employed in Criminal Justice

Virtually all industries experience discomfort as they look around at how their particular landscape has changed and then look off into the distance and try to make out the shape of things to come. Public safety personnel certainly fit this mold when considering a shift of some core functions, or at least a sharing of law enforcement and corrections with private sector entities. National and personal views of competition and capitalism predispose many if not most Americans to the general notion of private provision of goods and services – even those viewed as traditionally the province of government institutions and employees.

In England and subsequently in the United States, the early years of organized policing involved a hybrid of publicly hired police and compensated private investigators and enforcers. Jail and prison facilities often allowed for private funding of some practices and profit for those using inmate labor. To be sure, these arrangements presented many problems and represented the lack of public agency resources or orientation to certain activities more than a mature policy on public policing or penal practices.

Today, private for-profit corporations once again vie for the chance to receive public dollars to house inmates or fight in overseas U.S. conflicts. As for the provision of policing services, a broad reading of the term will find everything from alarm monitoring, to armored car service, to uniformed security officers in business buildings or gated communities. Those who can afford security services take advantage of various arrangements; those lacking the finances are perhaps what Harvard professor Mark Moore loosely referred to as the "police of the poor" (1990). What he meant by this was a prediction that public law enforcement would increasingly handle duties on public avenues and property while many affluent citizens relied on private employees for provision of security arrangements. Twenty-five years on, private companies and public officials continue to work through the daily coordination of providing security to people and places, layered with newer concerns of homeland security-driven critical infrastructure and key resources (CIKR) protection.

Private contractors are able to use some force as they restrain a shoplifter or break up a fight at a private establishment. Overstepping their limited force authority can result in criminal charges or civil litigation, as with public law enforcement and corrections. When actions by criminal justice agency employees seems to run counter to public or political sensibilities, various media, advocacy, or citizen–politician interest groups may get involved to change the policy direction that gave rise to undesirable practices. When the actions cross a threshold of legal or ethical propriety to a crime or tort, other mechanisms of a democracy can come into play.

In considering what some see as the militarization of the already paramilitary, there are observers who question the level of equipment possessed by some agencies, as well as the low- or no-cost acquisition from the U.S. government's 20-year-old 1033 program. At the same time we see members of the public openly carrying firearms in various states. Many in law enforcement are quite nervous about large numbers of essentially untrained civilians with firearms carried openly or concealed. Law enforcement officers are trained to handle and know *when* to use firearms. They respond to calls that are dangerous. They walk up to cars in the middle of the night. They scuffle and fight with people who might take their gun. The vast majority of citizens do not understand the second-to-second pulse of actual threat assessment and danger. With many current state laws, this deficiency in grasping when it might be necessary to end the life of another human is often washed away with an assertion that "I was in fear of my life." This statement is often made when there is little to no objective evidence that a threat had reached lethal likelihood or that the citizen could not have bowed out of the dance of confrontation before deciding to kill someone. There is a large concern in the trend of using force in the 21st century, regarding the increasing number of private security companies and employees. While these private sector agents use force, they are not restricted by the same rules and laws as law enforcement or corrections officers.

Sparrow (2014) provides his view of the contemporary paradigm:

> Private security and private policing have become inescapable. It is no longer useful for public police to hang on to their own regrets about these trends, bemoan their loss of market share, or pretend that public/private partnerships cannot be useful. There are too many reasons to embrace the idea that private contributions can and should contribute to public purposes.
>
> *(p. 20)*

Procedural and Organizational Justice

An important component of assessing the performance of employees and the overall organization is how that agency is run and what the culture is like. Criminal justice organizations are bureaucracies. This is not stated pejoratively. Rather, it is an observation that the rules and procedures that help officers effectively meet the demands of the various missions of criminal justice, foster their well-being, and also help ensure accountability to the public through a transparent and orderly set of processes (Trinkner, Tyler, and Goff, 2016; Schulhofer, Tyler, and Huq, 2011). This type of clarity should extend to the organization's values and leadership priorities which are intentionally espoused to employees and manifested in general acceptance and support of department goals (Bennett and Schmitt, 2002). Procedural justice is the rubric for approaches that recognize "the public is concerned that police decisions are made fairly and evenhandedly, that citizens are treated respectfully and given a chance to voice their views, and that officers are thought to abide by the rules that govern their behavior" (Skogan, Van Craen, and Hennessy, 2015, p. 320). Fairness in dealing with employees can pay it forward to citizens, of both the free and the incarcerated varieties. Procedural justice as a foundational element of a public safety/service organization can support many structural elements and do much for the health of an agency's internal culture and the external relationship with the public.

That the promise of community policing, three decades in the making, has not been realized in the form of an enlightened class of autonomous super-generalists adroitly resolving each and every daily challenge that compels a citizen to contact the police, is far from a condemnation of the paradigm. Community policing initiatives have brought agencies closer to their citizenry and an orientation of partnership. Turning over errant citizens to a "corrections" subsystem to provide an environment for reflection, upgrade, and redemption has also not taken the place of the volume-driven, budget-restricted practice of human warehousing. The field of public administration has grown and matured on a comparable timeline to criminal justice. Both of these applied disciplines are important to structure an effective workplace that recognizes internal and external organizational factors while navigating the (usually foreseeable) hazards of reform implementation (Skogan, 2008). Informed and intelligent managers and administrators must consistently work to align the individual goals of current generation officers with organizational goals, which include public trust and cooperation. The hard work and investment of competent and "good" management can pay dividends in community recognition of police legitimacy (Mazerolle, Antrobus, Bennett, and Tyler, 2013; Wolfe and Piquero, 2011) and the enhancement of safety this may bring (Goff, Epstein, Mentovich, and Reddy, 2013).

Employees within the criminal justice system have been shown as supportive of due process reforms throughout the years, and indeed derive some of their sense of self-legitimacy from efforts of organizational procedural justice (Taxman and Gordon, 2009; Bradford and Quinton, 2014; Pickett and Ryon, 2017). Due process support and appropriate restraint in the use of force, derives in part from the perception that the agency is run well and that supervisors are fair and model appropriate behavior (Van Craen and Skogan, 2017). This mindset likely contributes to and is also derived from a general outlook of procedural fairness. This is desirable from a moral and ethical standpoint but also pragmatically, as organizations realize the importance of employee satisfaction and productive work behaviors (Cohen-Charash and Spector, 2001). Like the public safety professional, the average citizen seeks to be treated fairly in dealings with the criminal justice system, and that in turn fosters a more positive view of the courts, corrections, and law enforcement (Friedrichs, 2003). In future, the procedural justice focus by agencies may help mitigate public concerns and possibly lead to improved and embraced practices on the part of officers.

Summary

The diversity of U.S. society creates a rich tapestry of life. Some fraying at the edges of this fabric can present challenges for law enforcement as members navigate the frictions that may arise. Officers using force is inevitable. But at the margins, most industries can improve their processes. Improving the criminal justice responses process with increased attention to training and procedures for officers, an optimistic and procedurally fair organization, and more transparency and inclusion of community members, is both an assessment of needed elements and necessary.

Reporting use of force is important. Supervisors and agencies cannot ensure proper use of procedures and compliance with policy if officers do not report force usage as required by those procedures and policies. Officers and agencies cannot expect the full confidence of the public without consistent, thorough, and transparent force reporting. Training cannot fulfill its function if it does not proceed from supplying complete information about force usage circumstances.

Policies must be thorough, must be reviewed in a timely and consistent manner, must be communicated effectively to employees, and must be an integral component of training. But it is never just policy that needs clarifying or communicating, and it is never just officers who need to do better work in the area of response and force usage.

Data without insight is, at the least, distracting. An important data source that may provide insights into reform efforts in many agencies has been the consent decree initiatives of the federal government. It is likely that the emphasis on such federal efforts will diminish over the short term, cutting off the mandate-and-monitor function of a powerful external mechanism, and leaving such efforts to return to local and/or internal ones.

The reliance on local control that has been ingrained in the American experience, similar to the English concept of "policing by consent," brings a strong need to trust public safety officials. Legitimacy of an agency is not solely a statutory fact established by law, but in a democratic society requires the confidence of community members. Procedural justice as seen externally by citizens boosts confidence and cooperation. Fairness and organizational justice seen internally by officers is critical to views of self-legitimacy and commitment to organizational goals.

KEY TERMS

Autonomous technology
Defensive tactics
Procedural justice

Discussion Questions

1. How frequent are force usage events by public safety employees? Why might the general public believe otherwise?
2. Describe the challenges and benefits of using body-worn cameras.
3. Discuss why there is confusion among the terms "force," "excessive force," and "brutality."
4. Will technology eliminate the need for human officers to ever use force? Why or why not?
5. How does the management of a criminal justice agency impact public and employee perceptions of legitimacy?

TRY THIS

Perform an Internet search for use of force cases in news stories. Examine several and assess how much context is provided.

References

Ariel, B., Farrar, W., and Sutherland, A. (2015). The effect of police body-worn cameras on use of force and citizens' complaints against the police: a randomized controlled trial. *Journal of Quantitative Criminology*, 31(3), 509–535.

Bennett, R. R. and Schmitt, E. L. (2002). The effect of work environment on level of police cynicism: a comparative study. *Police Quarterly*, 5(4), 493–522.

Bradford, B. and Quinton, P. (2014). Self-legitimacy, police culture and support for democratic policing in an English constabulary. *British Journal of Criminology*, 54(6), 1023–1046.

Christopher, M. S., Goerling, R. J., Rogers, B. S., Hunsinger, M., Baron, G., Bergman, A. L., and Zava, D. T. (2016). A pilot study evaluating the effectiveness of a mindfulness-based intervention on cortisol awakening response and health outcomes among law enforcement officers. *Journal of Police and Criminal Psychology*, 31(1), 15–29.

Cohen-Charash, Y. and Spector, P. E. (2001). The role of justice in organizations: a meta analysis. *Organizational Behavior and Human Decision Processes*, 86(2), 278–321.

Culhane, S. E., Boman, J. H., and Schweitzer, K. (2016). Public perceptions of the justifiability of police shootings: the role of body cameras in a pre- and post-Ferguson experiment. *Police Quarterly*, 19, 251–274.

Dowler, K. and Zawilski, V. (2007). Public perceptions of police misconduct and discriminations: examining the impact of media consumption. *Journal of Criminal Justice*, 35(2), 193–203.

Friedrichs, D. O. (2003). Review: Trust in the Law: Encouraging Public Cooperation with the Police and Courts, by Tom R. Tyler and Huen J. Huo. *American Journal of Sociology*, 109(2), 553–555.

Gettinger, D. (2017). *Drones at home: public safety drones*. Annandale, NY: Center for the Study of the Drone at Bard College.

Goff, P. A., Epstein, L. M., Mentovich, A., and Reddy, K. S. (2013). Illegitimacy is dangerous: how authorities experience and react to illegitimacy. *Psychology*, 4(3), 340–344.

Graham v. Connor, 490 U.S. 386 (1989).

Hough, R. M. (2017). *Event termination response: when the cars stop*. Unpublished manuscript.

Hough, R. M. and Tatum, K. M. (2014). Murder investigation and media: mutual goals. *Law Enforcement Executive Forum*, 14(3), 71–84.

International Association of Chiefs of Police. (2012). *Emerging use of force issues: balancing public and officer safety*. Alexandria, VA: Author.

International Association of Chiefs of Police. (2014). Technology policy framework. January. Alexandria, VA: Author.

Lee, C. (2016). Race, policing, and lethal force: remedying shooter bias with martial arts training. *Law and Contemporary Problems*, 79(3), 145–172.

McTackett, L. J. and Thomas, S. M. (2017). Police perceptions of irrational unstable behaviours and use of force. *Journal of Police and Criminal Psychology*, 32(2), 163.

Mazerolle, L., Antrobus, E., Bennett, S., and Tyler, T. R. (2013). Shaping citizen perceptions of police legitimacy: a randomized field trial of procedural justice. *Criminology*, 51(1), 33–63.

Moore, Mark (1990). Classroom presentation at Harvard Kennedy School of Government.

Nix, J., Campbell, B. A., Byers, E. H., and Alpert, G. P. (2017). A bird's eye view of civilians killed by police in 2015: further evidence of shooter bias. *Criminology and Public Policy*, 16(1), 1–32.

Nix, J. and Wolfe, S. E. (2017). The impact of negative publicity on police self-legitimacy. *Justice Quarterly*, 34(1), 84–108.

Pickett, J. T. and Ryon, S. B. (2017). Procedurally just cooperation: explaining support for due process reforms in policing. *Journal of Criminal Justice*, 48, 9–20.

Police Executive Research Forum (PERF). (2016). *Integrating communications, assessment, and tactics (ICAT)*. Washington, DC: Author.

President's Task Force on 21st Century Policing. (2015). *Final report of the President's Task Force on 21st Century Policing*. Washington, DC: Office of Community Oriented Policing Services.

Schulhofer, S. J., Tyler, T. R., and Huq, A. Z. (2011). American policing at a crossroads: unsustainable policies and the procedural justice alternative. *The Journal of Criminal Law and Criminology*, 101(2), 335–374.

Shane, J. M. (2016). Improving police use of force: a policy essay on national data collection. *Criminal Justice Policy Review*. doi:10.1177/0887403416662504

Skogan, W. G. (2008). Why reforms fail. *Policing and Society*, 18(1), 23–34.

Skogan, W. G., Van Craen M., and Hennessy, C. (2015). Training police for procedural justice. *Journal of Experimental Criminology*, 11(3), 319–335.

Sparrow, M. K. (2014). *Managing the boundary between public and private policing*. NCJ 247182. New Perspectives in Policing Bulletin. Washington, DC: U.S. Department of Justice, National Institute of Justice.

Squires, P.and KennisonP. (2010)*Shooting to kill? Policing, firearms and armed response.* Chichester UK and New York:Wiley-Blackwell.

Straub, J. (2014). Unmanned aerial systems: consideration of the use of force for law enforcement applications. *Technology in Society*, 39, 100–109.

Taxman, F. S. and Gordon, J. A. (2009). Do fairness and equity matter? An examination of organizational justice among correctional officers in adult prisons. *Criminal Justice and Behavior*, 36(7), 695–711.

Trinkner, R., Tyler, T. R., and Goff, P. A. (2016). Justice from within: the relations between a procedurally just organizational climate and police organizational efficiency, endorsement of democratic policing, and officer well-being. *Psychology, Public Policy, and Law*, 22(2), 158–172.

Van Craen, M. and Skogan, W. G. (2017). Officer support for use of force policy: the role of fair supervision. *Criminal Justice and Behavior*, 44(6), 843.

Wolfe, S. E. and Piquero, A. R. (2011). Organizational justice and police misconduct. *Criminal Justice and Behavior*, 38(4), 332–353.

Yokum, D., Ravishankar, A., and Coppock, A. (2017). Evaluating the effects of police body-worn cameras: a randomized controlled trial. Working paper. Washington, DC: The Lab @ DC, Office of the City Administrator, Executive Office of the Mayor.

INDEX